THE BOOK OF FIVE RINGS

THE BOOK OF

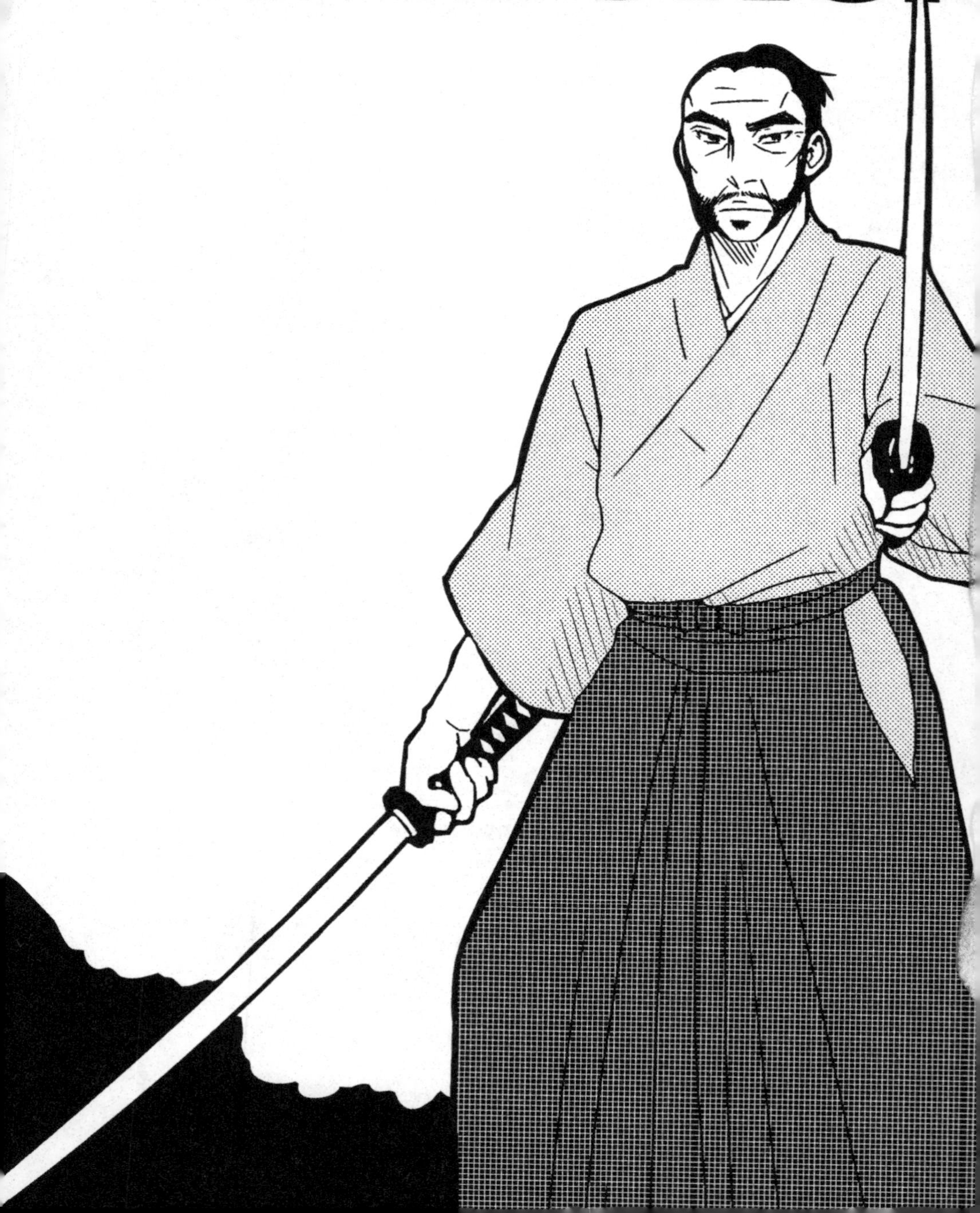

FIVE RINGS

A GRAPHIC NOVEL

From the book by **Miyamoto Musashi**

Based on the translation by **William Scott Wilson**

Adapted by **Sean Michael Wilson**

Illustrated by **Chie Kutsuwada**

With an Afterword by **William Scott Wilson**

SHAMBHALA
Boulder | 2012

Based on *The Book of Five Rings* by Miyamoto Musashi, translated by William Scott Wilson, © 2002, published by Shambhala Publications.

Shambhala Publications, Inc.
2129 13th Street
Boulder, Colorado 80302
www.shambhala.com

14 13 12 11 10 9 8 7

Printed in the United States of America
Shambhala Publications makes every effort to print on acid-free, recycled paper.

Shambhala Publications is distributed worldwide by
Penguin Random House, Inc., and its subsidiaries.

Library of Congress Cataloging-in-Publication Data
Wilson, Sean Michael.
[Gorin no sho. English]
The book of five rings: a graphic novel/from the book by Miyamoto Musashi; adapted by Sean Michael Wilson; illustrated by Chie Kutsuwada; with an afterword by William Scott Wilson.
p. cm.
ISBN 978-1-61180-012-8 (pbk.: alk. paper)
1. Military art and science—Early works to 1800—Comic books, strips, etc.
2. Swordplay—Japan—Early works to 1800—Comic books, strips, etc. 3. Graphic novels. I. Miyamoto, Musashi, 1584–1645. Gorin no sho. English. II. Title.
U101.W73 2012

CONTENTS

I

EARTH

地

What is called the 'martial arts' is the standard of the military clans. Commanders, in particuar, should get it into practice, and common soldiers should know its Way as well. Yet there are no warriors who clearly understand the Way of Martial Arts in the world today.

First, as representatives of Ways, Buddhism is a Way of salvation for man, Confucianism venerates a Way of culture, and medicine is a Way of curing various diseases. Moreover, poets teach the Way of Japanese verse; and then there are tea masters, archers, and others who teach the various arts. All of these practice according to their own thoughts and relish what they do according to their own hearts. It is a rare person who relishes the Way of the Martial Arts.

What is most basic in the Way of practicing the martial arts is overcoming your opponent in a duel, or in being victorious in a fight with a number of men. There are many people who, even when studying the Way of the Martial Arts, think that these skills will not be useful in real situations. In fact, the true Way of the Martial Arts is to train so that these skills are useful at any time, and to teach these skills so that they will be useful in all things.

—*Miyamoto Musashi*

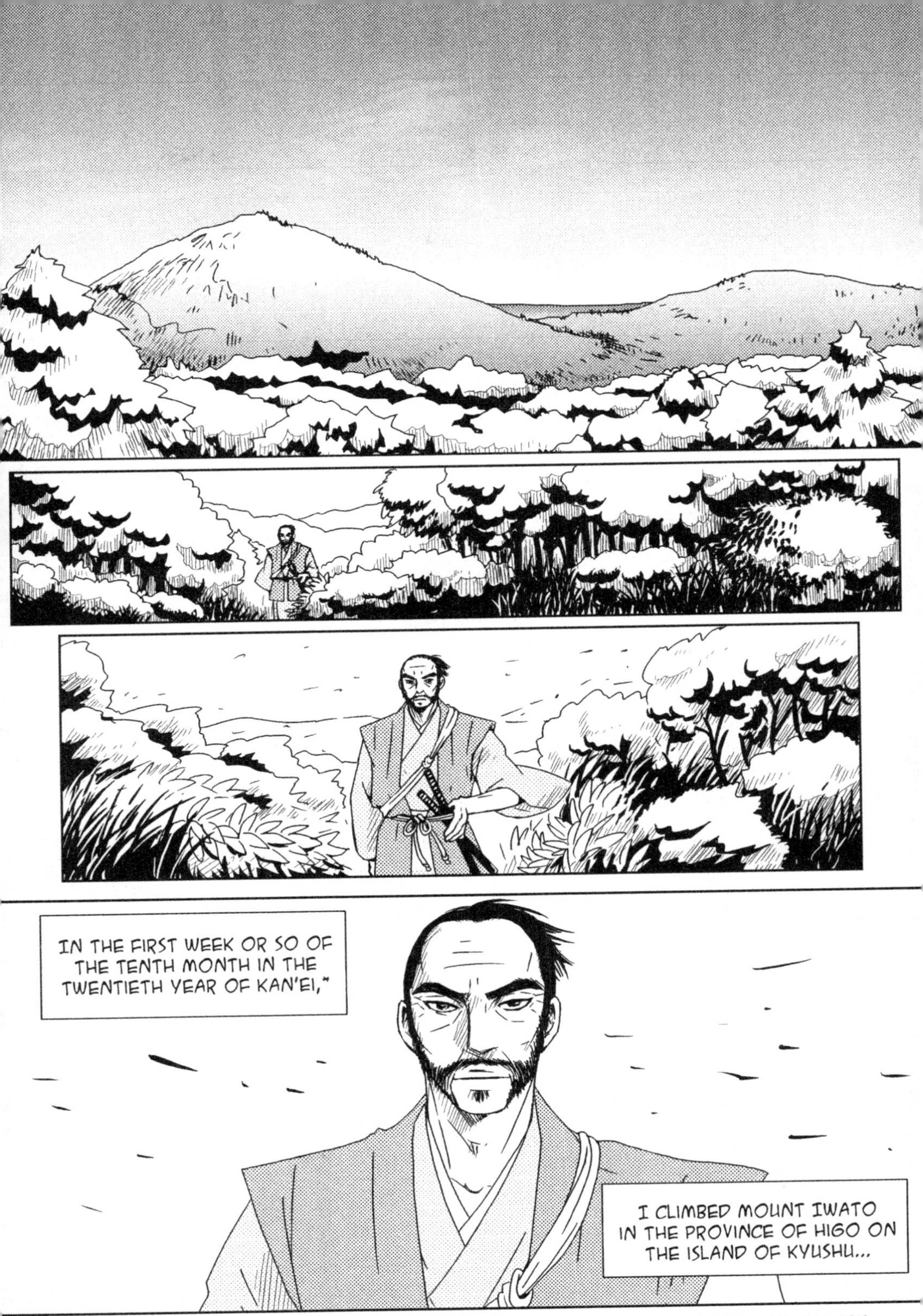
IN THE FIRST WEEK OR SO OF THE TENTH MONTH IN THE TWENTIETH YEAR OF KAN'EI,*
I CLIMBED MOUNT IWATO IN THE PROVINCE OF HIGO ON THE ISLAND OF KYUSHU...

* The Twentieth Year of Kan'ei is 1643.

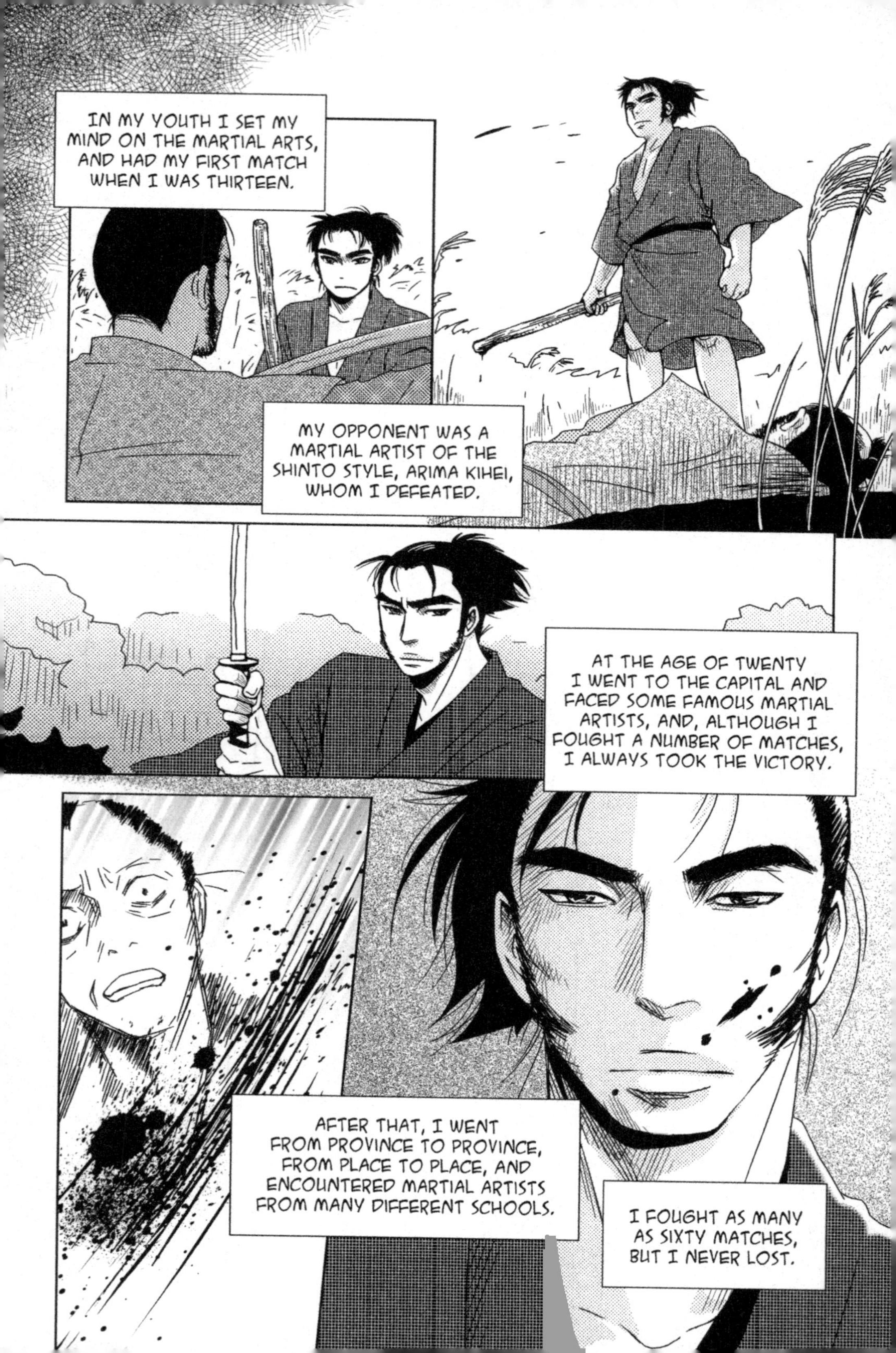
IN MY YOUTH I SET MY MIND ON THE MARTIAL ARTS, AND HAD MY FIRST MATCH WHEN I WAS THIRTEEN.
MY OPPONENT WAS A MARTIAL ARTIST OF THE SHINTO STYLE, ARIMA KIHEI, WHOM I DEFEATED.
AT THE AGE OF TWENTY I WENT TO THE CAPITAL AND FACED SOME FAMOUS MARTIAL ARTISTS, AND, ALTHOUGH I FOUGHT A NUMBER OF MATCHES, I ALWAYS TOOK THE VICTORY.
AFTER THAT, I WENT FROM PROVINCE TO PROVINCE, FROM PLACE TO PLACE, AND ENCOUNTERED MARTIAL ARTISTS FROM MANY DIFFERENT SCHOOLS.
I FOUGHT AS MANY AS SIXTY MATCHES, BUT I NEVER LOST.

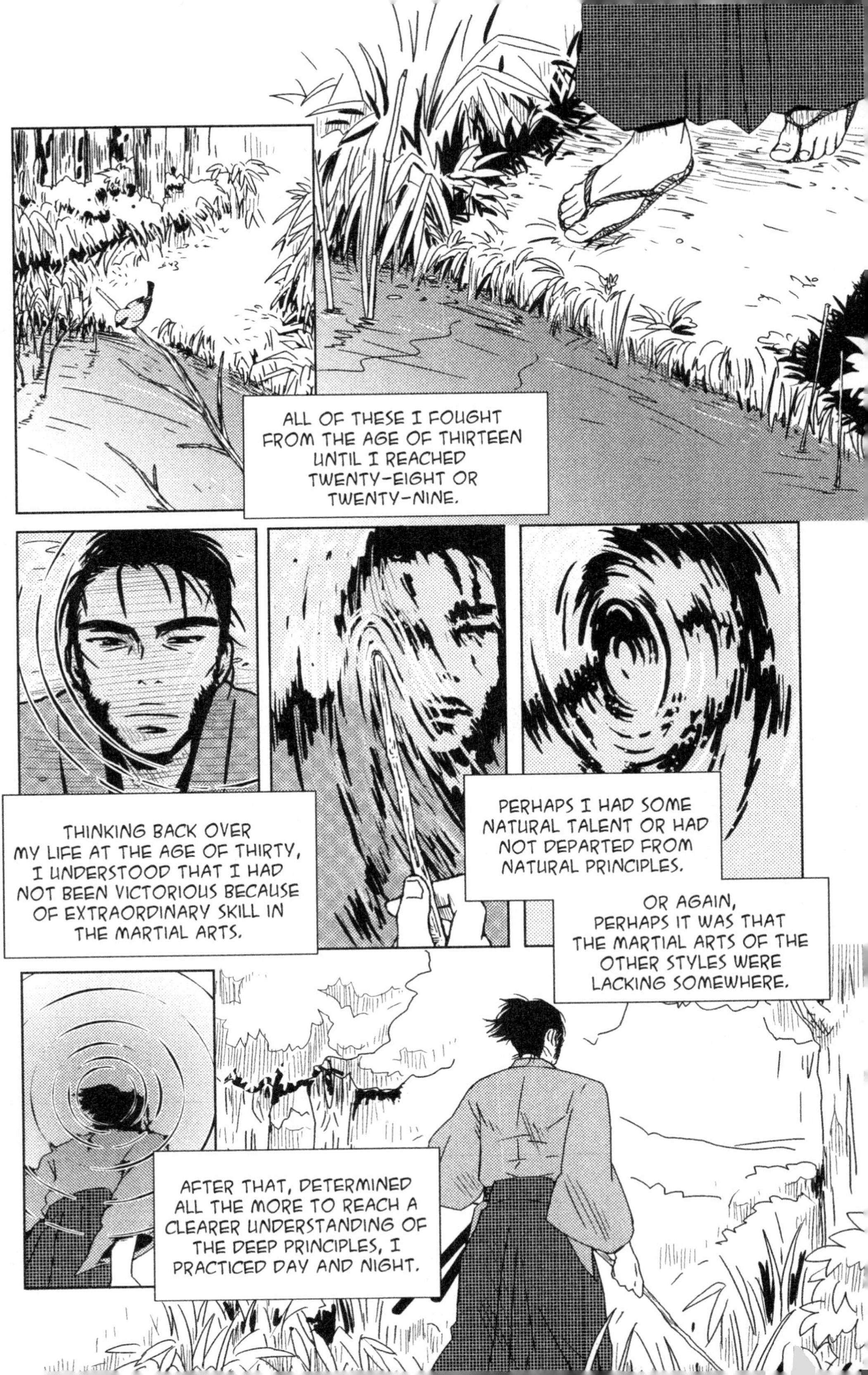
ALL OF THESE I FOUGHT FROM THE AGE OF THIRTEEN UNTIL I REACHED TWENTY-EIGHT OR TWENTY-NINE.
THINKING BACK OVER MY LIFE AT THE AGE OF THIRTY, I UNDERSTOOD THAT I HAD NOT BEEN VICTORIOUS BECAUSE OF EXTRAORDINARY SKILL IN THE MARTIAL ARTS.
PERHAPS I HAD SOME NATURAL TALENT OR HAD NOT DEPARTED FROM NATURAL PRINCIPLES.
OR AGAIN, PERHAPS IT WAS THAT THE MARTIAL ARTS OF THE OTHER STYLES WERE LACKING SOMEWHERE.
AFTER THAT, DETERMINED ALL THE MORE TO REACH A CLEARER UNDERSTANDING OF THE DEEP PRINCIPLES, I PRACTICED DAY AND NIGHT.

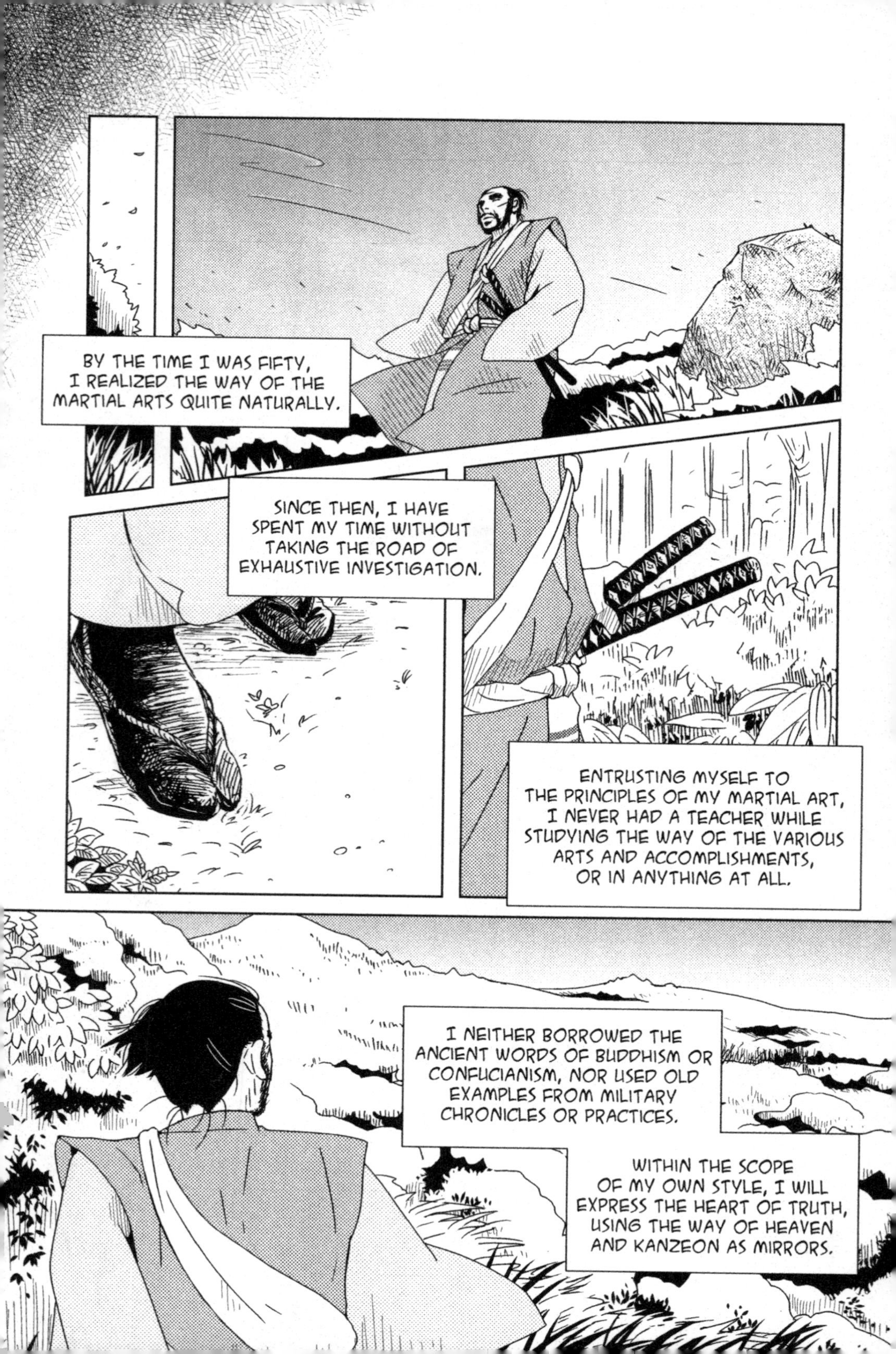
BY THE TIME I WAS FIFTY, I REALIZED THE WAY OF THE MARTIAL ARTS QUITE NATURALLY.
SINCE THEN, I HAVE SPENT MY TIME WITHOUT TAKING THE ROAD OF EXHAUSTIVE INVESTIGATION.
ENTRUSTING MYSELF TO THE PRINCIPLES OF MY MARTIAL ART, I NEVER HAD A TEACHER WHILE STUDYING THE WAY OF THE VARIOUS ARTS AND ACCOMPLISHMENTS, OR IN ANYTHING AT ALL.
I NEITHER BORROWED THE ANCIENT WORDS OF BUDDHISM OR CONFUCIANISM, NOR USED OLD EXAMPLES FROM MILITARY CHRONICLES OR PRACTICES.
WITHIN THE SCOPE OF MY OWN STYLE, I WILL EXPRESS THE HEART OF TRUTH, USING THE WAY OF HEAVEN AND KANZEON AS MIRRORS.

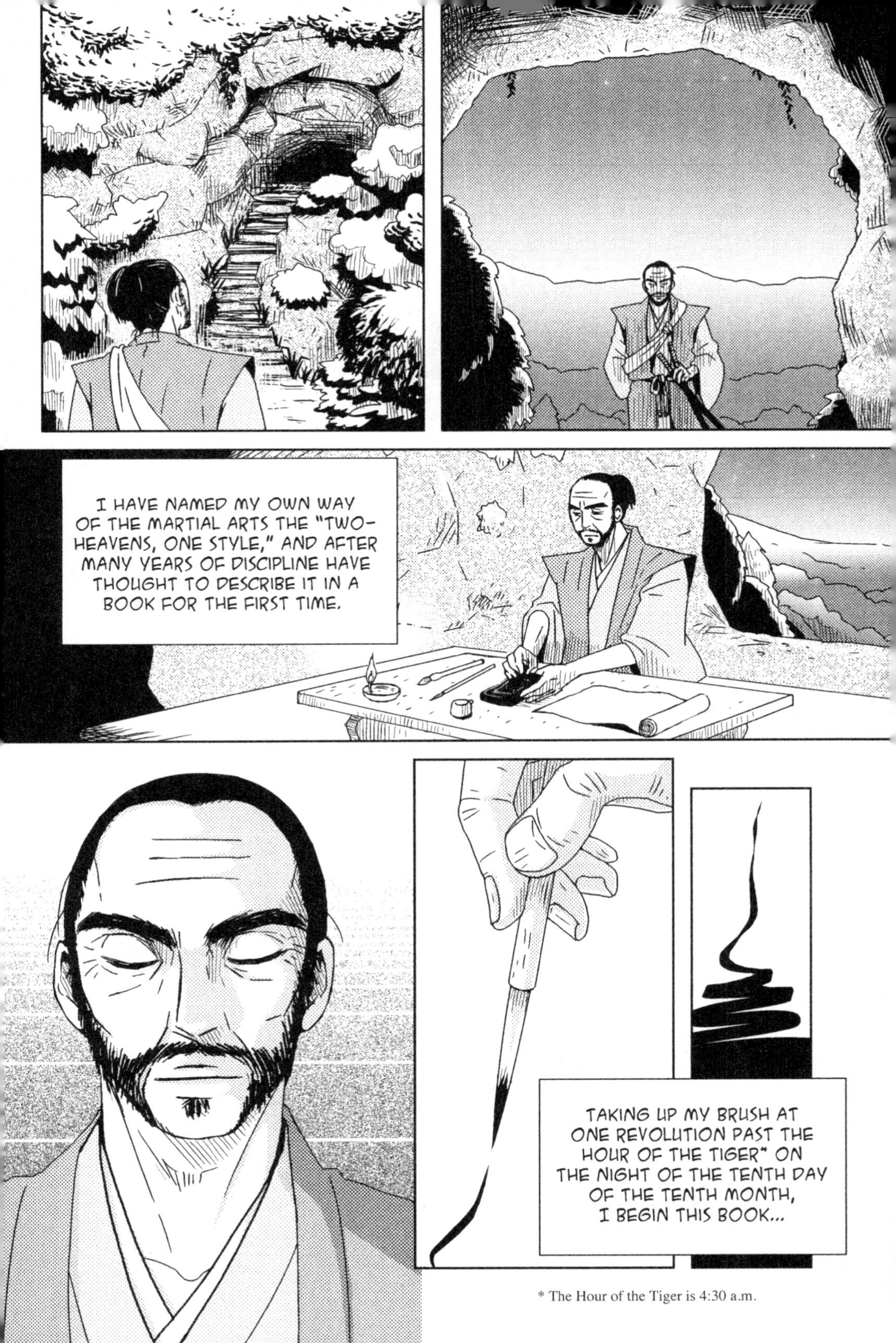
I HAVE NAMED MY OWN WAY OF THE MARTIAL ARTS THE "TWO-HEAVENS, ONE STYLE," AND AFTER MANY YEARS OF DISCIPLINE HAVE THOUGHT TO DESCRIBE IT IN A BOOK FOR THE FIRST TIME.
TAKING UP MY BRUSH AT ONE REVOLUTION PAST THE HOUR OF THE TIGER* ON THE NIGHT OF THE TENTH DAY OF THE TENTH MONTH, I BEGIN THIS BOOK...

* The Hour of the Tiger is 4:30 a.m.

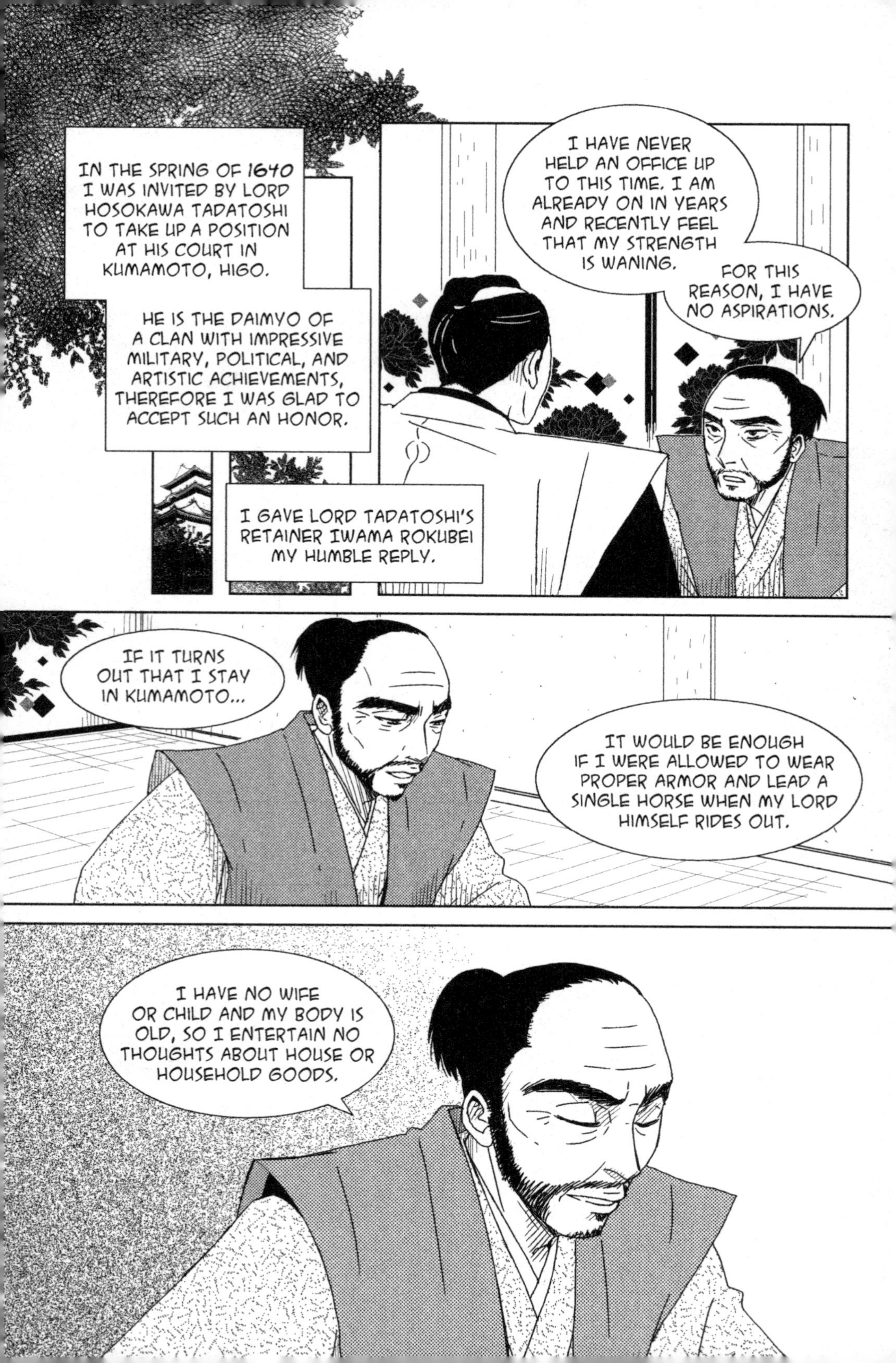
IN THE SPRING OF 1640 I WAS INVITED BY LORD HOSOKAWA TADATOSHI TO TAKE UP A POSITION AT HIS COURT IN KUMAMOTO, HIGO.
HE IS THE DAIMYO OF A CLAN WITH IMPRESSIVE MILITARY, POLITICAL, AND ARTISTIC ACHIEVEMENTS, THEREFORE I WAS GLAD TO ACCEPT SUCH AN HONOR.
I GAVE LORD TADATOSHI'S RETAINER IWAMA ROKUBEI MY HUMBLE REPLY.
I HAVE NEVER HELD AN OFFICE UP TO THIS TIME. I AM ALREADY ON IN YEARS AND RECENTLY FEEL THAT MY STRENGTH IS WANING.
FOR THIS REASON, I HAVE NO ASPIRATIONS.
IF IT TURNS OUT THAT I STAY IN KUMAMOTO...
IT WOULD BE ENOUGH IF I WERE ALLOWED TO WEAR PROPER ARMOR AND LEAD A SINGLE HORSE WHEN MY LORD HIMSELF RIDES OUT.
I HAVE NO WIFE OR CHILD AND MY BODY IS OLD, SO I ENTERTAIN NO THOUGHTS ABOUT HOUSE OR HOUSEHOLD GOODS.

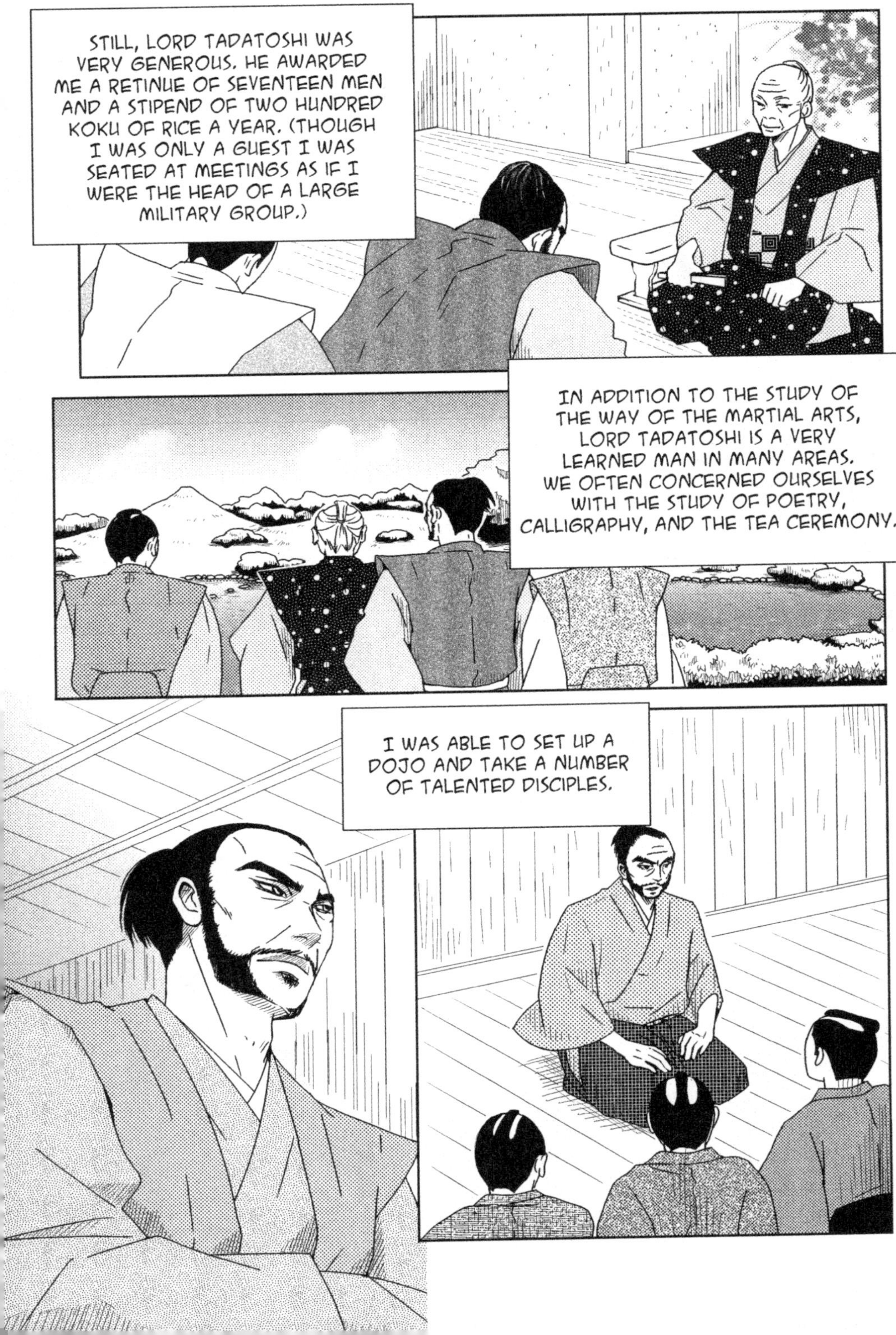
STILL, LORD TADATOSHI WAS VERY GENEROUS. HE AWARDED ME A RETINUE OF SEVENTEEN MEN AND A STIPEND OF TWO HUNDRED KOKU OF RICE A YEAR. (THOUGH I WAS ONLY A GUEST I WAS SEATED AT MEETINGS AS IF I WERE THE HEAD OF A LARGE MILITARY GROUP.)
IN ADDITION TO THE STUDY OF THE WAY OF THE MARTIAL ARTS, LORD TADATOSHI IS A VERY LEARNED MAN IN MANY AREAS. WE OFTEN CONCERNED OURSELVES WITH THE STUDY OF POETRY, CALLIGRAPHY, AND THE TEA CEREMONY.
I WAS ABLE TO SET UP A DOJO AND TAKE A NUMBER OF TALENTED DISCIPLES.

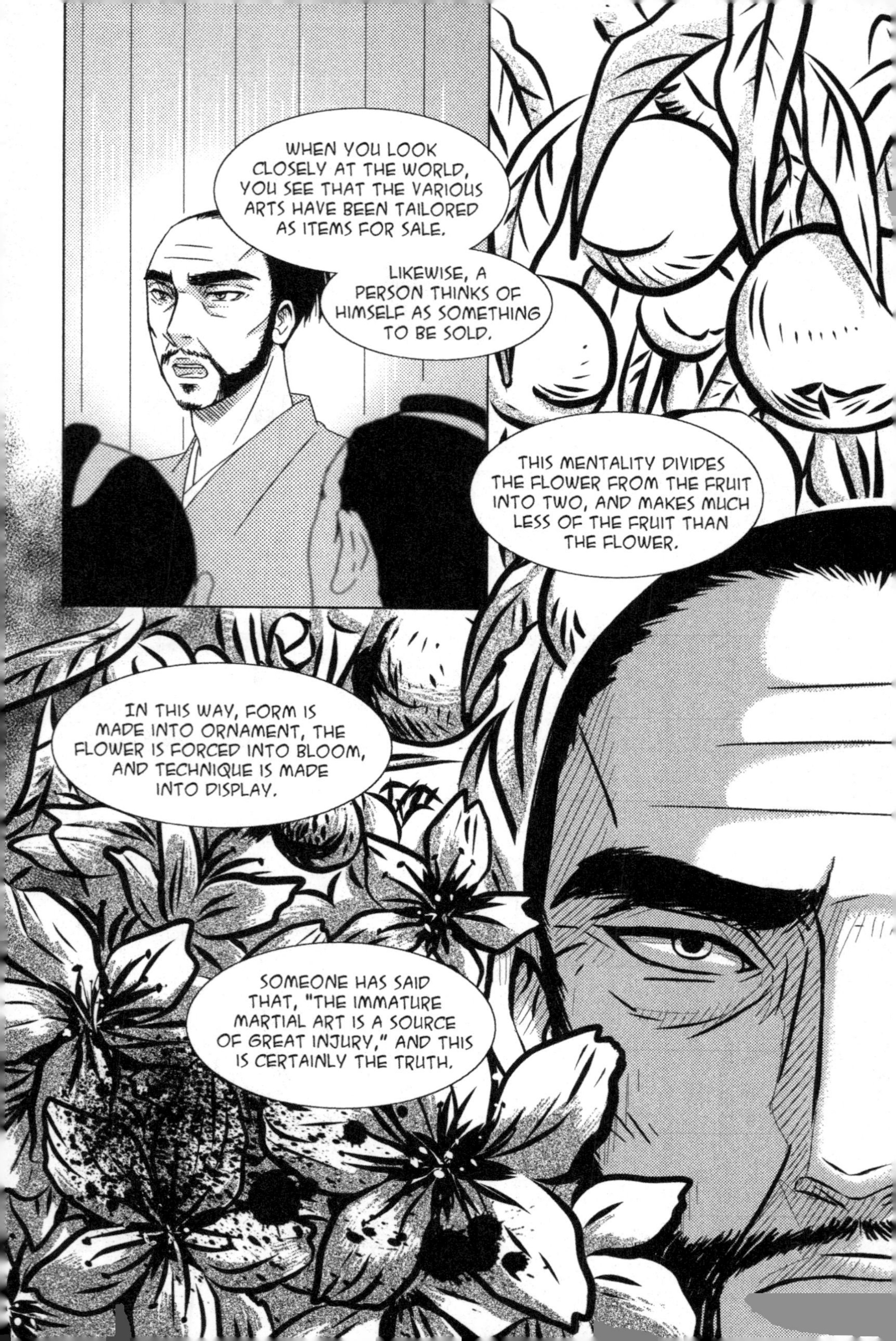
WHEN YOU LOOK CLOSELY AT THE WORLD, YOU SEE THAT THE VARIOUS ARTS HAVE BEEN TAILORED AS ITEMS FOR SALE.
LIKEWISE, A PERSON THINKS OF HIMSELF AS SOMETHING TO BE SOLD.
THIS MENTALITY DIVIDES THE FLOWER FROM THE FRUIT INTO TWO, AND MAKES MUCH LESS OF THE FRUIT THAN THE FLOWER.
IN THIS WAY, FORM IS MADE INTO ORNAMENT, THE FLOWER IS FORCED INTO BLOOM, AND TECHNIQUE IS MADE INTO DISPLAY.
SOMEONE HAS SAID THAT, "THE IMMATURE MARTIAL ART IS A SOURCE OF GREAT INJURY," AND THIS IS CERTAINLY THE TRUTH.

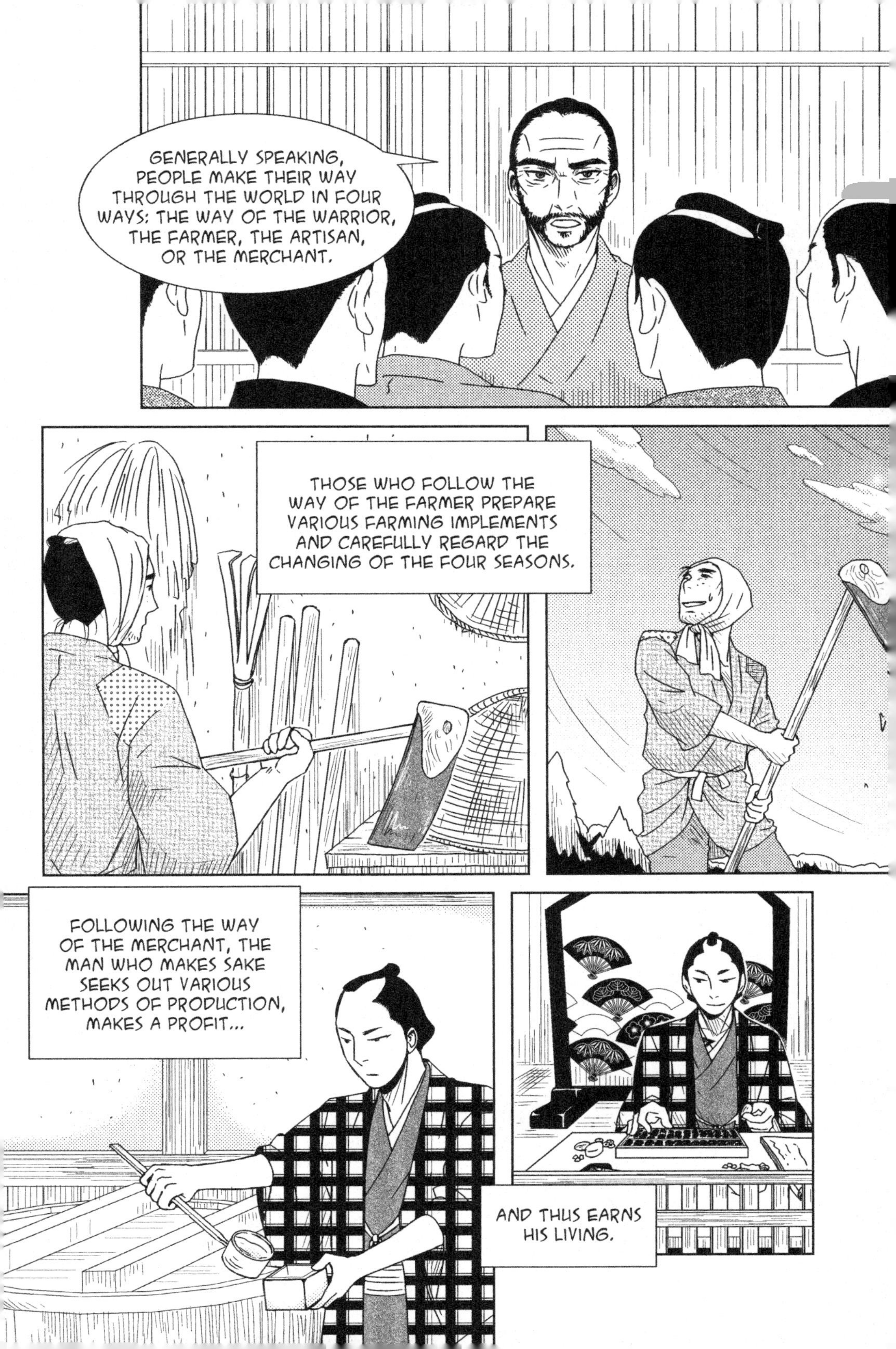
GENERALLY SPEAKING, PEOPLE MAKE THEIR WAY THROUGH THE WORLD IN FOUR WAYS: THE WAY OF THE WARRIOR, THE FARMER, THE ARTISAN, OR THE MERCHANT.
THOSE WHO FOLLOW THE WAY OF THE FARMER PREPARE VARIOUS FARMING IMPLEMENTS AND CAREFULLY REGARD THE CHANGING OF THE FOUR SEASONS.
FOLLOWING THE WAY OF THE MERCHANT, THE MAN WHO MAKES SAKE SEEKS OUT VARIOUS METHODS OF PRODUCTION, MAKES A PROFIT...
AND THUS EARNS HIS LIVING.

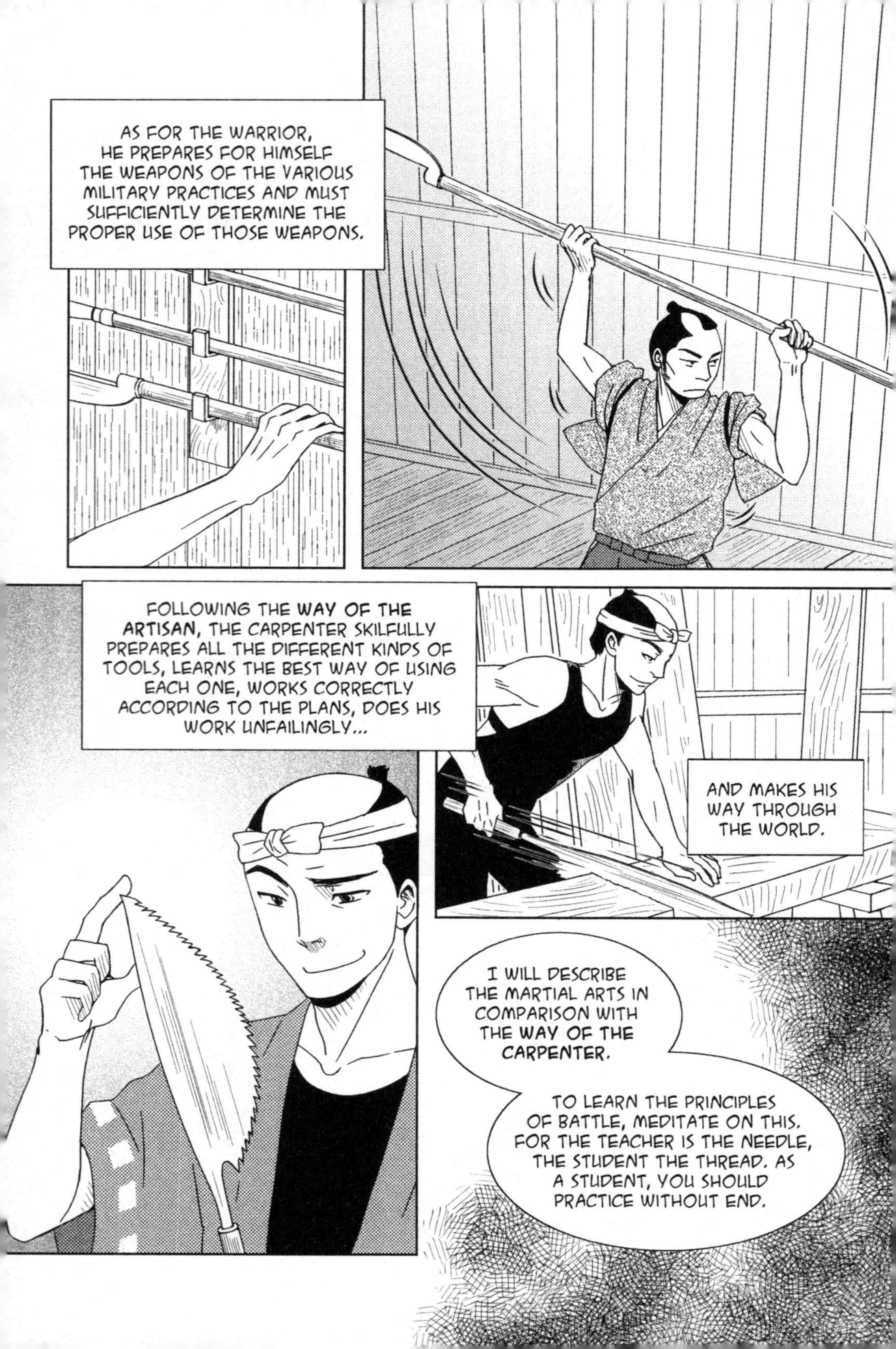
AS FOR THE WARRIOR, HE PREPARES FOR HIMSELF THE WEAPONS OF THE VARIOUS MILITARY PRACTICES AND MUST SUFFICIENTLY DETERMINE THE PROPER USE OF THOSE WEAPONS.
FOLLOWING THE WAY OF THE ARTISAN, THE CARPENTER SKILFULLY PREPARES ALL THE DIFFERENT KINDS OF TOOLS, LEARNS THE BEST WAY OF USING EACH ONE, WORKS CORRECTLY ACCORDING TO THE PLANS, DOES HIS WORK UNFAILINGLY...
AND MAKES HIS WAY THROUGH THE WORLD.
I WILL DESCRIBE THE MARTIAL ARTS IN COMPARISON WITH THE WAY OF THE CARPENTER.
TO LEARN THE PRINCIPLES OF BATTLE, MEDITATE ON THIS. FOR THE TEACHER IS THE NEEDLE, THE STUDENT THE THREAD. AS A STUDENT, YOU SHOULD PRACTICE WITHOUT END.

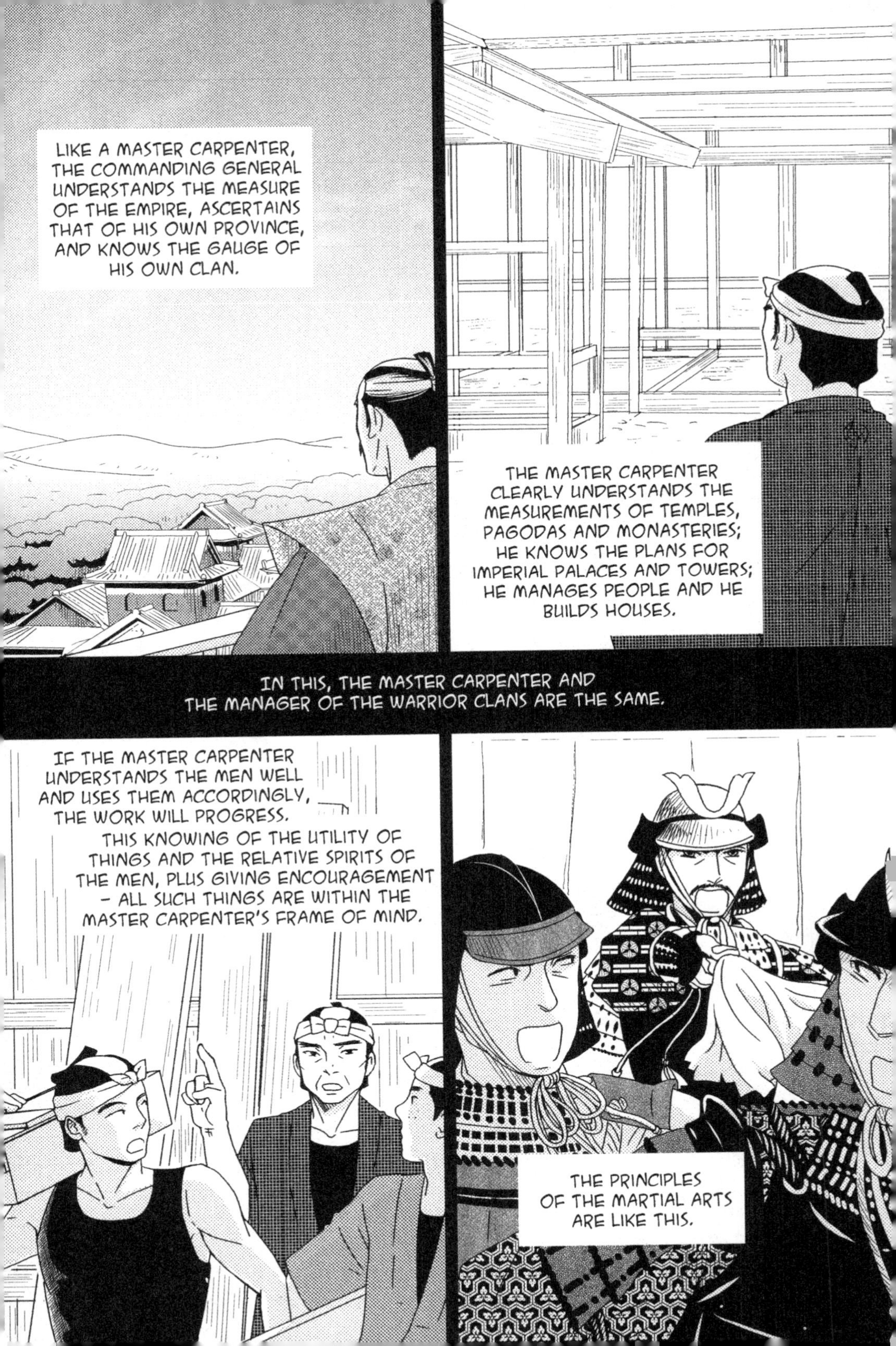
LIKE A MASTER CARPENTER, THE COMMANDING GENERAL UNDERSTANDS THE MEASURE OF THE EMPIRE, ASCERTAINS THAT OF HIS OWN PROVINCE, AND KNOWS THE GAUGE OF HIS OWN CLAN.
THE MASTER CARPENTER CLEARLY UNDERSTANDS THE MEASUREMENTS OF TEMPLES, PAGODAS AND MONASTERIES; HE KNOWS THE PLANS FOR IMPERIAL PALACES AND TOWERS; HE MANAGES PEOPLE AND HE BUILDS HOUSES.
IN THIS, THE MASTER CARPENTER AND THE MANAGER OF THE WARRIOR CLANS ARE THE SAME.
IF THE MASTER CARPENTER UNDERSTANDS THE MEN WELL AND USES THEM ACCORDINGLY, THE WORK WILL PROGRESS.
THIS KNOWING OF THE UTILITY OF THINGS AND THE RELATIVE SPIRITS OF THE MEN, PLUS GIVING ENCOURAGEMENT – ALL SUCH THINGS ARE WITHIN THE MASTER CARPENTER'S FRAME OF MIND.
THE PRINCIPLES OF THE MARTIAL ARTS ARE LIKE THIS.

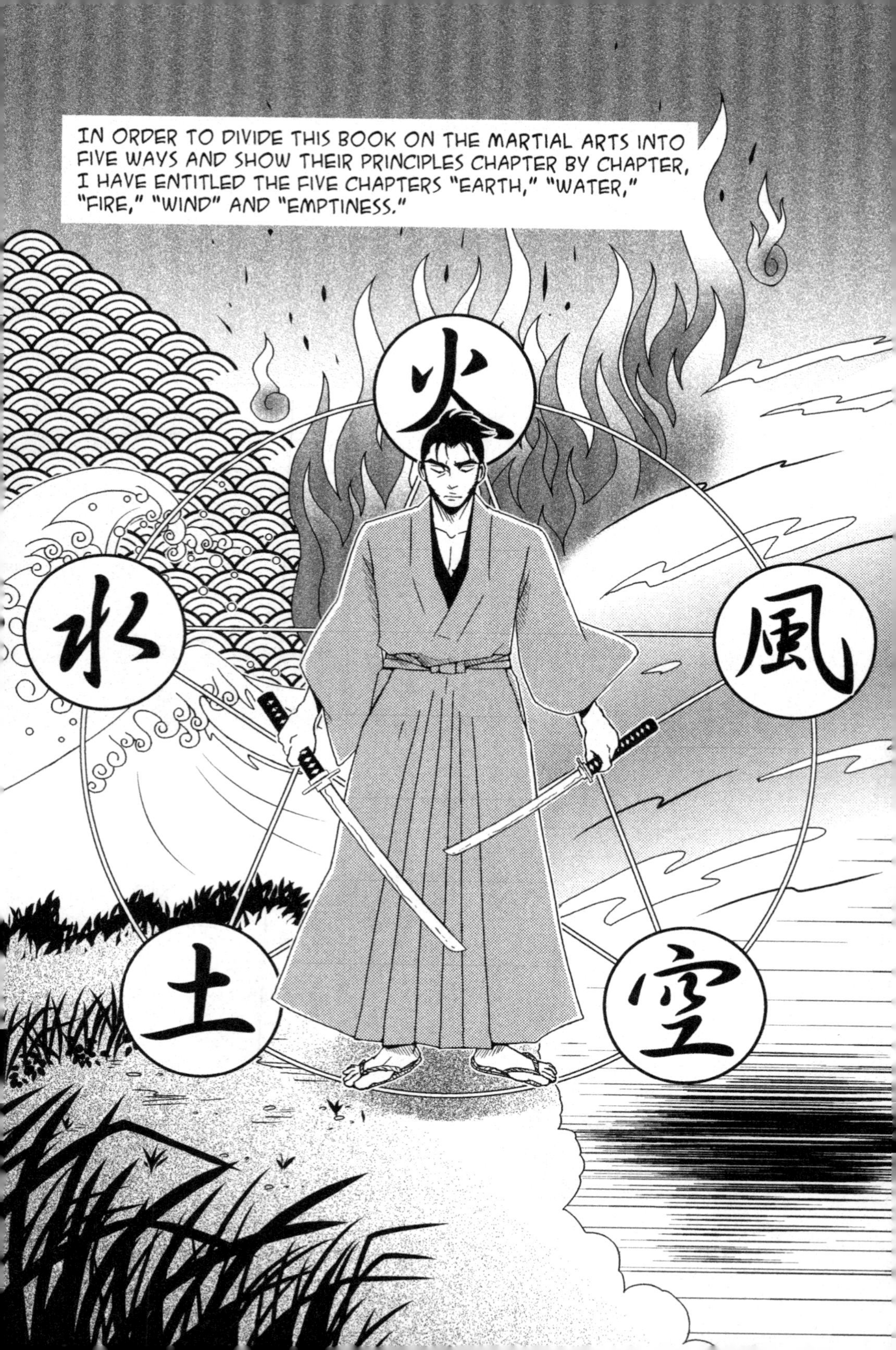
IN ORDER TO DIVIDE THIS BOOK ON THE MARTIAL ARTS INTO FIVE WAYS AND SHOW THEIR PRINCIPLES CHAPTER BY CHAPTER, I HAVE ENTITLED THE FIVE CHAPTERS "EARTH," "WATER," "FIRE," "WIND" AND "EMPTINESS."
火
水
風
土
空

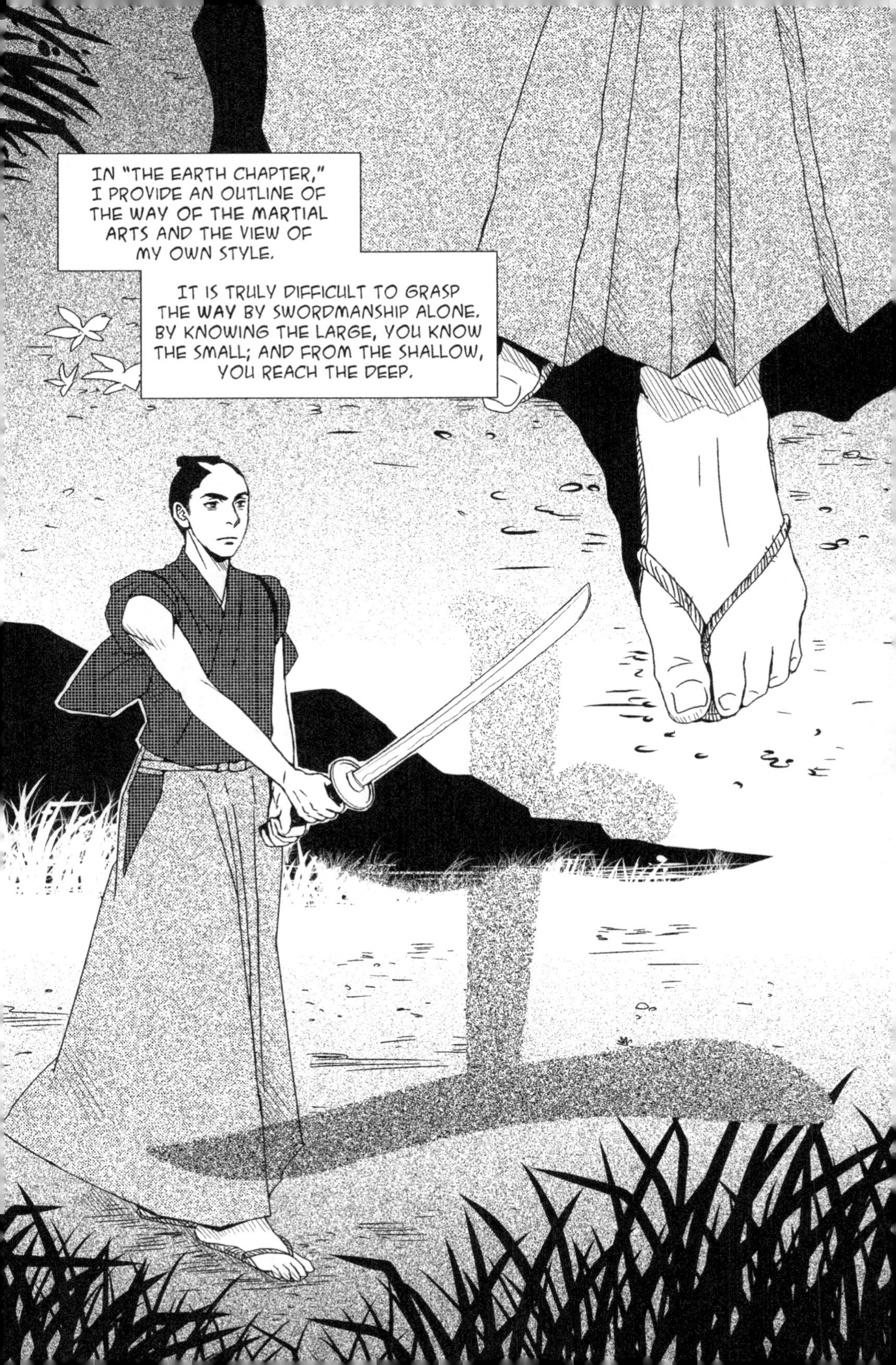
IN "THE EARTH CHAPTER," I PROVIDE AN OUTLINE OF THE WAY OF THE MARTIAL ARTS AND THE VIEW OF MY OWN STYLE.
IT IS TRULY DIFFICULT TO GRASP THE WAY BY SWORDMANSHIP ALONE. BY KNOWING THE LARGE, YOU KNOW THE SMALL; AND FROM THE SHALLOW, YOU REACH THE DEEP.

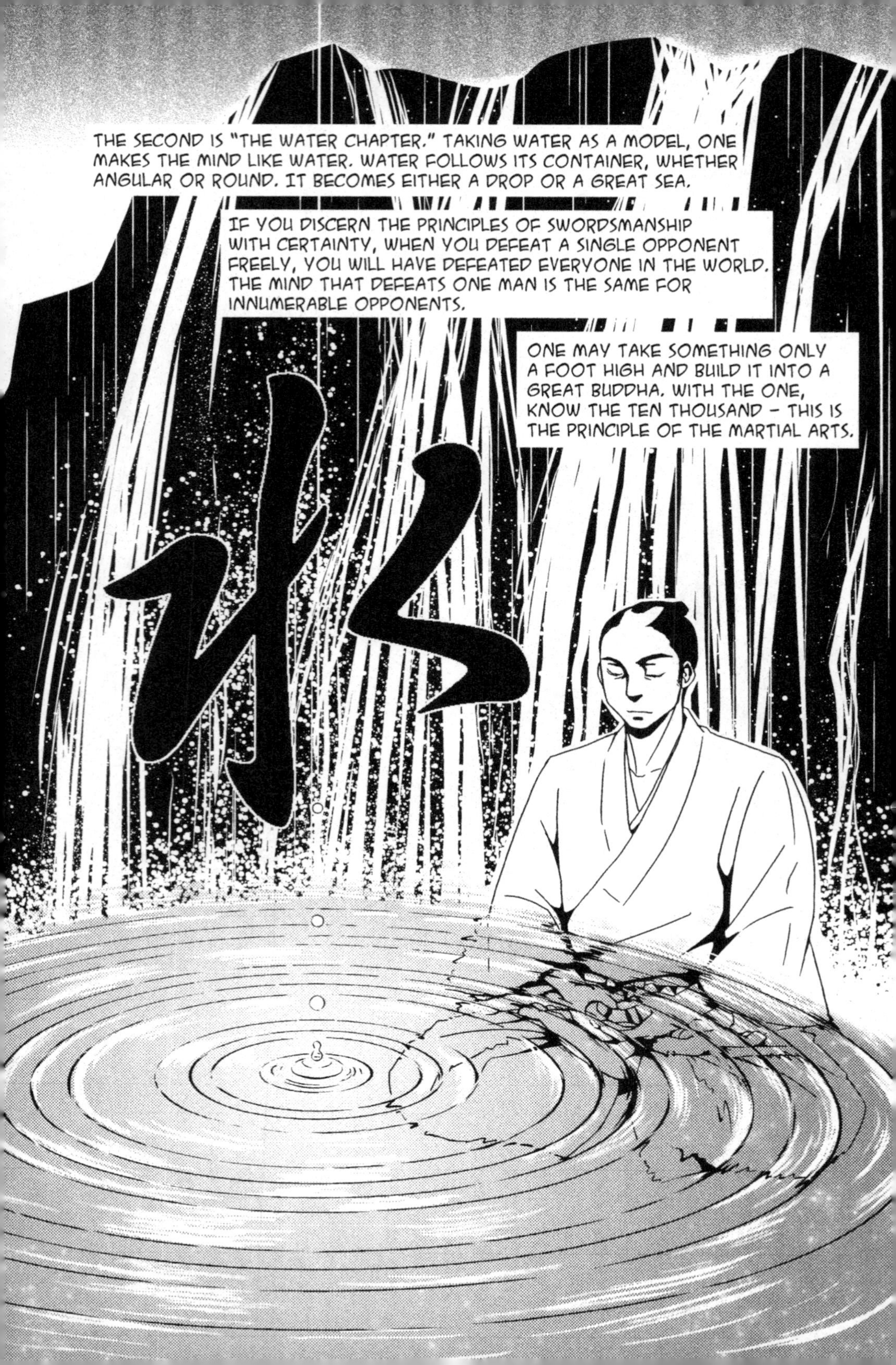
THE SECOND IS "THE WATER CHAPTER." TAKING WATER AS A MODEL, ONE MAKES THE MIND LIKE WATER. WATER FOLLOWS ITS CONTAINER, WHETHER ANGULAR OR ROUND. IT BECOMES EITHER A DROP OR A GREAT SEA.
IF YOU DISCERN THE PRINCIPLES OF SWORDSMANSHIP WITH CERTAINTY, WHEN YOU DEFEAT A SINGLE OPPONENT FREELY, YOU WILL HAVE DEFEATED EVERYONE IN THE WORLD. THE MIND THAT DEFEATS ONE MAN IS THE SAME FOR INNUMERABLE OPPONENTS.
ONE MAY TAKE SOMETHING ONLY A FOOT HIGH AND BUILD IT INTO A GREAT BUDDHA. WITH THE ONE, KNOW THE TEN THOUSAND – THIS IS THE PRINCIPLE OF THE MARTIAL ARTS.
水

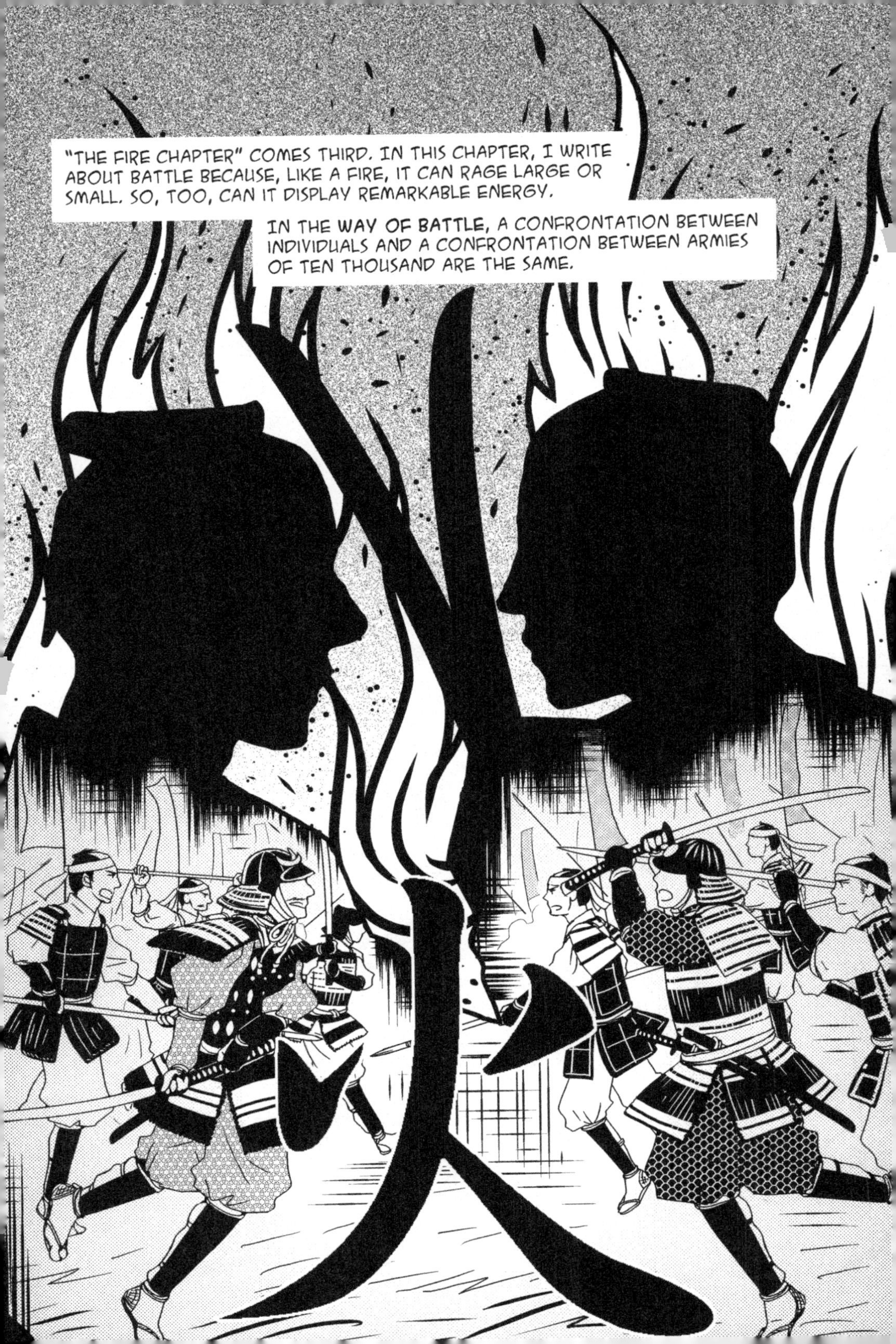
"THE FIRE CHAPTER" COMES THIRD. IN THIS CHAPTER, I WRITE ABOUT BATTLE BECAUSE, LIKE A FIRE, IT CAN RAGE LARGE OR SMALL. SO, TOO, CAN IT DISPLAY REMARKABLE ENERGY.
IN THE WAY OF BATTLE, A CONFRONTATION BETWEEN INDIVIDUALS AND A CONFRONTATION BETWEEN ARMIES OF TEN THOUSAND ARE THE SAME.

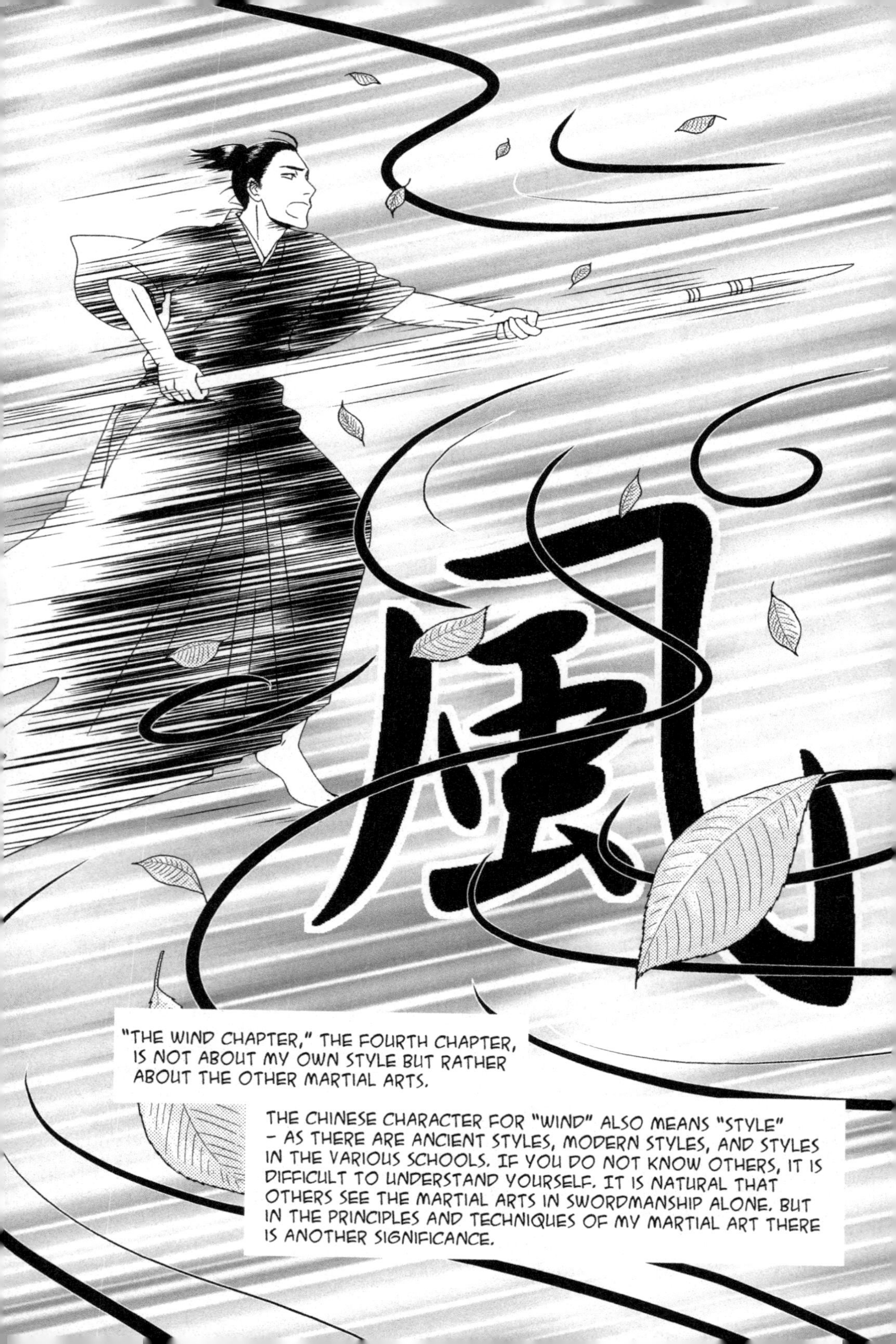
風
"THE WIND CHAPTER," THE FOURTH CHAPTER, IS NOT ABOUT MY OWN STYLE BUT RATHER ABOUT THE OTHER MARTIAL ARTS.
THE CHINESE CHARACTER FOR "WIND" ALSO MEANS "STYLE" – AS THERE ARE ANCIENT STYLES, MODERN STYLES, AND STYLES IN THE VARIOUS SCHOOLS. IF YOU DO NOT KNOW OTHERS, IT IS DIFFICULT TO UNDERSTAND YOURSELF. IT IS NATURAL THAT OTHERS SEE THE MARTIAL ARTS IN SWORDMANSHIP ALONE. BUT IN THE PRINCIPLES AND TECHNIQUES OF MY MARTIAL ART THERE IS ANOTHER SIGNIFICANCE.

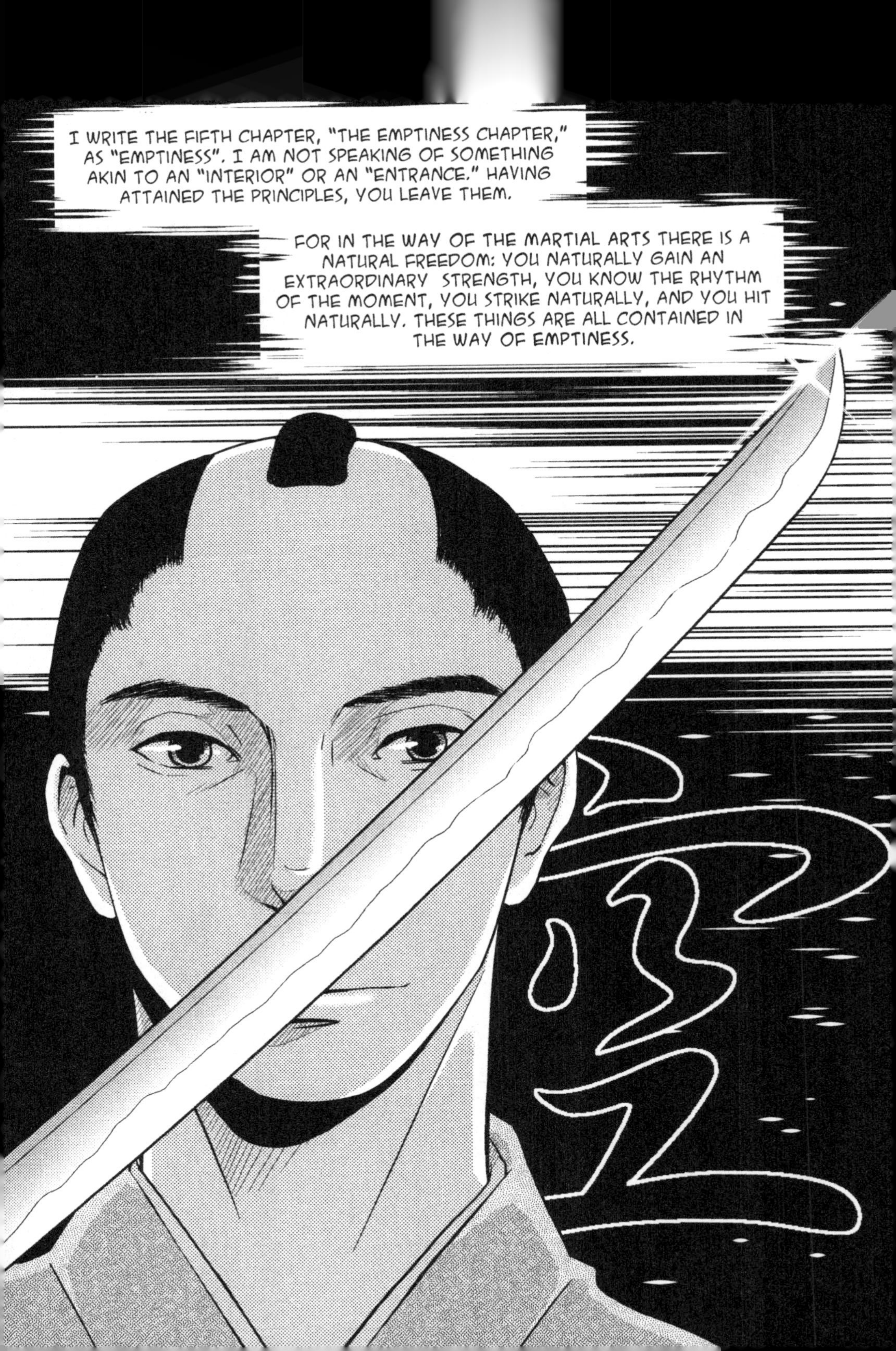
I WRITE THE FIFTH CHAPTER, "THE EMPTINESS CHAPTER," AS "EMPTINESS". I AM NOT SPEAKING OF SOMETHING AKIN TO AN "INTERIOR" OR AN "ENTRANCE." HAVING ATTAINED THE PRINCIPLES, YOU LEAVE THEM.
FOR IN THE WAY OF THE MARTIAL ARTS THERE IS A NATURAL FREEDOM: YOU NATURALLY GAIN AN EXTRAORDINARY STRENGTH, YOU KNOW THE RHYTHM OF THE MOMENT, YOU STRIKE NATURALLY, AND YOU HIT NATURALLY. THESE THINGS ARE ALL CONTAINED IN THE WAY OF EMPTINESS.

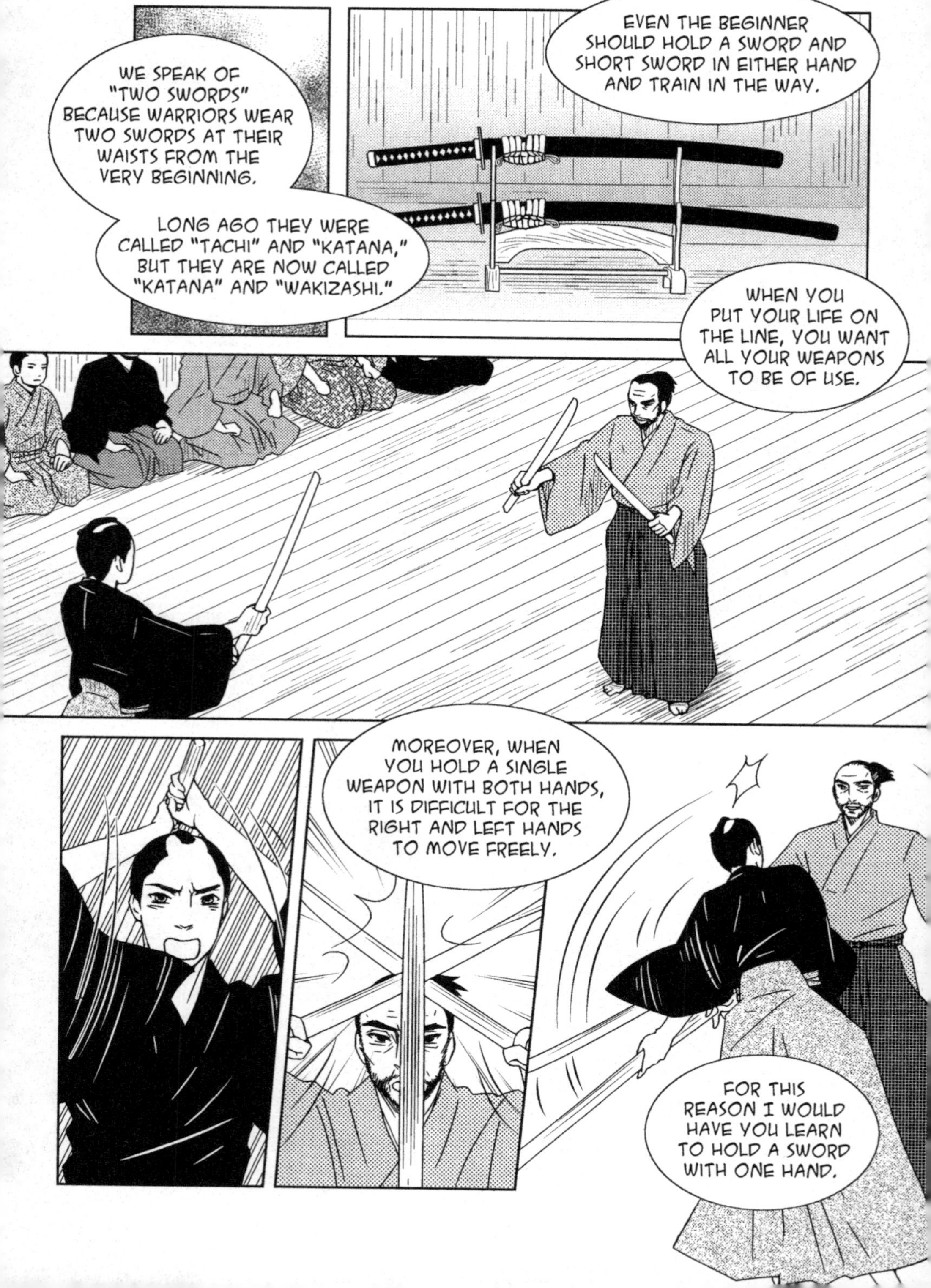
WE SPEAK OF "TWO SWORDS" BECAUSE WARRIORS WEAR TWO SWORDS AT THEIR WAISTS FROM THE VERY BEGINNING.
LONG AGO THEY WERE CALLED "TACHI" AND "KATANA," BUT THEY ARE NOW CALLED "KATANA" AND "WAKIZASHI."
EVEN THE BEGINNER SHOULD HOLD A SWORD AND SHORT SWORD IN EITHER HAND AND TRAIN IN THE WAY.
WHEN YOU PUT YOUR LIFE ON THE LINE, YOU WANT ALL YOUR WEAPONS TO BE OF USE.
MOREOVER, WHEN YOU HOLD A SINGLE WEAPON WITH BOTH HANDS, IT IS DIFFICULT FOR THE RIGHT AND LEFT HANDS TO MOVE FREELY.
FOR THIS REASON I WOULD HAVE YOU LEARN TO HOLD A SWORD WITH ONE HAND.

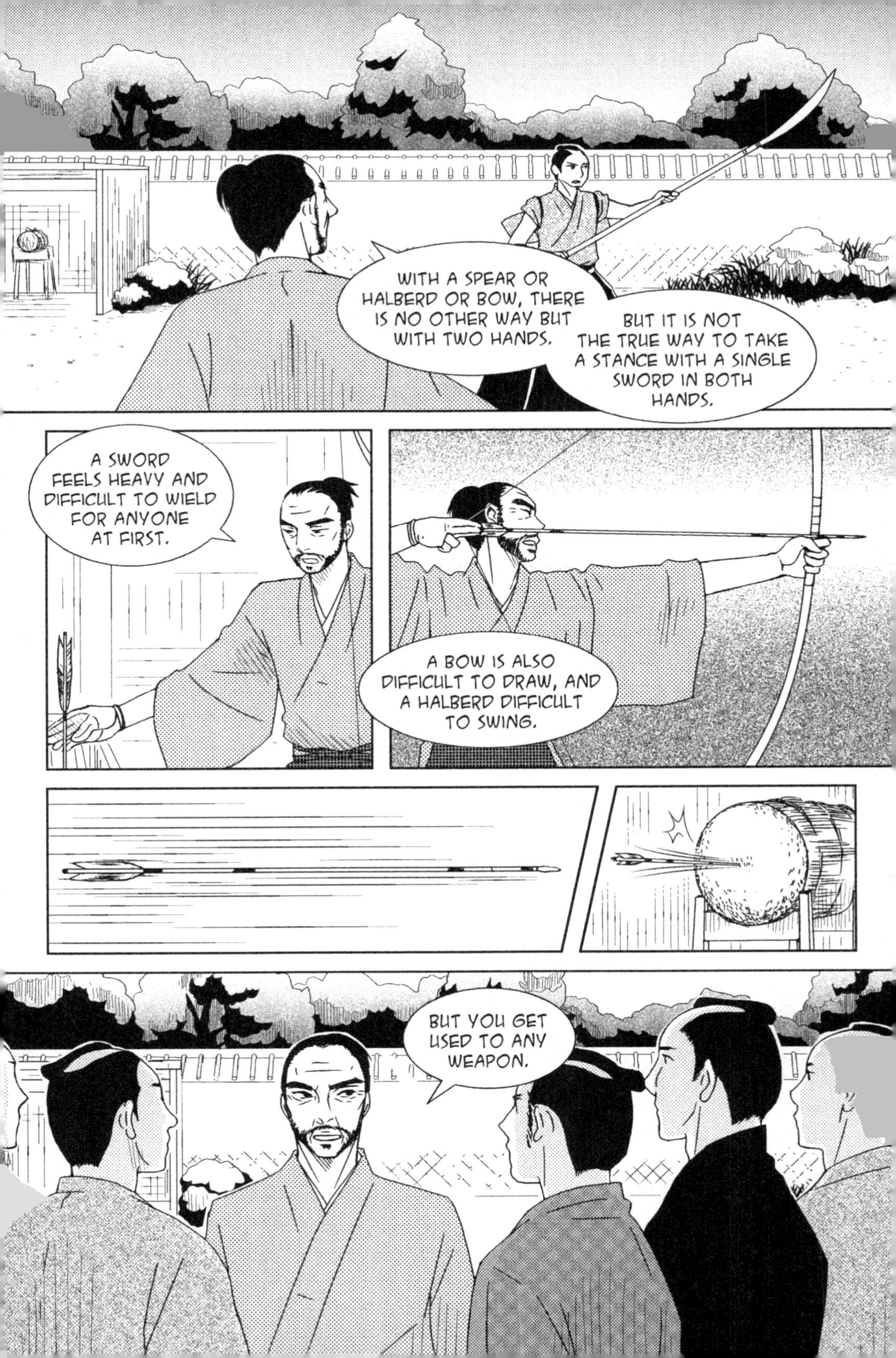
WITH A SPEAR OR HALBERD OR BOW, THERE IS NO OTHER WAY BUT WITH TWO HANDS.
BUT IT IS NOT THE TRUE WAY TO TAKE A STANCE WITH A SINGLE SWORD IN BOTH HANDS.
A SWORD FEELS HEAVY AND DIFFICULT TO WIELD FOR ANYONE AT FIRST.
A BOW IS ALSO DIFFICULT TO DRAW, AND A HALBERD DIFFICULT TO SWING.
BUT YOU GET USED TO ANY WEAPON.

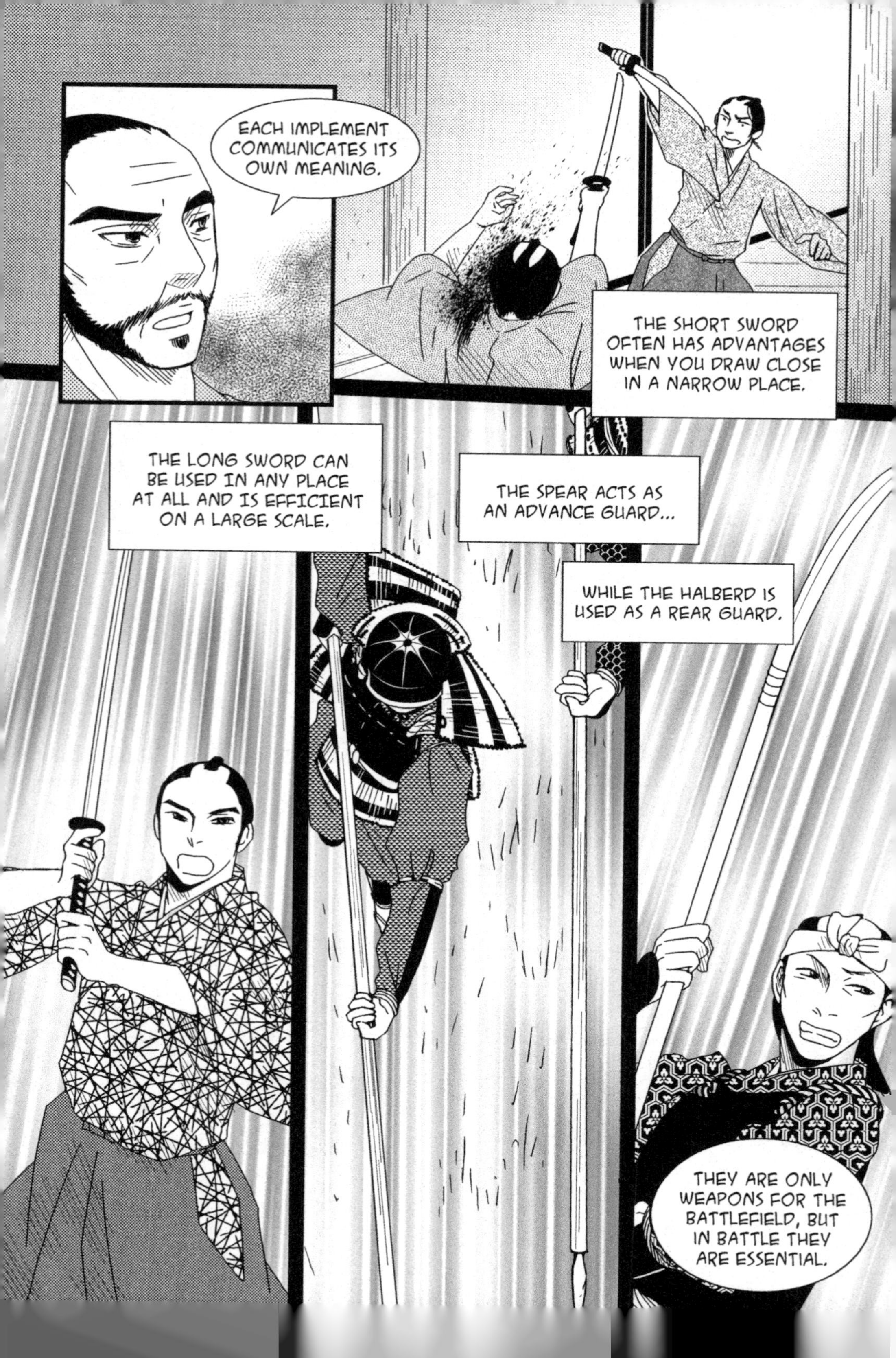
EACH IMPLEMENT COMMUNICATES ITS OWN MEANING.
THE SHORT SWORD OFTEN HAS ADVANTAGES WHEN YOU DRAW CLOSE IN A NARROW PLACE.
THE LONG SWORD CAN BE USED IN ANY PLACE AT ALL AND IS EFFICIENT ON A LARGE SCALE.
THE SPEAR ACTS AS AN ADVANCE GUARD...
WHILE THE HALBERD IS USED AS A REAR GUARD.
THEY ARE ONLY WEAPONS FOR THE BATTLEFIELD, BUT IN BATTLE THEY ARE ESSENTIAL.

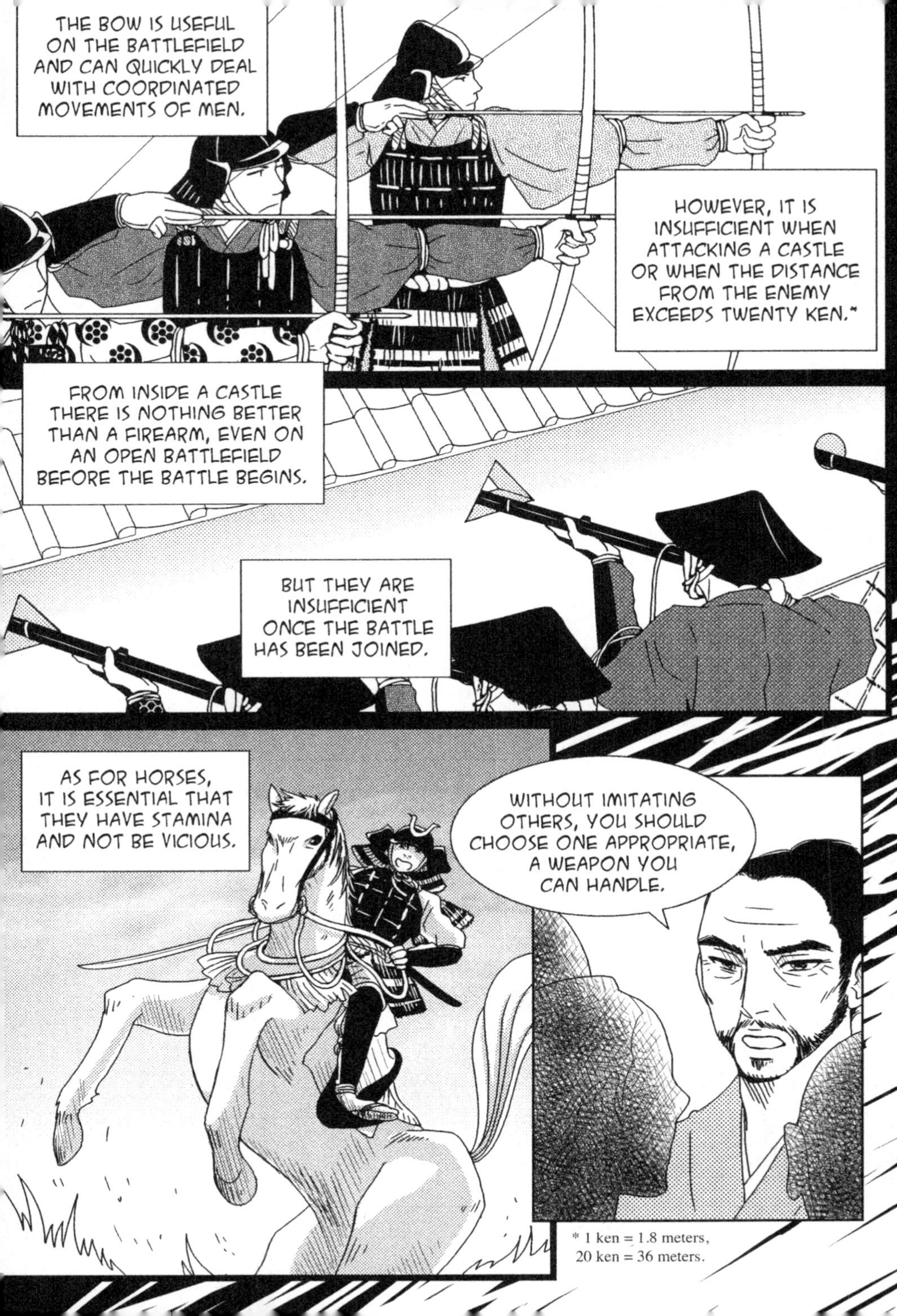
THE BOW IS USEFUL ON THE BATTLEFIELD AND CAN QUICKLY DEAL WITH COORDINATED MOVEMENTS OF MEN.
HOWEVER, IT IS INSUFFICIENT WHEN ATTACKING A CASTLE OR WHEN THE DISTANCE FROM THE ENEMY EXCEEDS TWENTY KEN.*
FROM INSIDE A CASTLE THERE IS NOTHING BETTER THAN A FIREARM, EVEN ON AN OPEN BATTLEFIELD BEFORE THE BATTLE BEGINS.
BUT THEY ARE INSUFFICIENT ONCE THE BATTLE HAS BEEN JOINED.
AS FOR HORSES, IT IS ESSENTIAL THAT THEY HAVE STAMINA AND NOT BE VICIOUS.
WITHOUT IMITATING OTHERS, YOU SHOULD CHOOSE ONE APPROPRIATE, A WEAPON YOU CAN HANDLE.

* 1 ken = 1.8 meters, 20 ken = 36 meters.

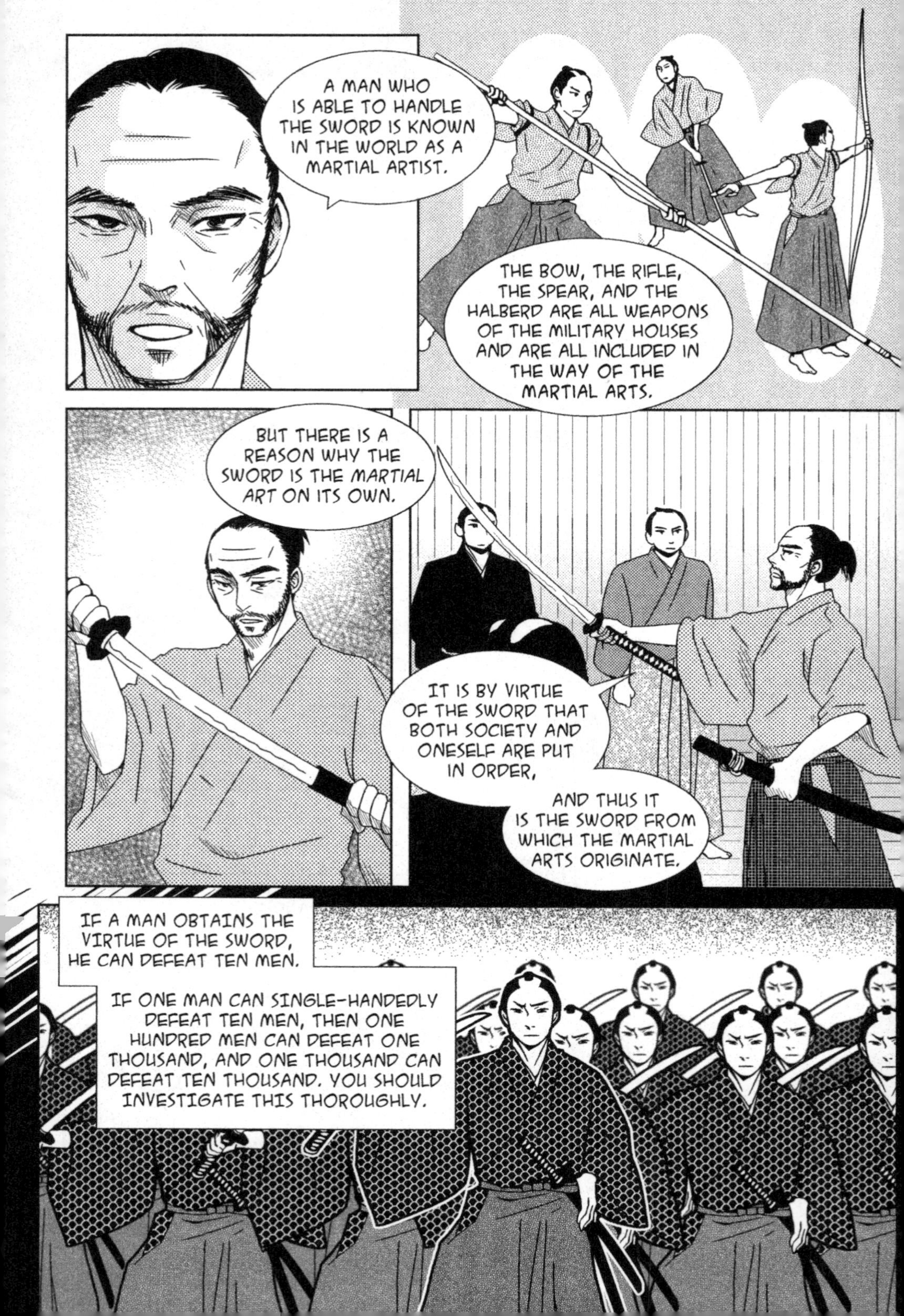
A MAN WHO IS ABLE TO HANDLE THE SWORD IS KNOWN IN THE WORLD AS A MARTIAL ARTIST.
THE BOW, THE RIFLE, THE SPEAR, AND THE HALBERD ARE ALL WEAPONS OF THE MILITARY HOUSES AND ARE ALL INCLUDED IN THE WAY OF THE MARTIAL ARTS.
BUT THERE IS A REASON WHY THE SWORD IS THE *MARTIAL ART* ON ITS OWN.
IT IS BY VIRTUE OF THE SWORD THAT BOTH SOCIETY AND ONESELF ARE PUT IN ORDER,
AND THUS IT IS THE SWORD FROM WHICH THE MARTIAL ARTS ORIGINATE.
IF A MAN OBTAINS THE VIRTUE OF THE SWORD, HE CAN DEFEAT TEN MEN.
IF ONE MAN CAN SINGLE-HANDEDLY DEFEAT TEN MEN, THEN ONE HUNDRED MEN CAN DEFEAT ONE THOUSAND, AND ONE THOUSAND CAN DEFEAT TEN THOUSAND. YOU SHOULD INVESTIGATE THIS THOROUGHLY.

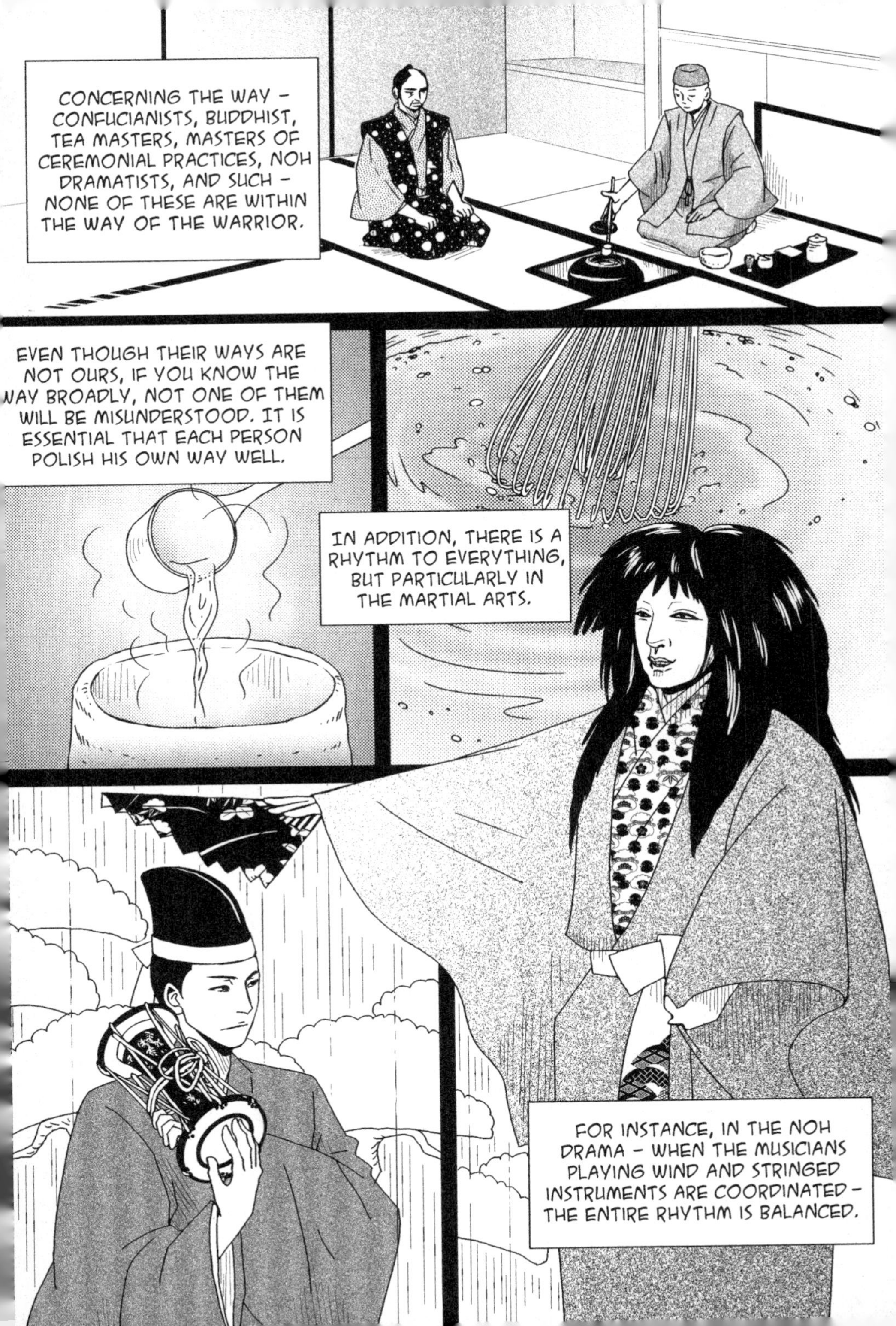
CONCERNING THE WAY – CONFUCIANISTS, BUDDHIST, TEA MASTERS, MASTERS OF CEREMONIAL PRACTICES, NOH DRAMATISTS, AND SUCH – NONE OF THESE ARE WITHIN THE WAY OF THE WARRIOR.
EVEN THOUGH THEIR WAYS ARE NOT OURS, IF YOU KNOW THE WAY BROADLY, NOT ONE OF THEM WILL BE MISUNDERSTOOD. IT IS ESSENTIAL THAT EACH PERSON POLISH HIS OWN WAY WELL.
IN ADDITION, THERE IS A RHYTHM TO EVERYTHING, BUT PARTICULARLY IN THE MARTIAL ARTS.
FOR INSTANCE, IN THE NOH DRAMA – WHEN THE MUSICIANS PLAYING WIND AND STRINGED INSTRUMENTS ARE COORDINATED – THE ENTIRE RHYTHM IS BALANCED.

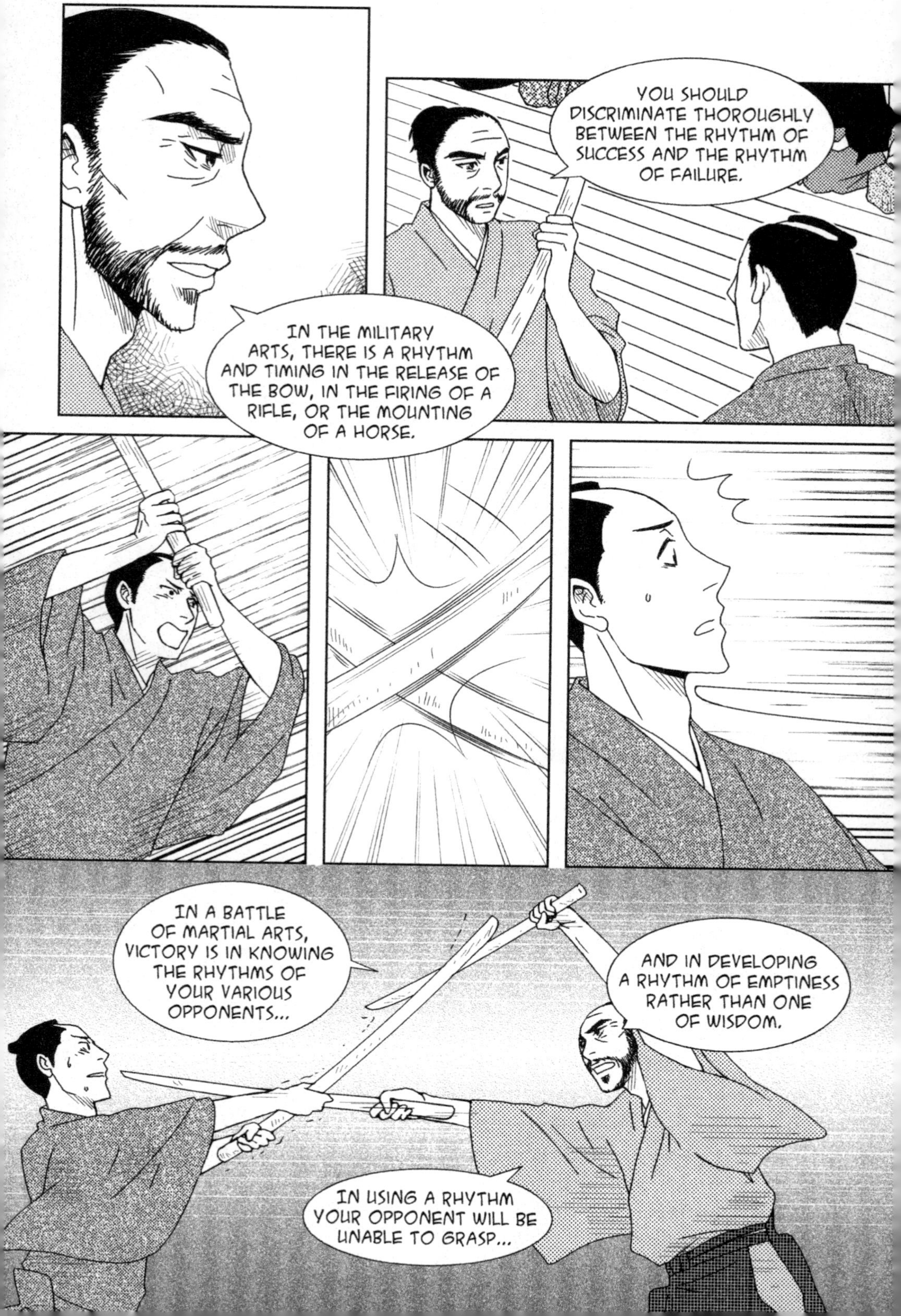
YOU SHOULD DISCRIMINATE THOROUGHLY BETWEEN THE RHYTHM OF SUCCESS AND THE RHYTHM OF FAILURE.
IN THE MILITARY ARTS, THERE IS A RHYTHM AND TIMING IN THE RELEASE OF THE BOW, IN THE FIRING OF A RIFLE, OR THE MOUNTING OF A HORSE.
IN A BATTLE OF MARTIAL ARTS, VICTORY IS IN KNOWING THE RHYTHMS OF YOUR VARIOUS OPPONENTS...
AND IN DEVELOPING A RHYTHM OF EMPTINESS RATHER THAN ONE OF WISDOM.
IN USING A RHYTHM YOUR OPPONENT WILL BE UNABLE TO GRASP...

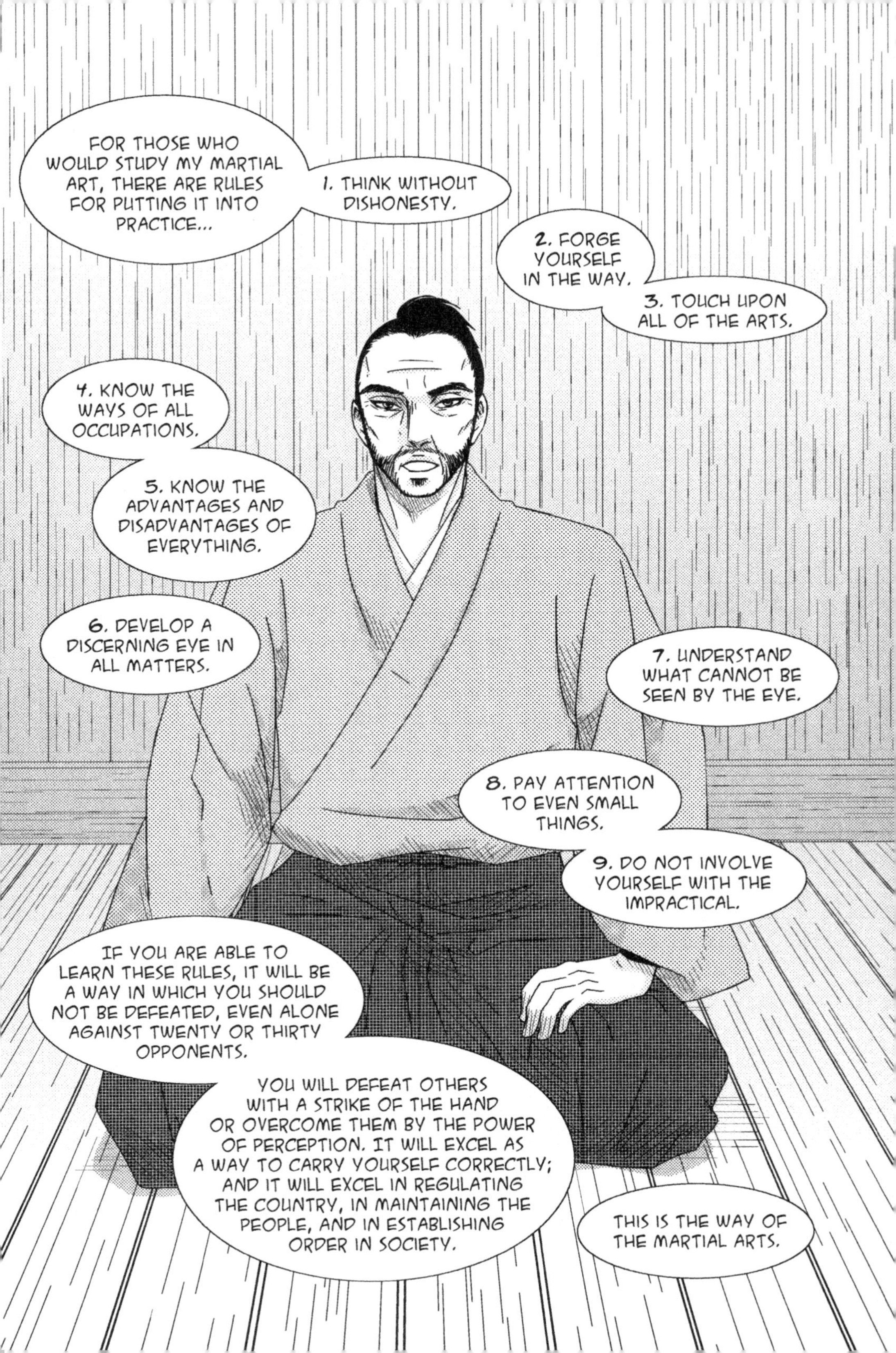
FOR THOSE WHO WOULD STUDY MY MARTIAL ART, THERE ARE RULES FOR PUTTING IT INTO PRACTICE...
1. THINK WITHOUT DISHONESTY.
2. FORGE YOURSELF IN THE WAY.
3. TOUCH UPON ALL OF THE ARTS.
4. KNOW THE WAYS OF ALL OCCUPATIONS.
5. KNOW THE ADVANTAGES AND DISADVANTAGES OF EVERYTHING.
6. DEVELOP A DISCERNING EYE IN ALL MATTERS.
7. UNDERSTAND WHAT CANNOT BE SEEN BY THE EYE.
8. PAY ATTENTION TO EVEN SMALL THINGS.
9. DO NOT INVOLVE YOURSELF WITH THE IMPRACTICAL.
IF YOU ARE ABLE TO LEARN THESE RULES, IT WILL BE A WAY IN WHICH YOU SHOULD NOT BE DEFEATED, EVEN ALONE AGAINST TWENTY OR THIRTY OPPONENTS.
YOU WILL DEFEAT OTHERS WITH A STRIKE OF THE HAND OR OVERCOME THEM BY THE POWER OF PERCEPTION. IT WILL EXCEL AS A WAY TO CARRY YOURSELF CORRECTLY; AND IT WILL EXCEL IN REGULATING THE COUNTRY, IN MAINTAINING THE PEOPLE, AND IN ESTABLISHING ORDER IN SOCIETY.
THIS IS THE WAY OF THE MARTIAL ARTS.

2
WATER

水

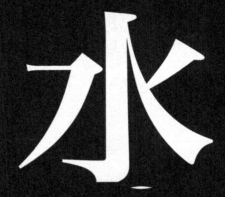

In the Way of Martial Arts, do not let your frame of mind be any different from your everyday mind. In both everyday and military events, your mind should not change in the least, but should be broad and straightforward, neither drawn too tight nor allowed to slacken even a little.

Keep your mind in the exact center, not allowing it to become sidetracked; let it sway peacefully, not allowing it to stop doing so for even a moment. You should investigate these things thoroughly.

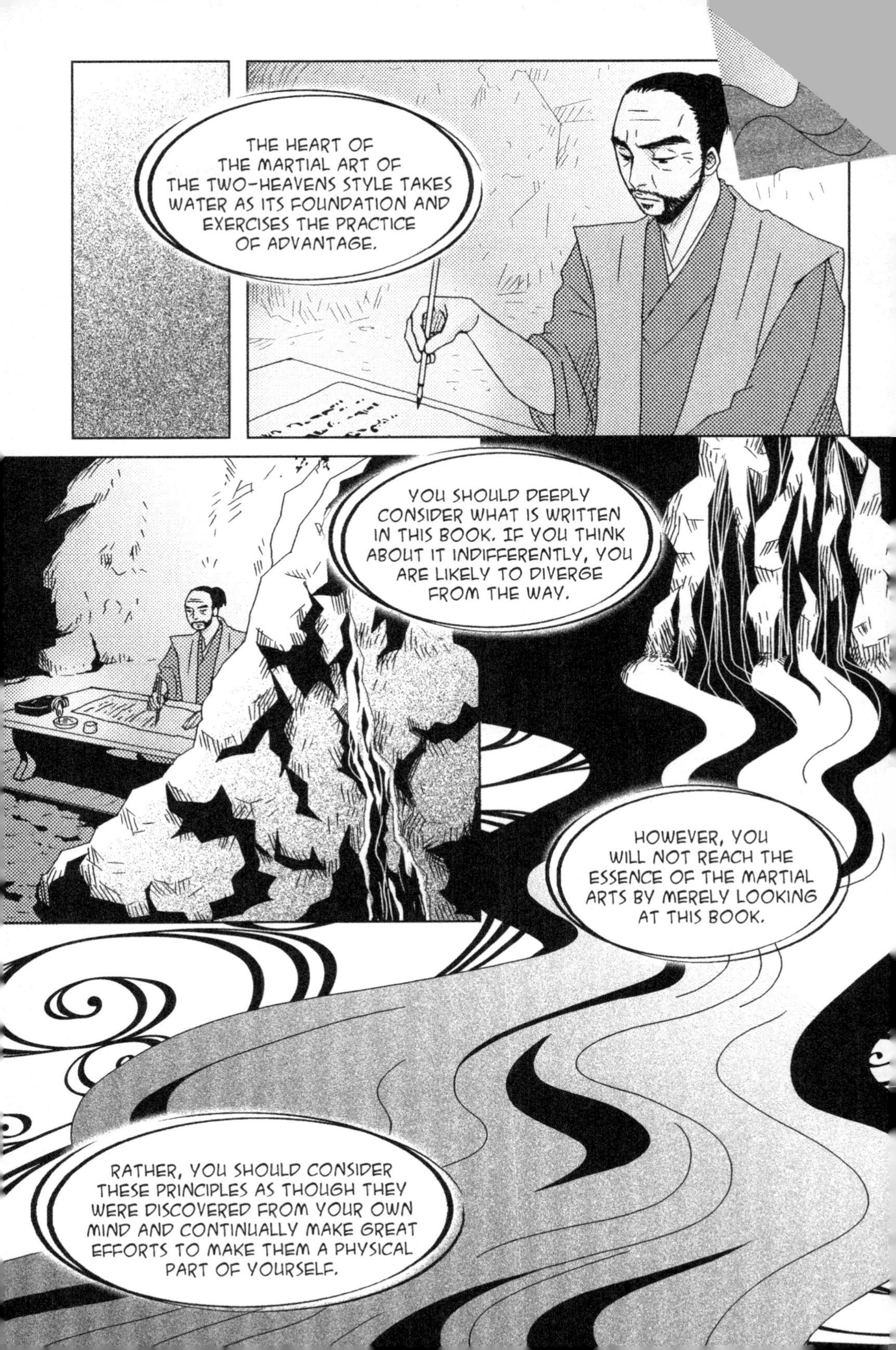
THE HEART OF THE MARTIAL ART OF THE TWO-HEAVENS STYLE TAKES WATER AS ITS FOUNDATION AND EXERCISES THE PRACTICE OF ADVANTAGE.
YOU SHOULD DEEPLY CONSIDER WHAT IS WRITTEN IN THIS BOOK. IF YOU THINK ABOUT IT INDIFFERENTLY, YOU ARE LIKELY TO DIVERGE FROM THE WAY.
HOWEVER, YOU WILL NOT REACH THE ESSENCE OF THE MARTIAL ARTS BY MERELY LOOKING AT THIS BOOK.
RATHER, YOU SHOULD CONSIDER THESE PRINCIPLES AS THOUGH THEY WERE DISCOVERED FROM YOUR OWN MIND AND CONTINUALLY MAKE GREAT EFFORTS TO MAKE THEM A PHYSICAL PART OF YOURSELF.

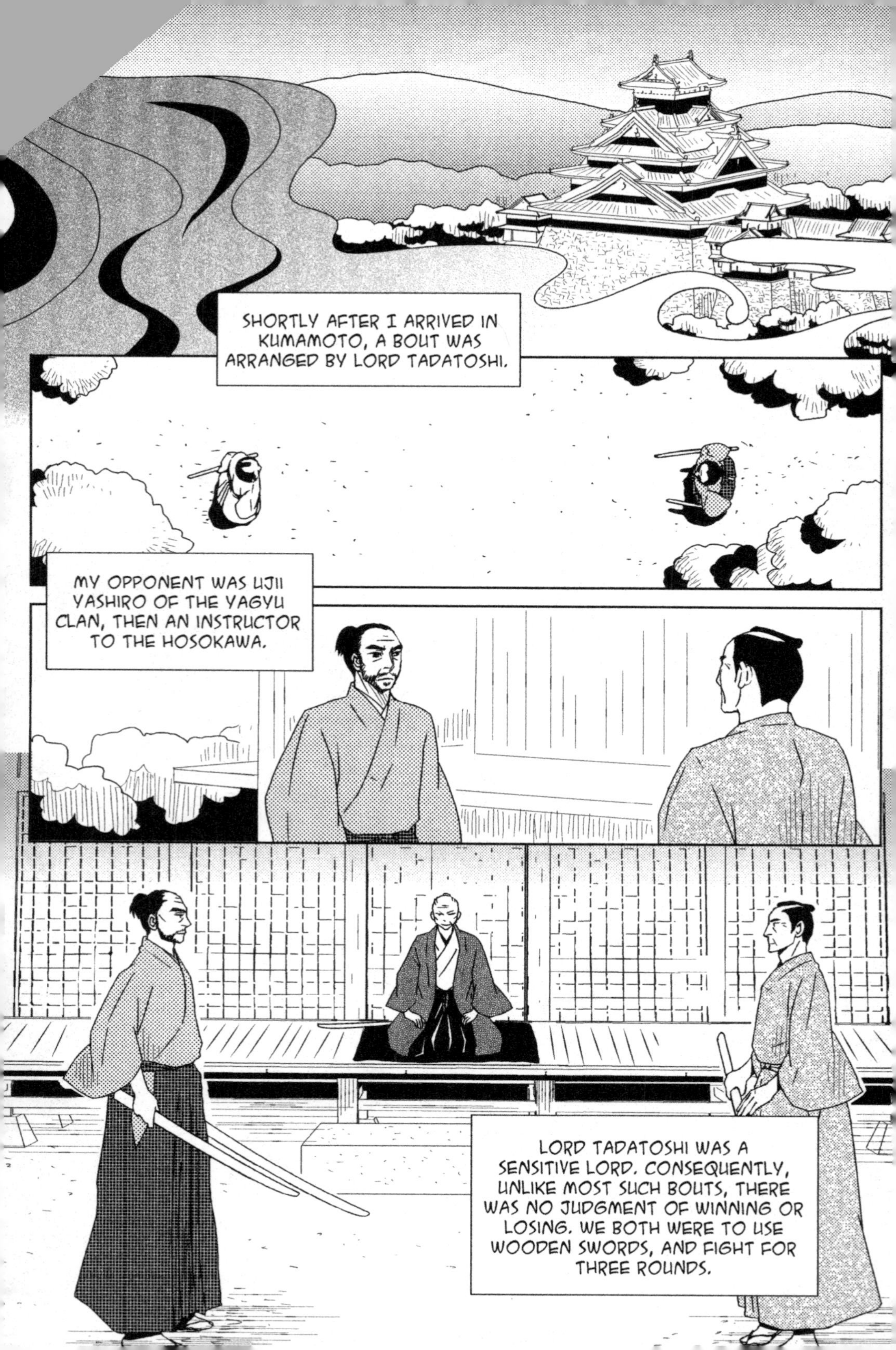
SHORTLY AFTER I ARRIVED IN KUMAMOTO, A BOUT WAS ARRANGED BY LORD TADATOSHI.
MY OPPONENT WAS UJII YASHIRO OF THE YAGYU CLAN, THEN AN INSTRUCTOR TO THE HOSOKAWA.
LORD TADATOSHI WAS A SENSITIVE LORD. CONSEQUENTLY, UNLIKE MOST SUCH BOUTS, THERE WAS NO JUDGMENT OF WINNING OR LOSING. WE BOTH WERE TO USE WOODEN SWORDS, AND FIGHT FOR THREE ROUNDS.

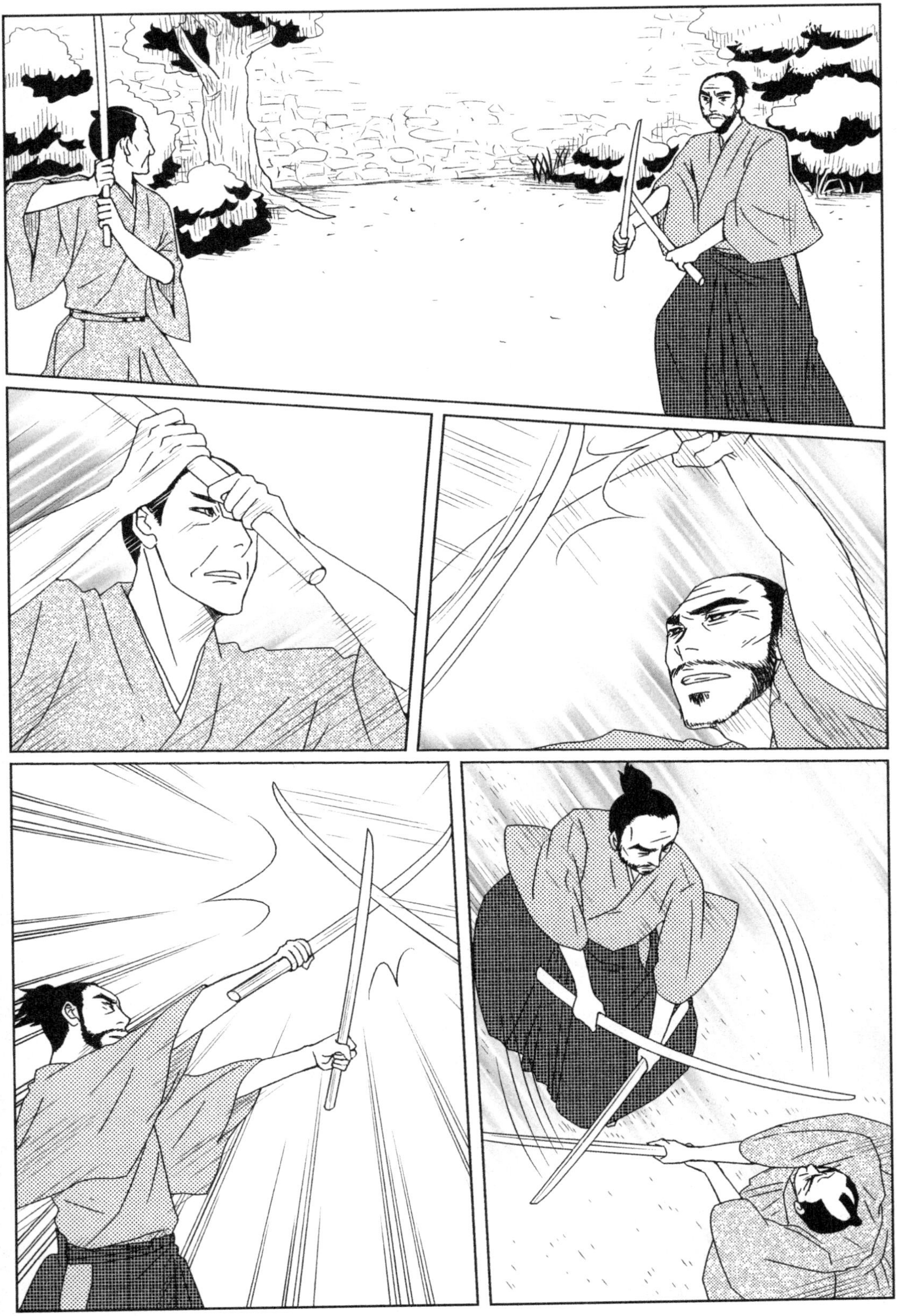

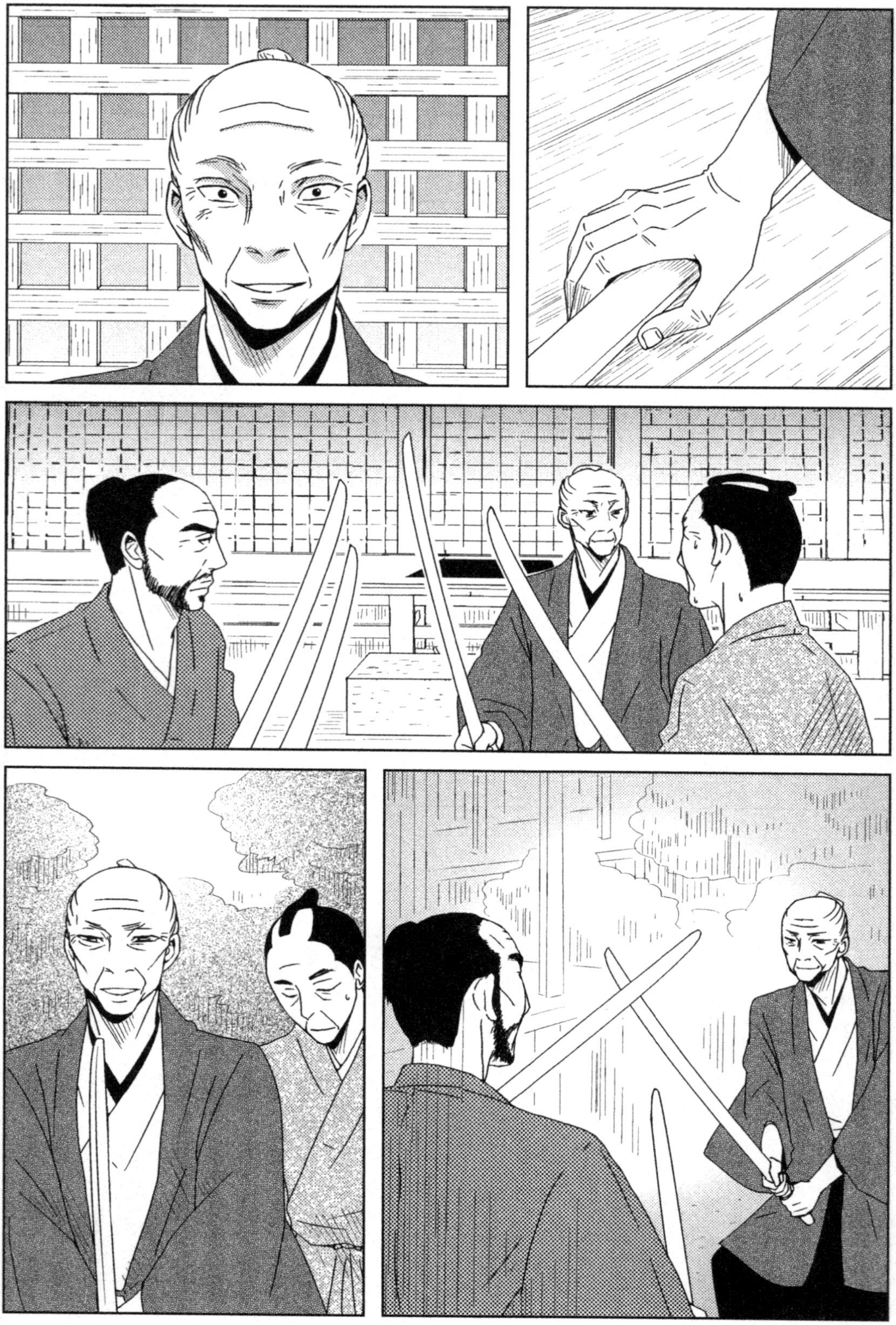

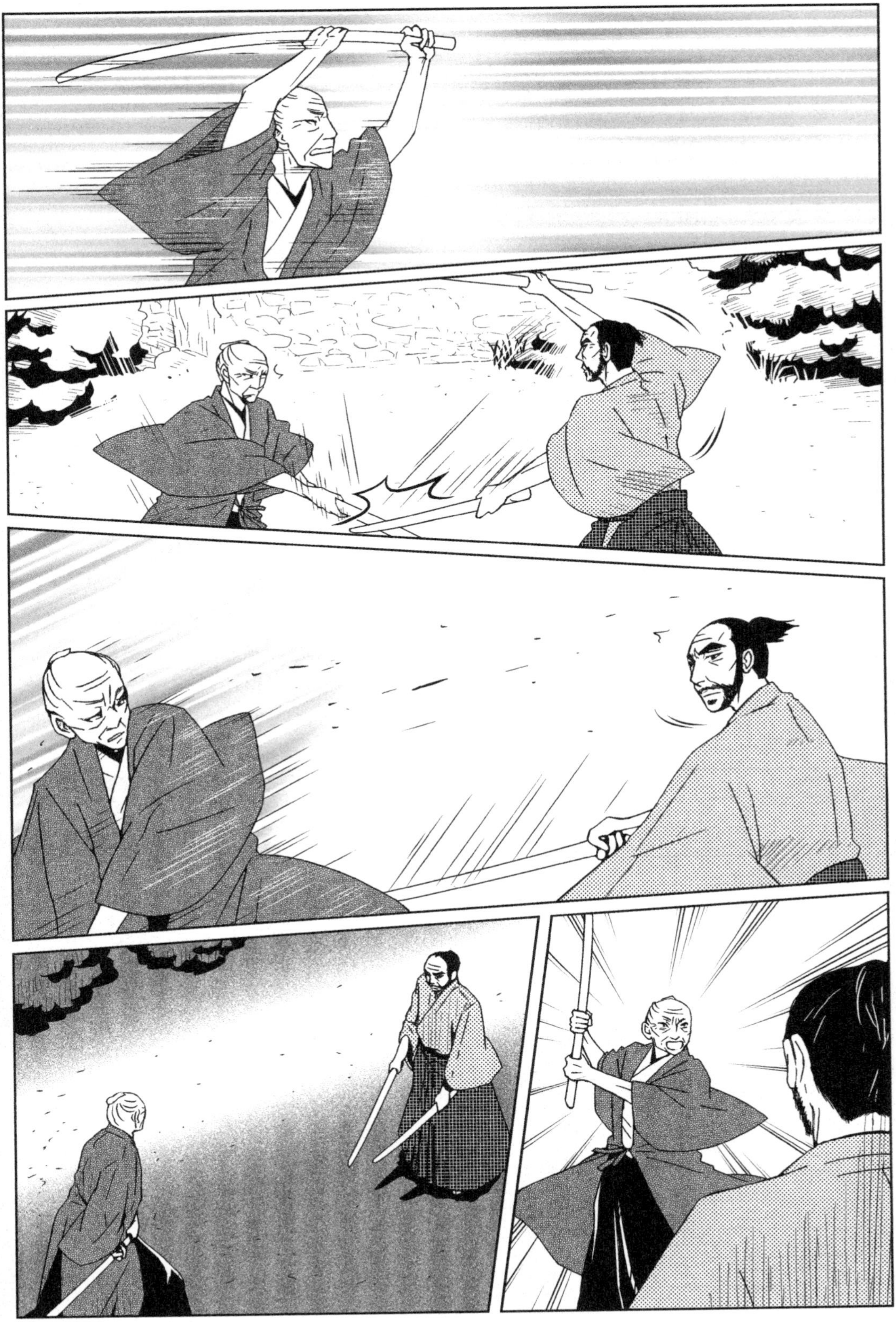

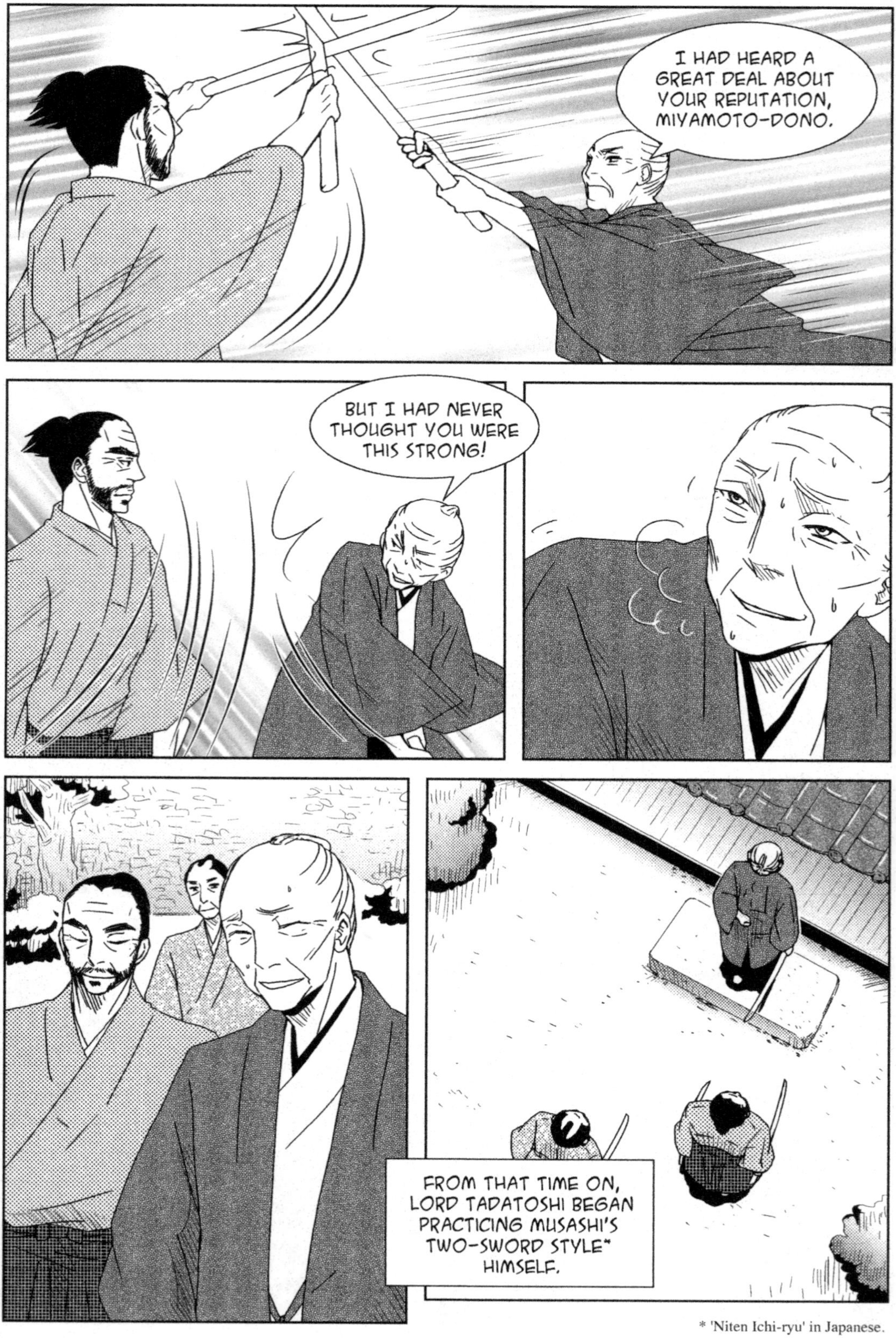
I HAD HEARD A GREAT DEAL ABOUT YOUR REPUTATION, MIYAMOTO-DONO.
BUT I HAD NEVER THOUGHT YOU WERE THIS STRONG!
FROM THAT TIME ON, LORD TADATOSHI BEGAN PRACTICING MUSASHI'S TWO-SWORD STYLE* HIMSELF.

* 'Niten Ichi-ryu' in Japanese.

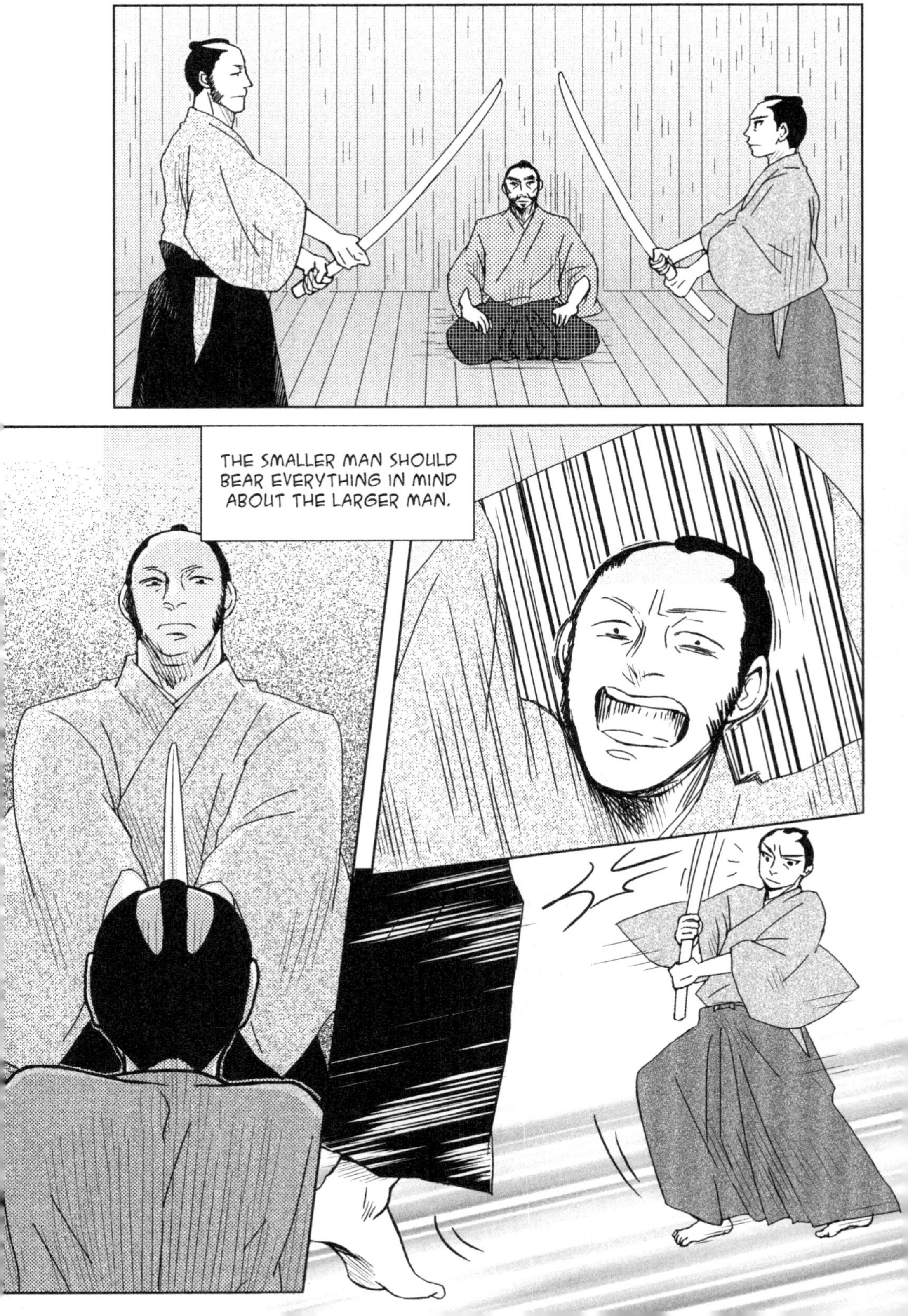
THE SMALLER MAN SHOULD BEAR EVERYTHING IN MIND ABOUT THE LARGER MAN.

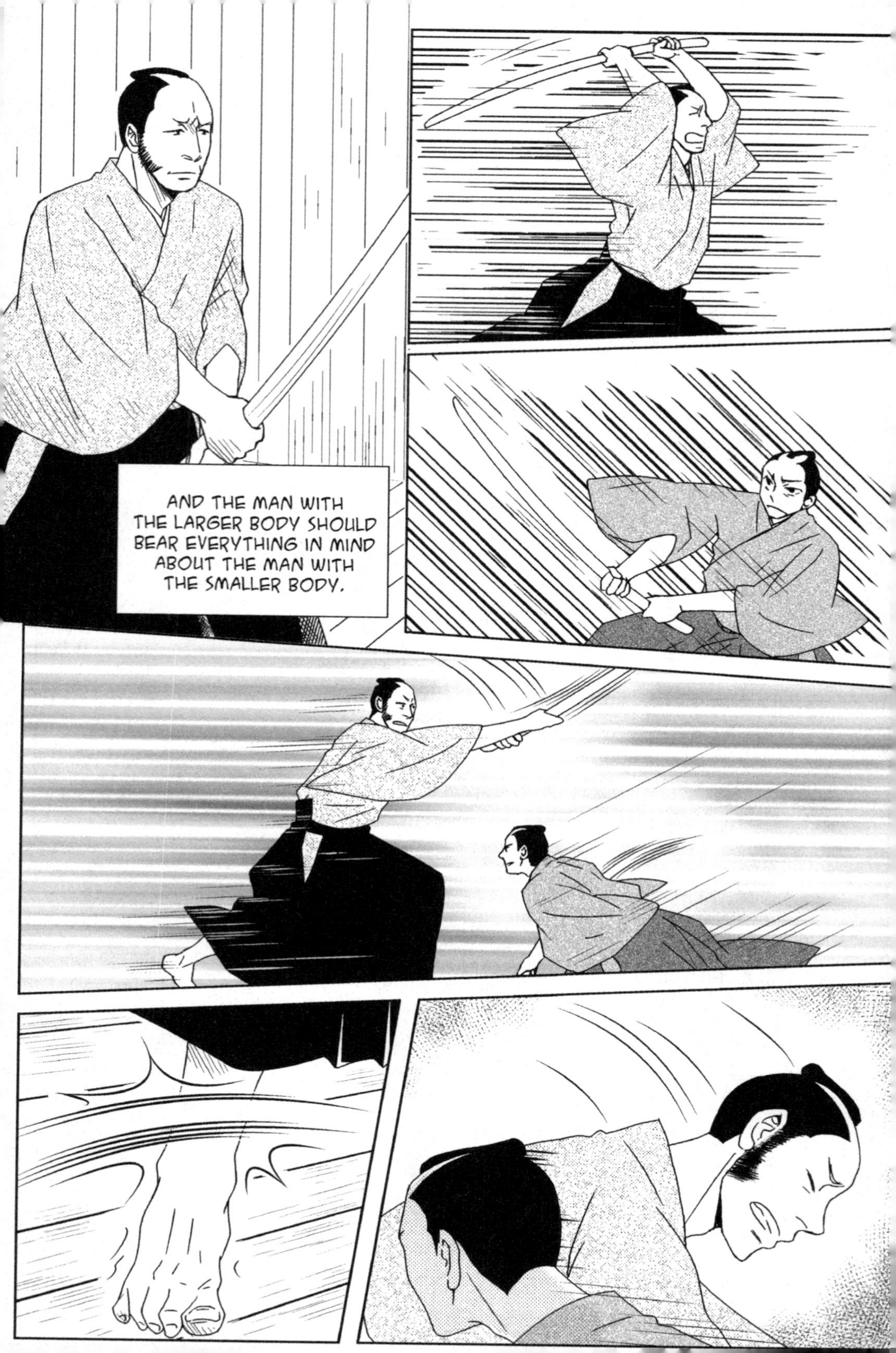
AND THE MAN WITH THE LARGER BODY SHOULD BEAR EVERYTHING IN MIND ABOUT THE MAN WITH THE SMALLER BODY.

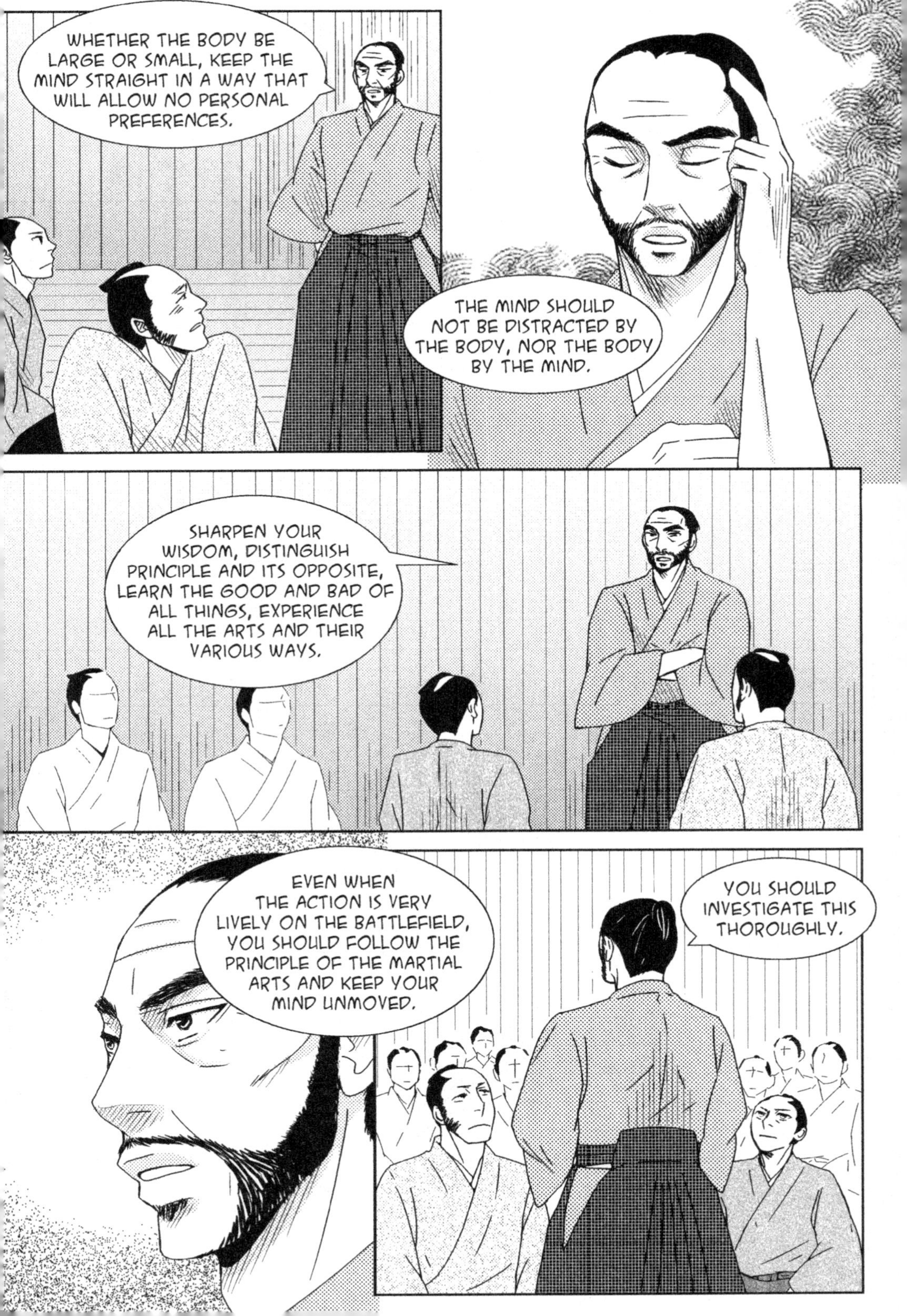
WHETHER THE BODY BE LARGE OR SMALL, KEEP THE MIND STRAIGHT IN A WAY THAT WILL ALLOW NO PERSONAL PREFERENCES.
THE MIND SHOULD NOT BE DISTRACTED BY THE BODY, NOR THE BODY BY THE MIND.
SHARPEN YOUR WISDOM, DISTINGUISH PRINCIPLE AND ITS OPPOSITE, LEARN THE GOOD AND BAD OF ALL THINGS, EXPERIENCE ALL THE ARTS AND THEIR VARIOUS WAYS.
EVEN WHEN THE ACTION IS VERY LIVELY ON THE BATTLEFIELD, YOU SHOULD FOLLOW THE PRINCIPLE OF THE MARTIAL ARTS AND KEEP YOUR MIND UNMOVED.
YOU SHOULD INVESTIGATE THIS THOROUGHLY.

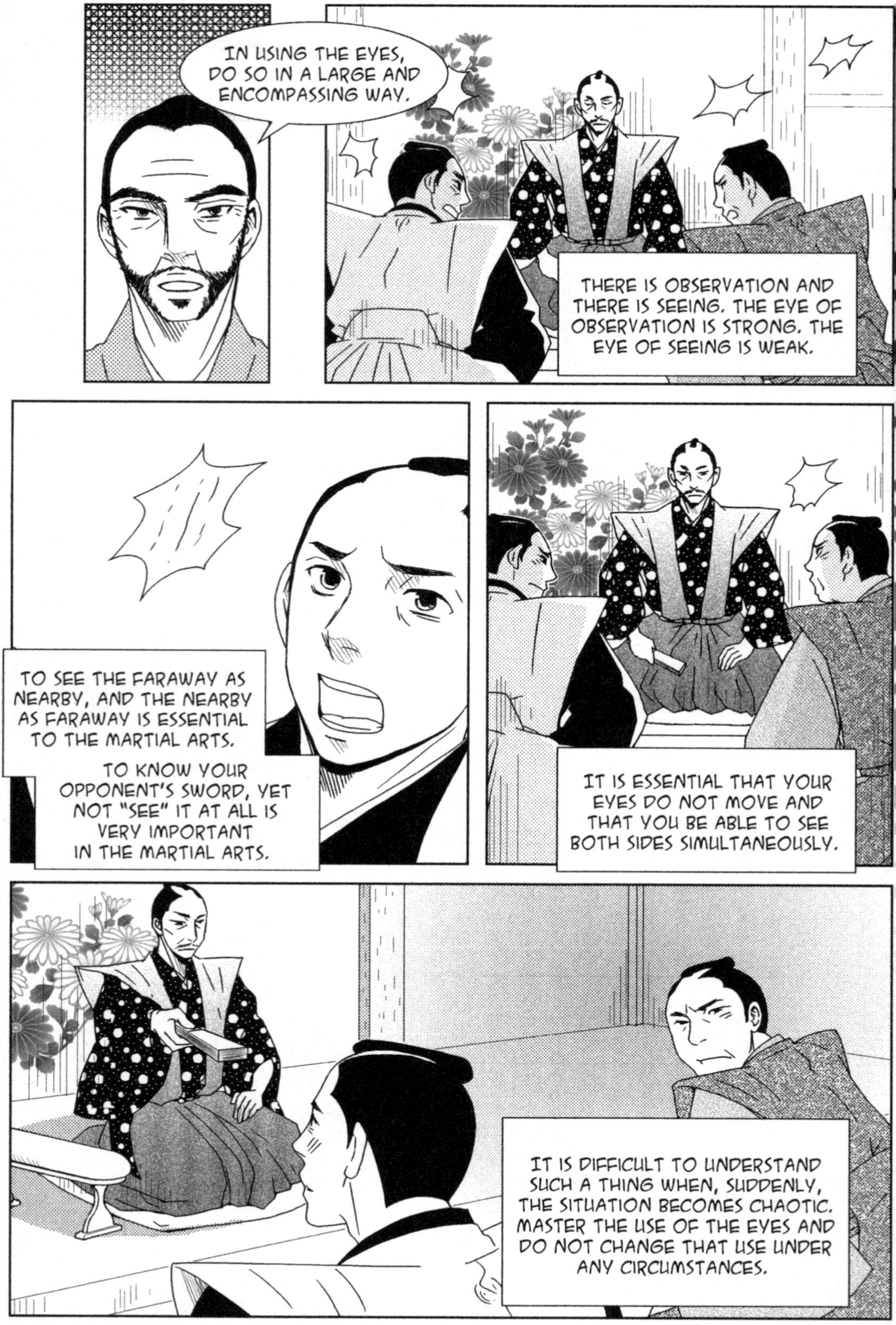

IN USING THE EYES, DO SO IN A LARGE AND ENCOMPASSING WAY.
THERE IS OBSERVATION AND THERE IS SEEING. THE EYE OF OBSERVATION IS STRONG. THE EYE OF SEEING IS WEAK.
TO SEE THE FARAWAY AS NEARBY, AND THE NEARBY AS FARAWAY IS ESSENTIAL TO THE MARTIAL ARTS.
TO KNOW YOUR OPPONENT'S SWORD, YET NOT "SEE" IT AT ALL IS VERY IMPORTANT IN THE MARTIAL ARTS.
IT IS ESSENTIAL THAT YOUR EYES DO NOT MOVE AND THAT YOU BE ABLE TO SEE BOTH SIDES SIMULTANEOUSLY.
IT IS DIFFICULT TO UNDERSTAND SUCH A THING WHEN, SUDDENLY, THE SITUATION BECOMES CHAOTIC. MASTER THE USE OF THE EYES AND DO NOT CHANGE THAT USE UNDER ANY CIRCUMSTANCES.

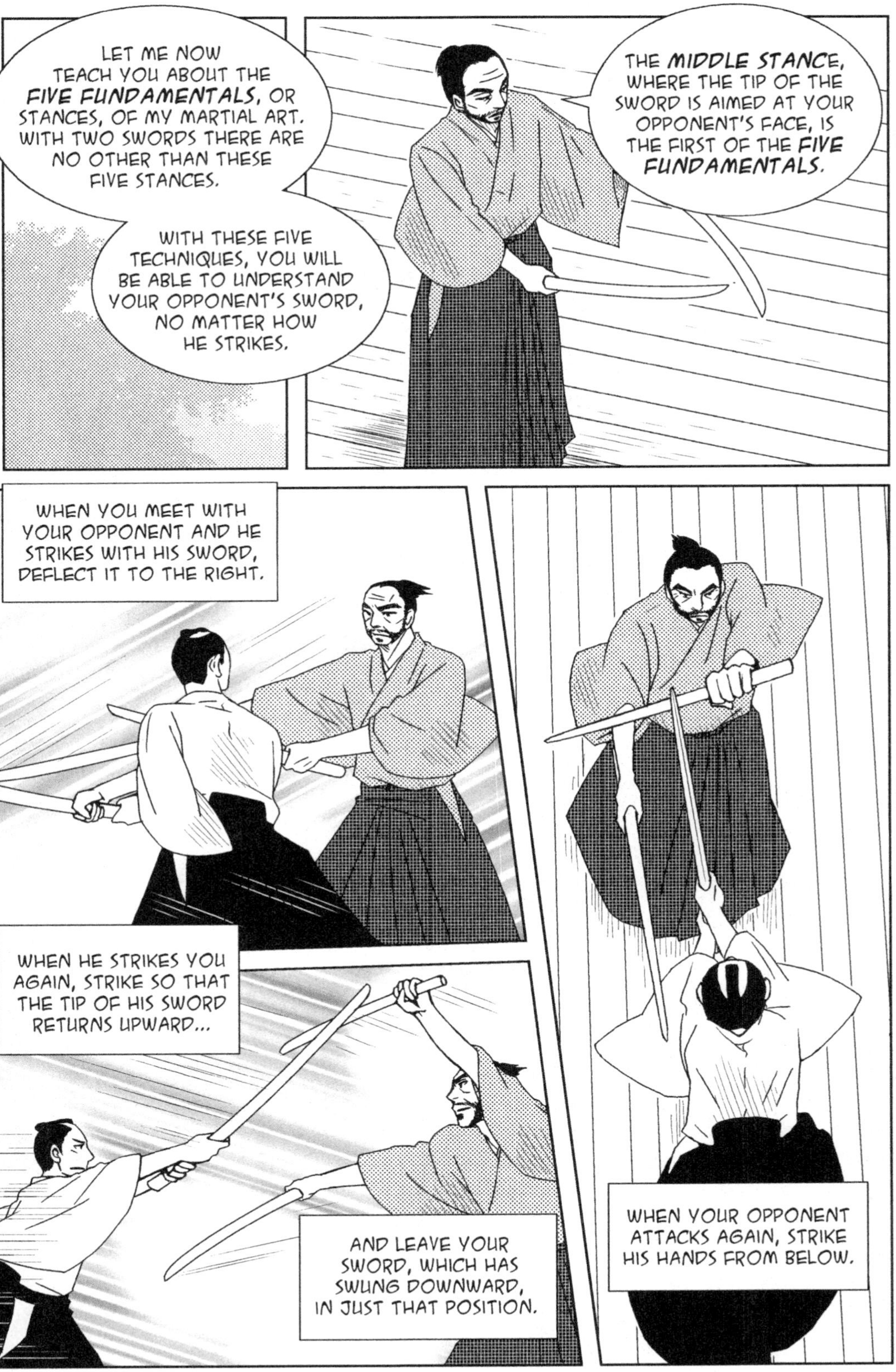
LET ME NOW TEACH YOU ABOUT THE ***FIVE FUNDAMENTALS***, OR STANCES, OF MY MARTIAL ART. WITH TWO SWORDS THERE ARE NO OTHER THAN THESE FIVE STANCES.
WITH THESE FIVE TECHNIQUES, YOU WILL BE ABLE TO UNDERSTAND YOUR OPPONENT'S SWORD, NO MATTER HOW HE STRIKES.
THE ***MIDDLE STANCE***, WHERE THE TIP OF THE SWORD IS AIMED AT YOUR OPPONENT'S FACE, IS THE FIRST OF THE ***FIVE FUNDAMENTALS***.
WHEN YOU MEET WITH YOUR OPPONENT AND HE STRIKES WITH HIS SWORD, DEFLECT IT TO THE RIGHT.
WHEN YOUR OPPONENT ATTACKS AGAIN, STRIKE HIS HANDS FROM BELOW.
WHEN HE STRIKES YOU AGAIN, STRIKE SO THAT THE TIP OF HIS SWORD RETURNS UPWARD...
AND LEAVE YOUR SWORD, WHICH HAS SWUNG DOWNWARD, IN JUST THAT POSITION.

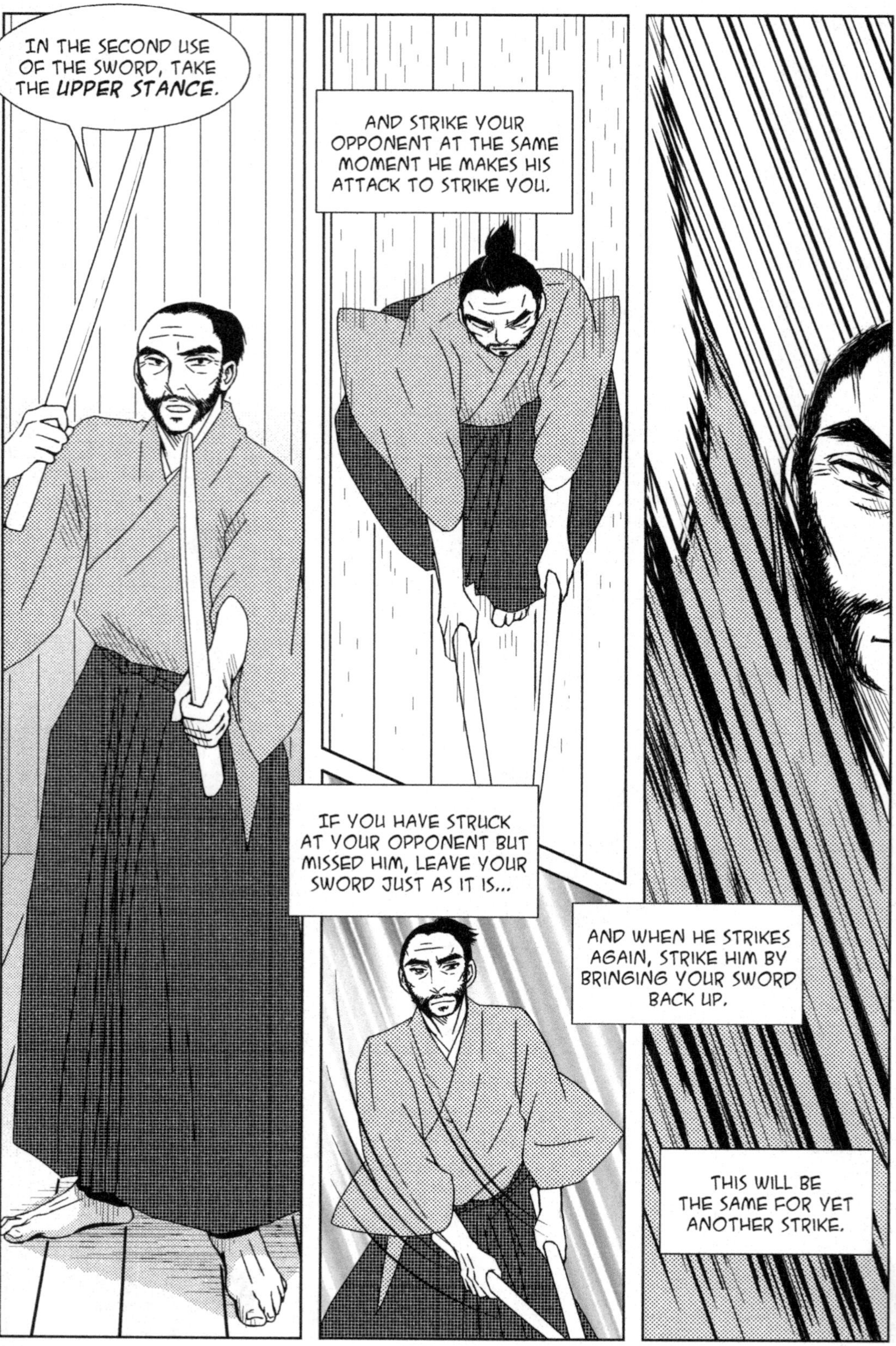
IN THE SECOND USE OF THE SWORD, TAKE THE UPPER STANCE.
AND STRIKE YOUR OPPONENT AT THE SAME MOMENT HE MAKES HIS ATTACK TO STRIKE YOU.
IF YOU HAVE STRUCK AT YOUR OPPONENT BUT MISSED HIM, LEAVE YOUR SWORD JUST AS IT IS...
AND WHEN HE STRIKES AGAIN, STRIKE HIM BY BRINGING YOUR SWORD BACK UP.
THIS WILL BE THE SAME FOR YET ANOTHER STRIKE.

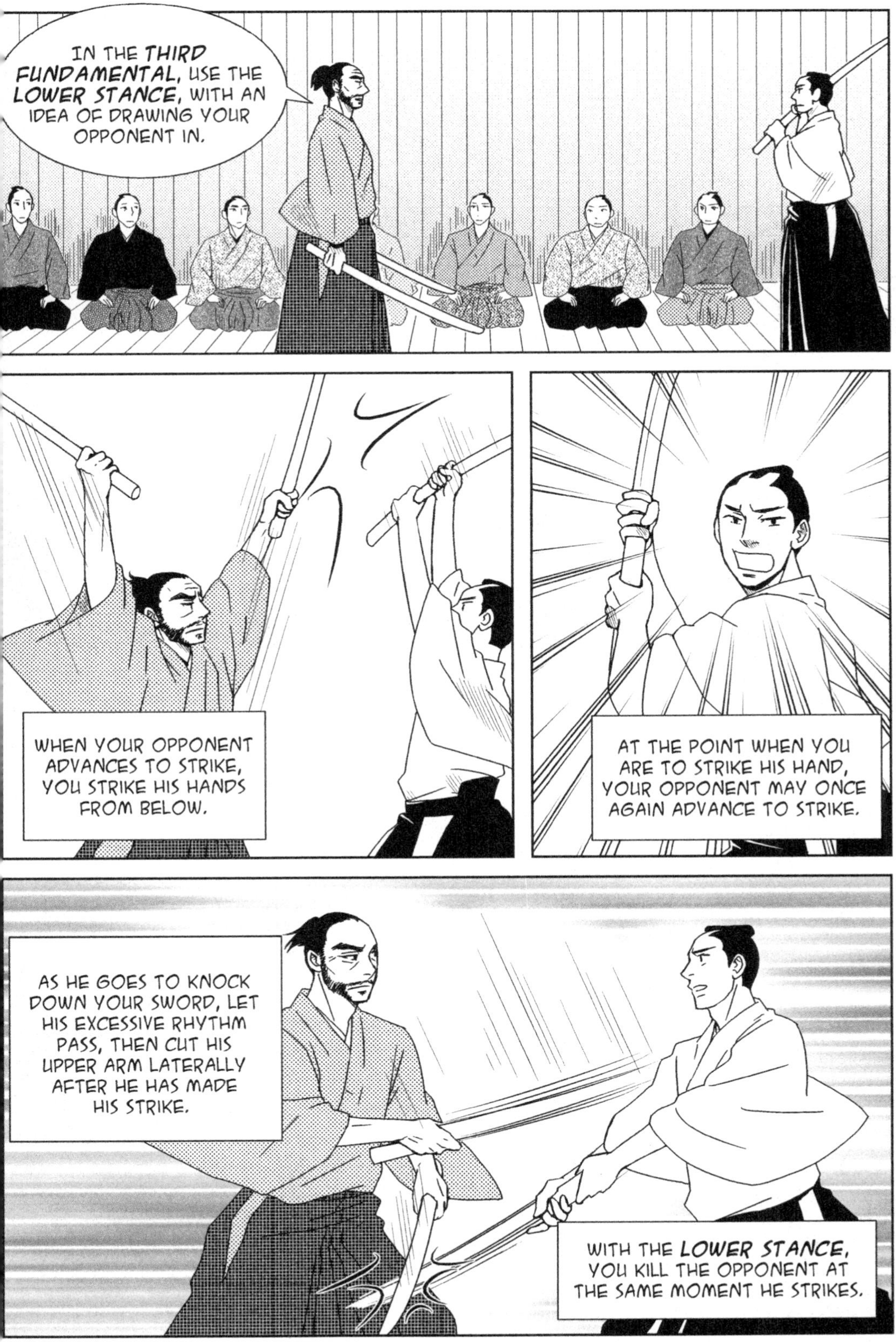
IN THE **THIRD FUNDAMENTAL,** USE THE **LOWER STANCE,** WITH AN IDEA OF DRAWING YOUR OPPONENT IN.
WHEN YOUR OPPONENT ADVANCES TO STRIKE, YOU STRIKE HIS HANDS FROM BELOW.
AT THE POINT WHEN YOU ARE TO STRIKE HIS HAND, YOUR OPPONENT MAY ONCE AGAIN ADVANCE TO STRIKE.
AS HE GOES TO KNOCK DOWN YOUR SWORD, LET HIS EXCESSIVE RHYTHM PASS, THEN CUT HIS UPPER ARM LATERALLY AFTER HE HAS MADE HIS STRIKE.
WITH THE **LOWER STANCE,** YOU KILL THE OPPONENT AT THE SAME MOMENT HE STRIKES.

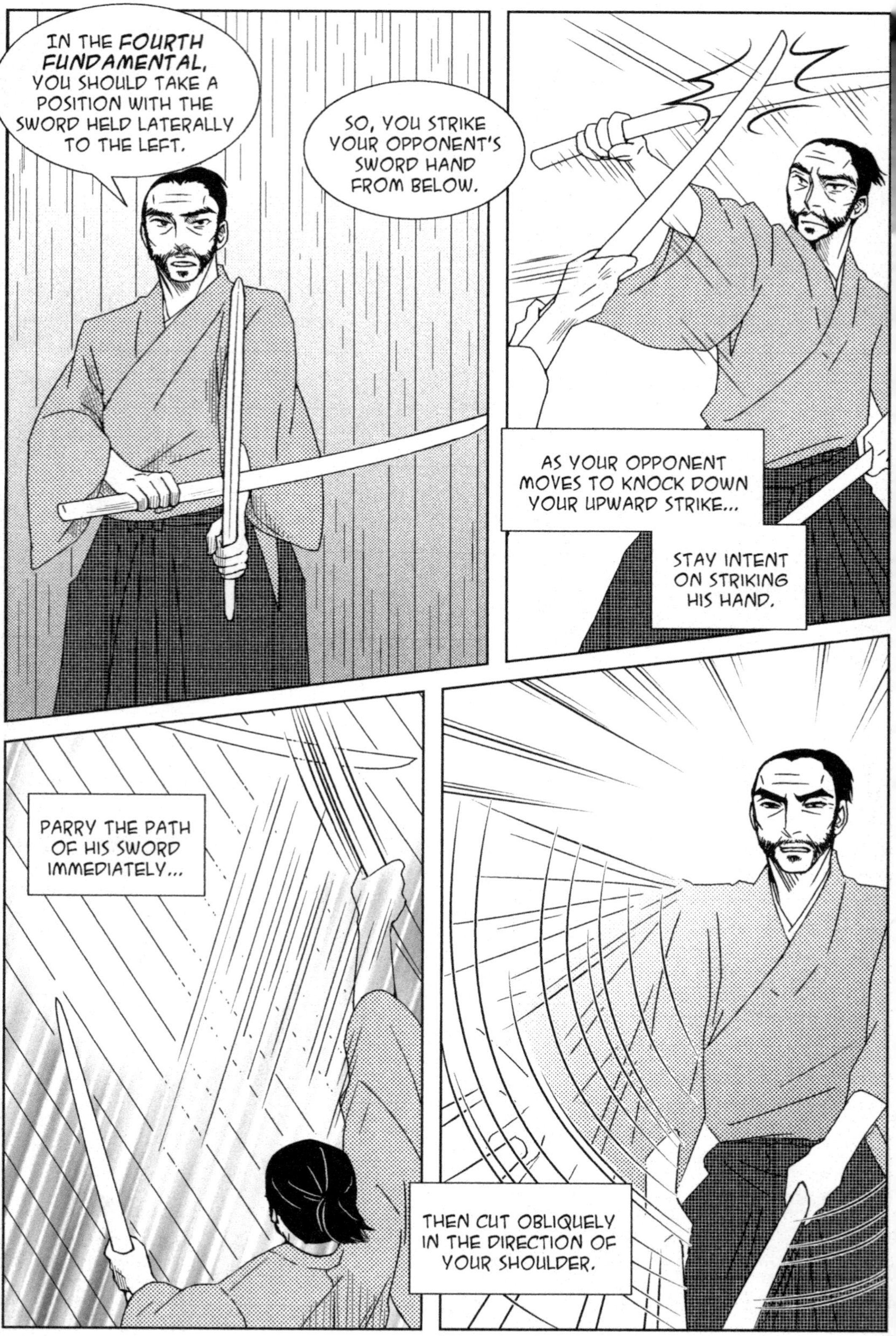
IN THE *FOURTH FUNDAMENTAL*, YOU SHOULD TAKE A POSITION WITH THE SWORD HELD LATERALLY TO THE LEFT.
SO, YOU STRIKE YOUR OPPONENT'S SWORD HAND FROM BELOW.
AS YOUR OPPONENT MOVES TO KNOCK DOWN YOUR UPWARD STRIKE...
STAY INTENT ON STRIKING HIS HAND.
PARRY THE PATH OF HIS SWORD IMMEDIATELY...
THEN CUT OBLIQUELY IN THE DIRECTION OF YOUR SHOULDER.

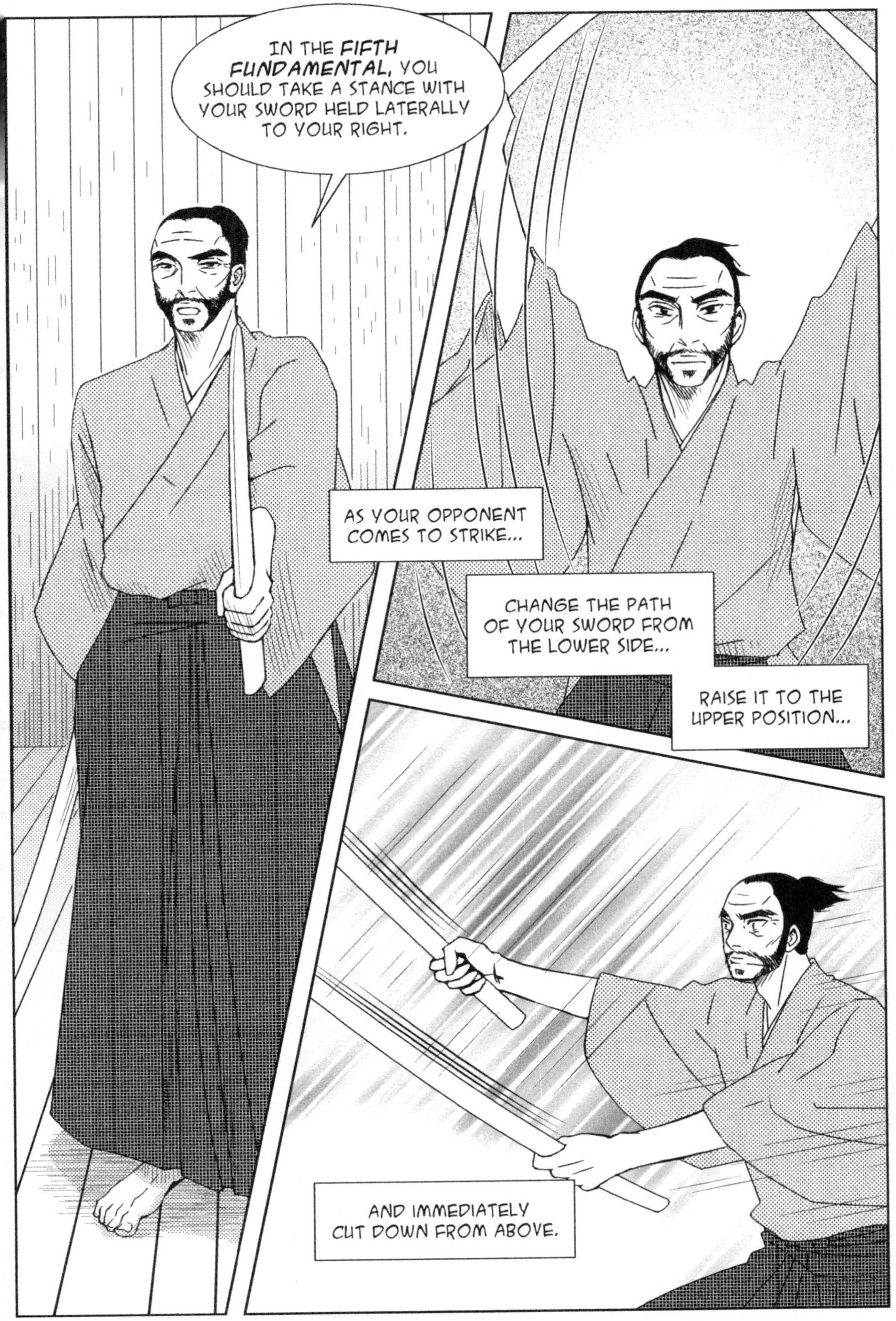
IN THE **FIFTH FUNDAMENTAL**, YOU SHOULD TAKE A STANCE WITH YOUR SWORD HELD LATERALLY TO YOUR RIGHT.
AS YOUR OPPONENT COMES TO STRIKE...
CHANGE THE PATH OF YOUR SWORD FROM THE LOWER SIDE...
RAISE IT TO THE UPPER POSITION...
AND IMMEDIATELY CUT DOWN FROM ABOVE.

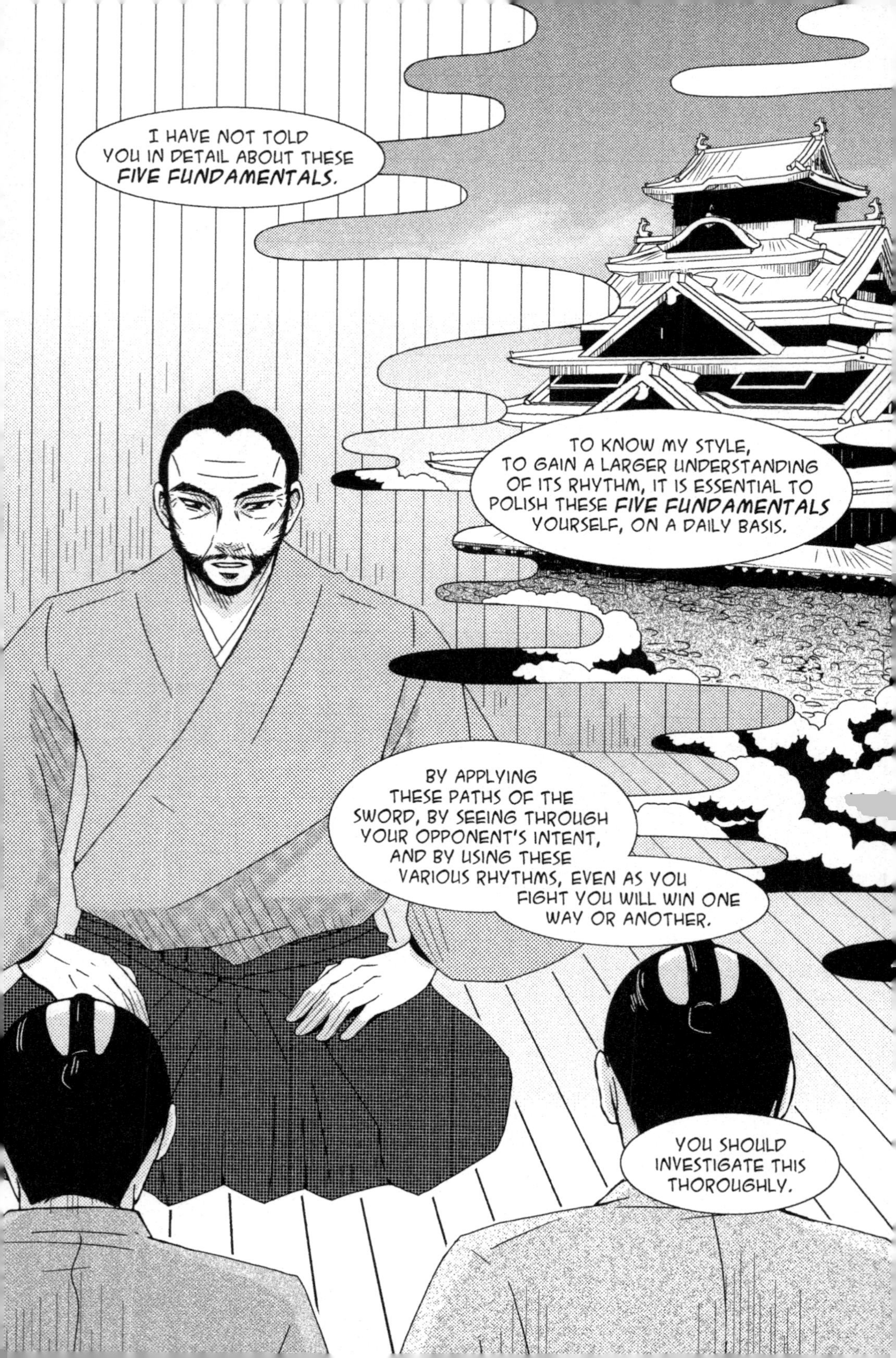
I HAVE NOT TOLD YOU IN DETAIL ABOUT THESE *FIVE FUNDAMENTALS.*
TO KNOW MY STYLE, TO GAIN A LARGER UNDERSTANDING OF ITS RHYTHM, IT IS ESSENTIAL TO POLISH THESE *FIVE FUNDAMENTALS* YOURSELF, ON A DAILY BASIS.
BY APPLYING THESE PATHS OF THE SWORD, BY SEEING THROUGH YOUR OPPONENT'S INTENT, AND BY USING THESE VARIOUS RHYTHMS, EVEN AS YOU FIGHT YOU WILL WIN ONE WAY OR ANOTHER.
YOU SHOULD INVESTIGATE THIS THOROUGHLY.

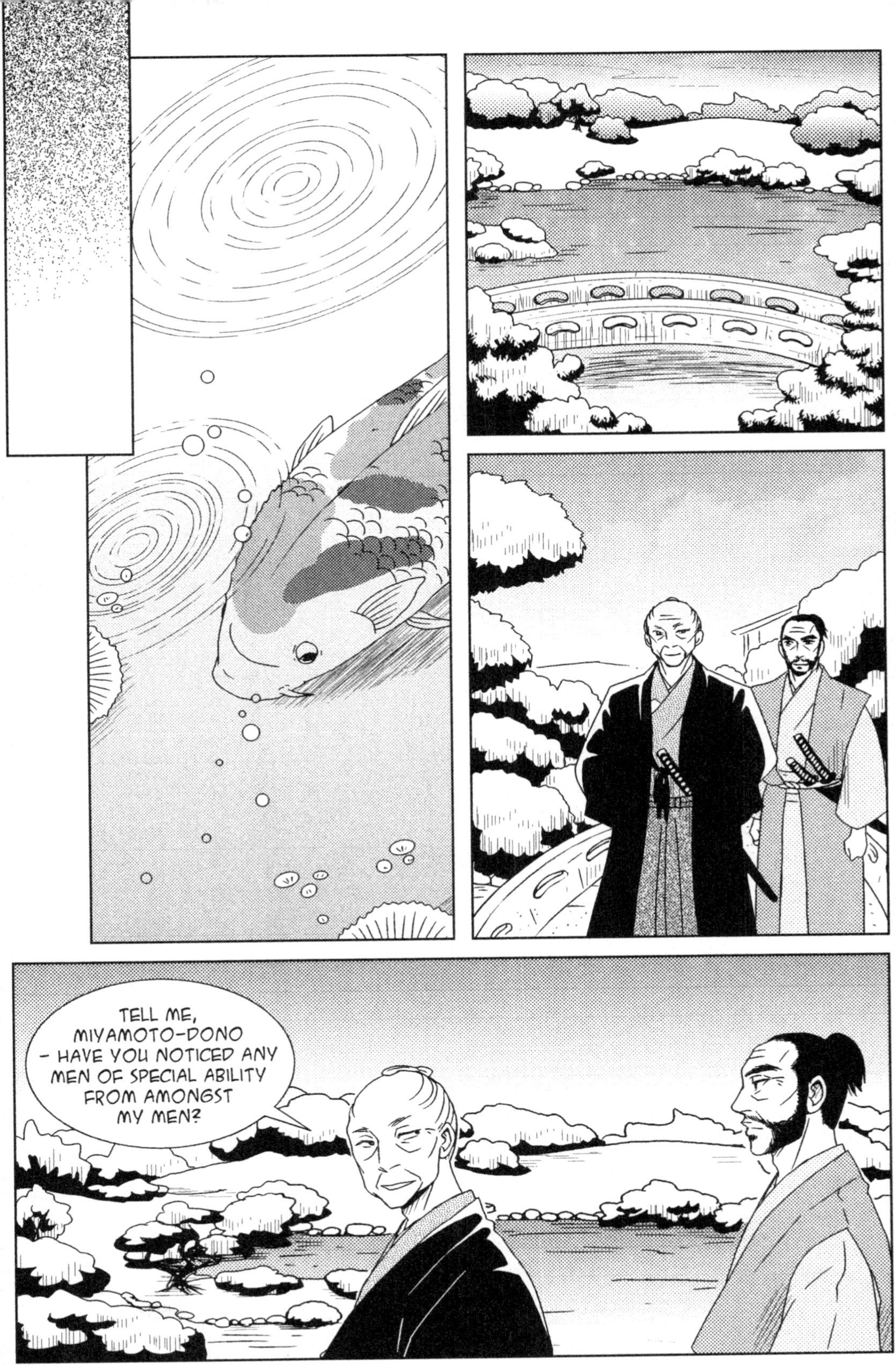
TELL ME, MIYAMOTO-DONO - HAVE YOU NOTICED ANY MEN OF SPECIAL ABILITY FROM AMONGST MY MEN?

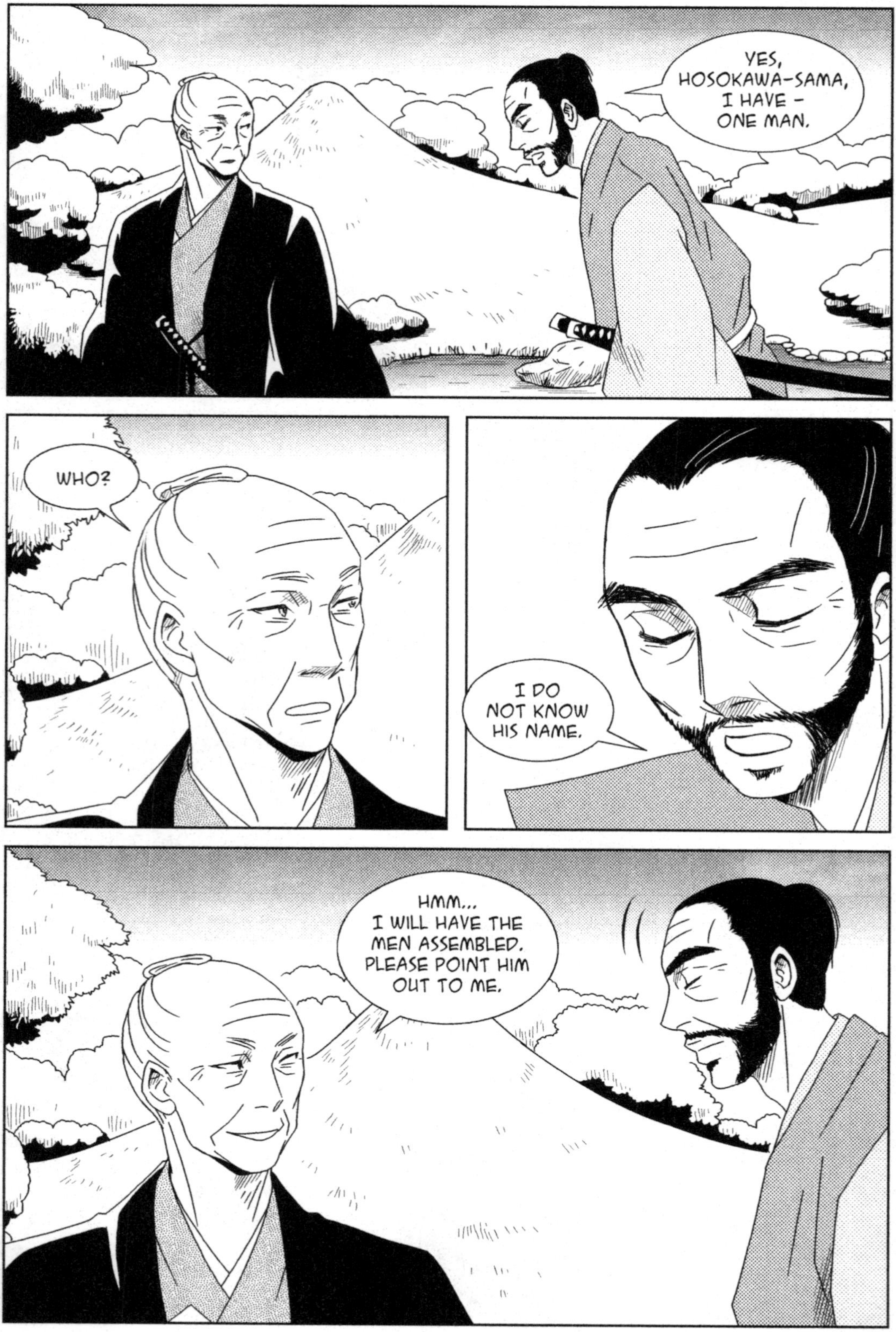
YES, HOSOKAWA-SAMA, I HAVE - ONE MAN.
WHO?
I DO NOT KNOW HIS NAME.
HMM... I WILL HAVE THE MEN ASSEMBLED. PLEASE POINT HIM OUT TO ME.

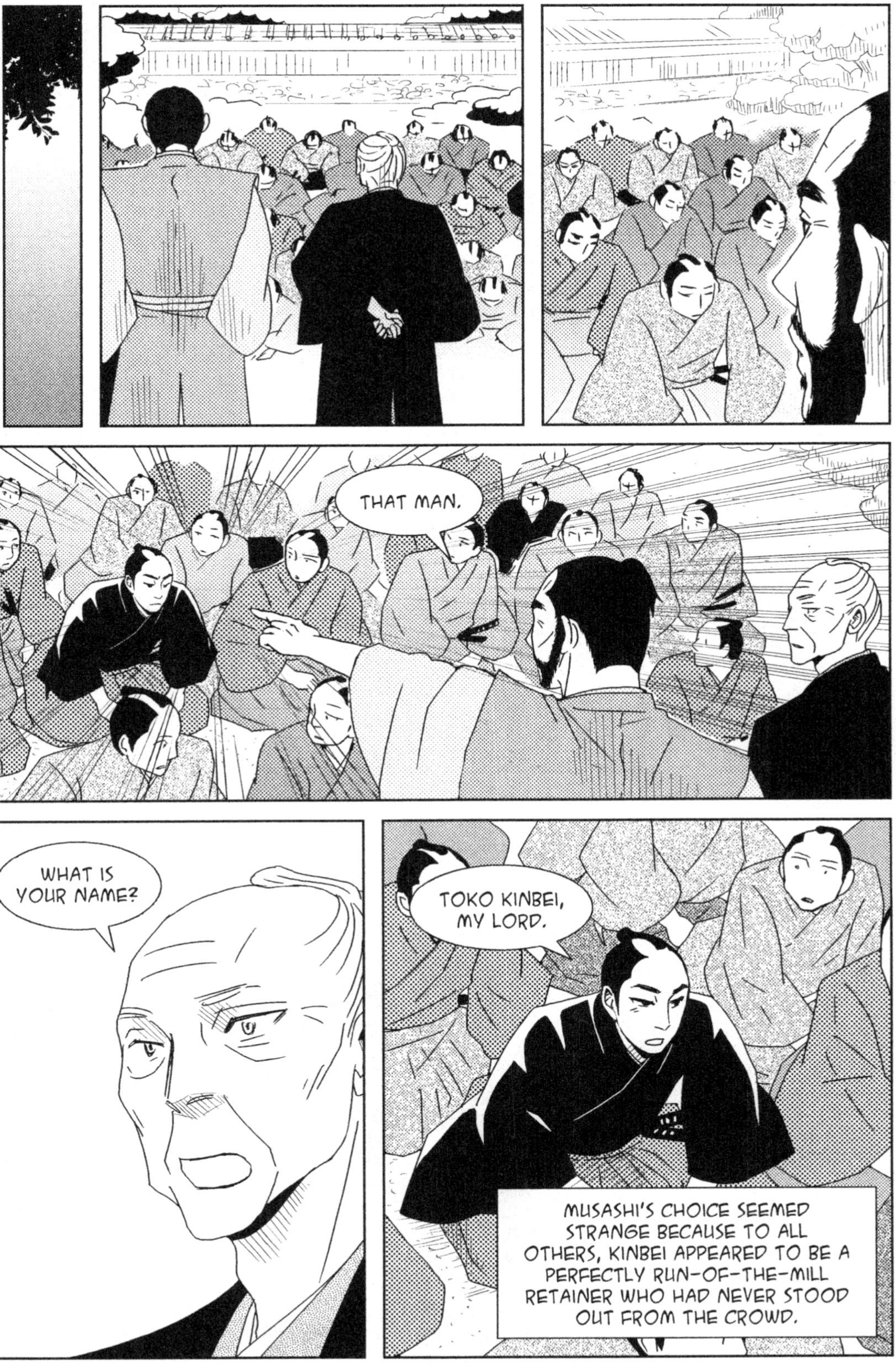
THAT MAN.
WHAT IS YOUR NAME?
TOKO KINBEI, MY LORD.
MUSASHI'S CHOICE SEEMED STRANGE BECAUSE TO ALL OTHERS, KINBEI APPEARED TO BE A PERFECTLY RUN-OF-THE-MILL RETAINER WHO HAD NEVER STOOD OUT FROM THE CROWD.

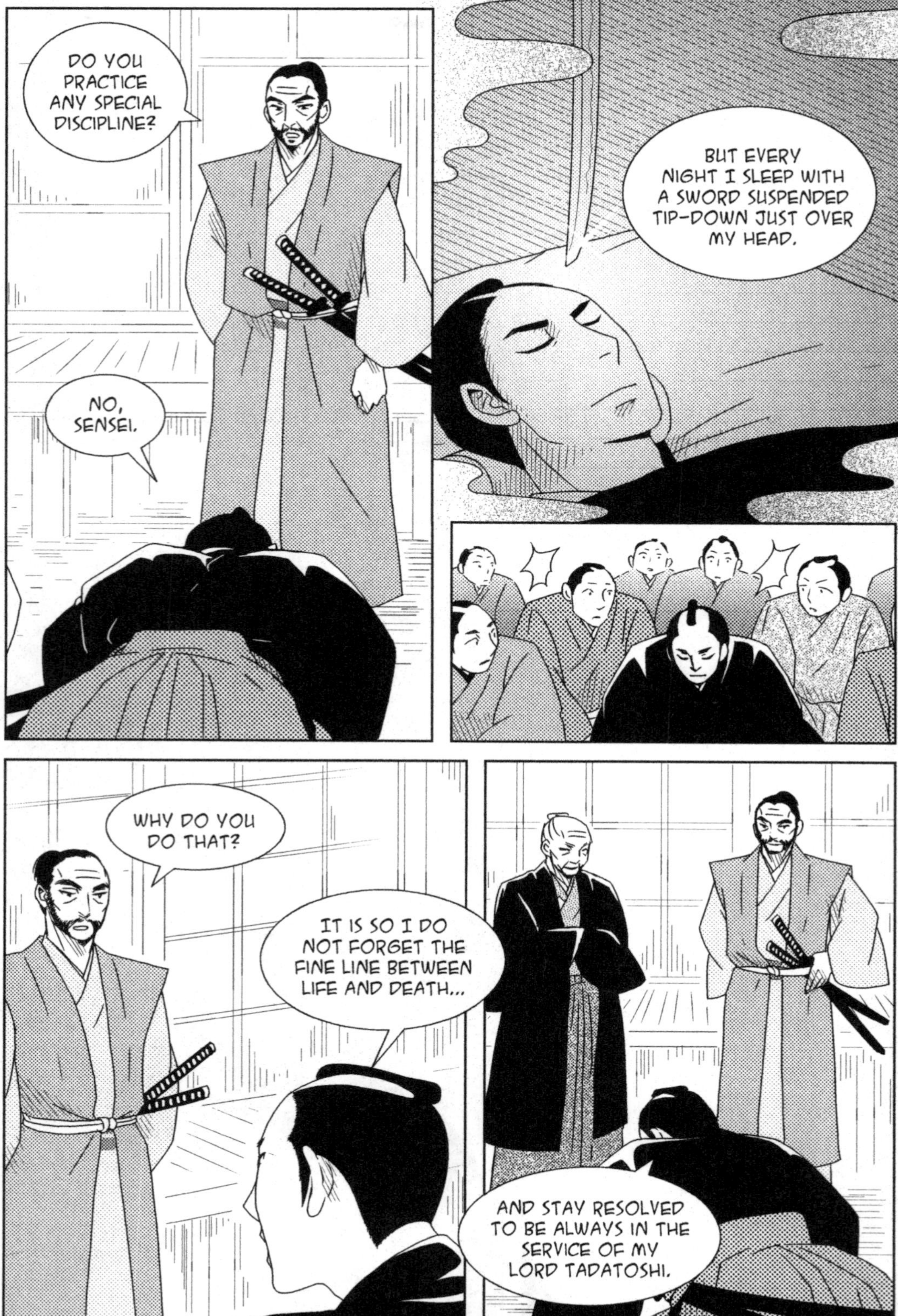
DO YOU PRACTICE ANY SPECIAL DISCIPLINE?
NO, SENSEI.
BUT EVERY NIGHT I SLEEP WITH A SWORD SUSPENDED TIP-DOWN JUST OVER MY HEAD.
WHY DO YOU DO THAT?
IT IS SO I DO NOT FORGET THE FINE LINE BETWEEN LIFE AND DEATH...
AND STAY RESOLVED TO BE ALWAYS IN THE SERVICE OF MY LORD TADATOSHI.

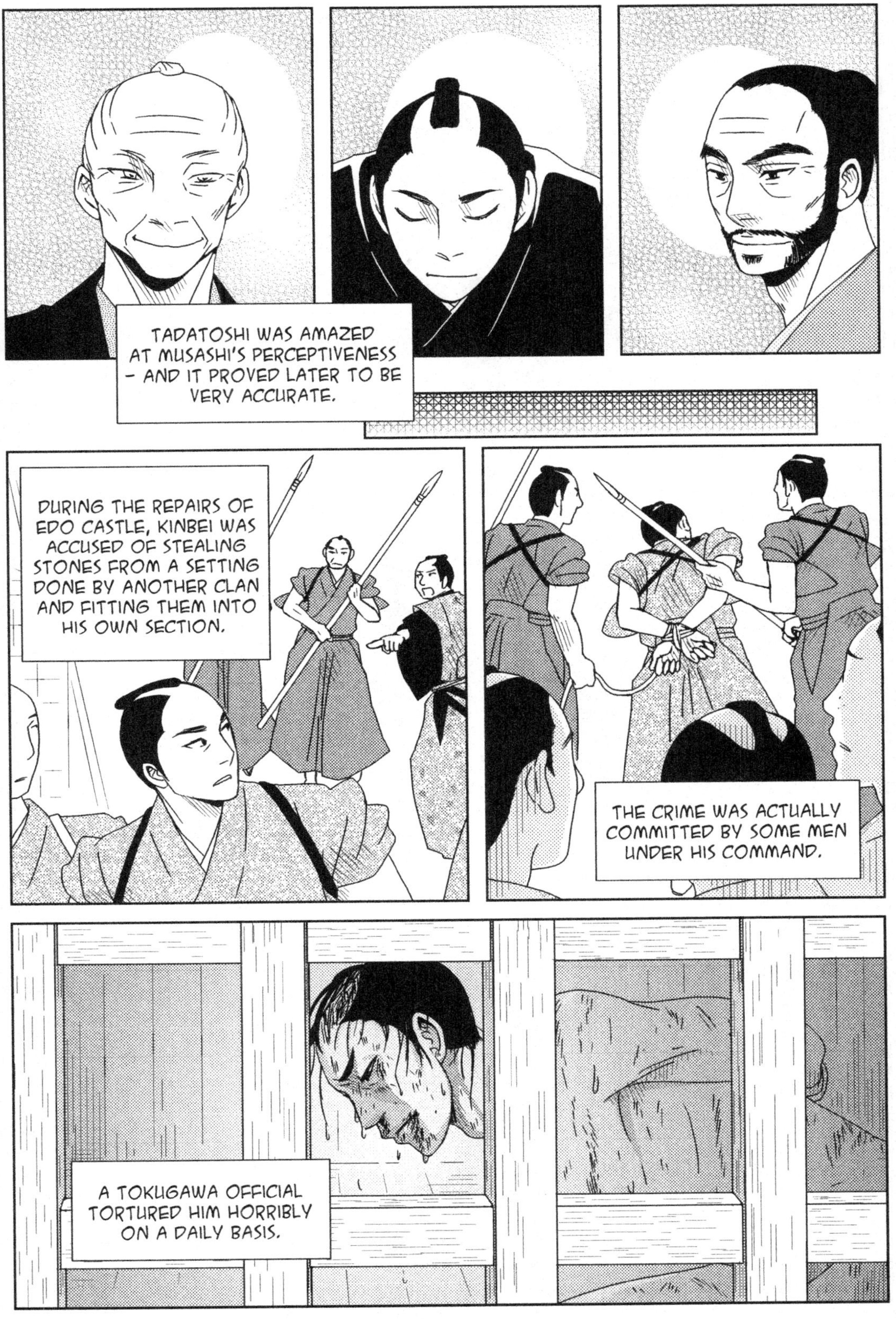
TADATOSHI WAS AMAZED AT MUSASHI'S PERCEPTIVENESS - AND IT PROVED LATER TO BE VERY ACCURATE.
DURING THE REPAIRS OF EDO CASTLE, KINBEI WAS ACCUSED OF STEALING STONES FROM A SETTING DONE BY ANOTHER CLAN AND FITTING THEM INTO HIS OWN SECTION.
THE CRIME WAS ACTUALLY COMMITTED BY SOME MEN UNDER HIS COMMAND.
A TOKUGAWA OFFICIAL TORTURED HIM HORRIBLY ON A DAILY BASIS.

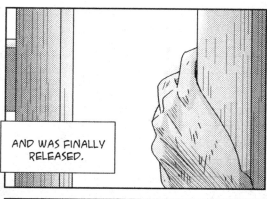

YET KINBEI CALMLY CONTINUED TO DECLARE HIS INNOCENCE...

AND WAS FINALLY RELEASED.

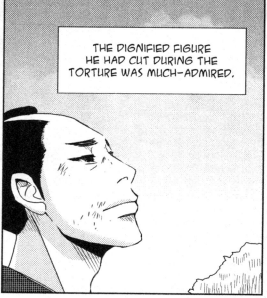

THE DIGNIFIED FIGURE HE HAD CUT DURING THE TORTURE WAS MUCH-ADMIRED.

HE WAS CONSIDERED EXTRAORDINARILY MANLY AND HEROIC.

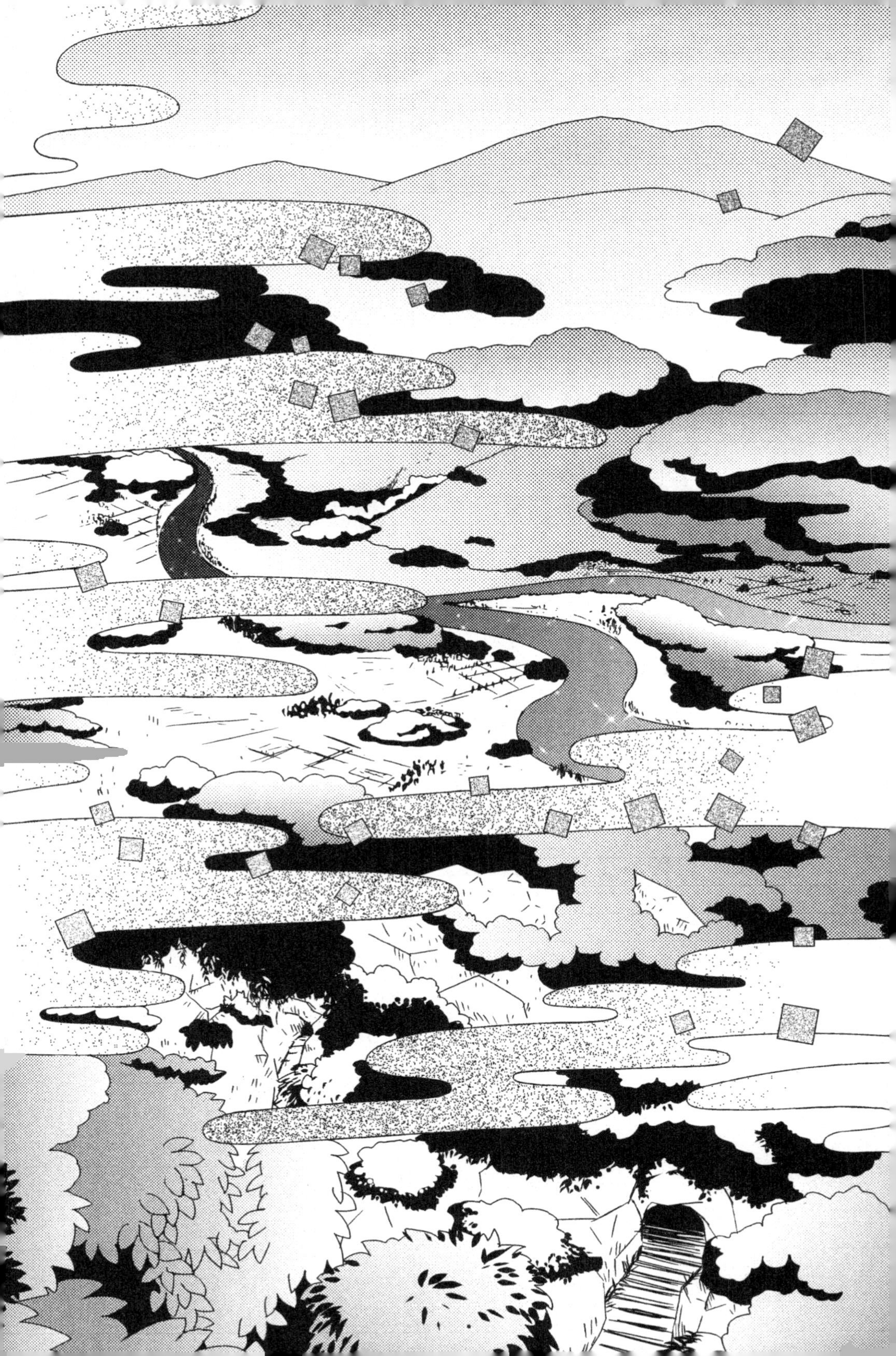

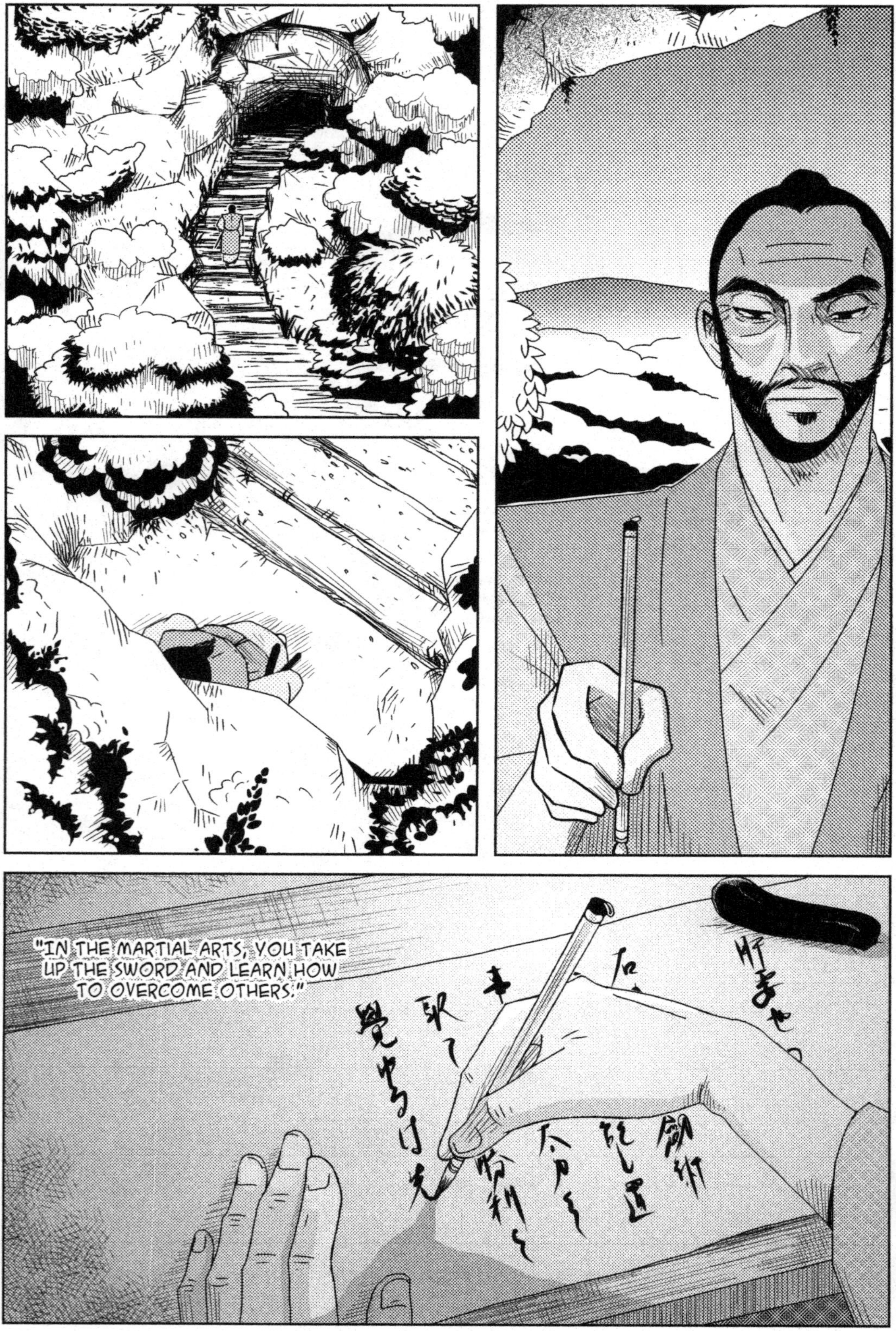
"IN THE MARTIAL ARTS, YOU TAKE UP THE SWORD AND LEARN HOW TO OVERCOME OTHERS."

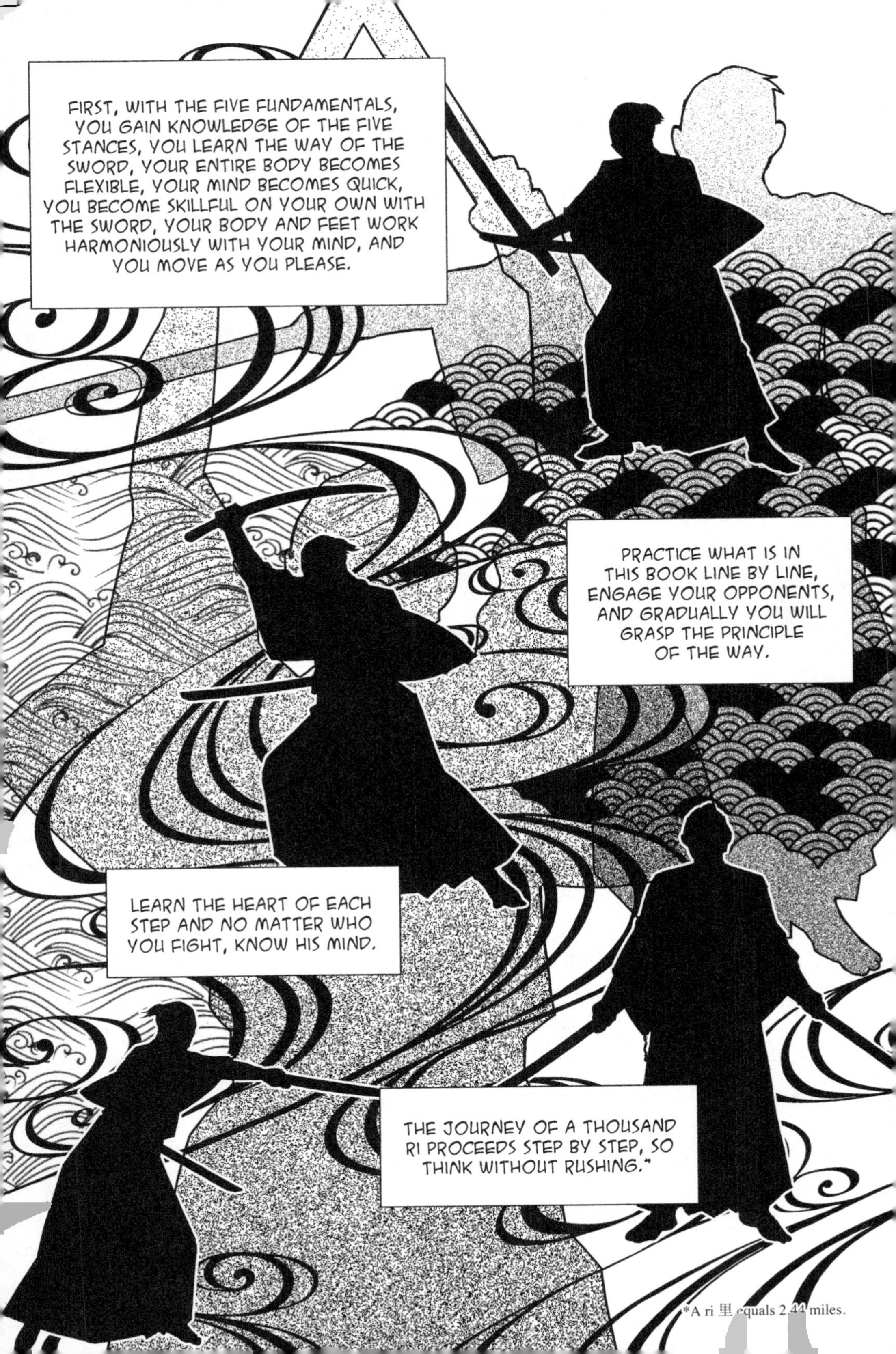
FIRST, WITH THE FIVE FUNDAMENTALS, YOU GAIN KNOWLEDGE OF THE FIVE STANCES, YOU LEARN THE WAY OF THE SWORD, YOUR ENTIRE BODY BECOMES FLEXIBLE, YOUR MIND BECOMES QUICK, YOU BECOME SKILLFUL ON YOUR OWN WITH THE SWORD, YOUR BODY AND FEET WORK HARMONIOUSLY WITH YOUR MIND, AND YOU MOVE AS YOU PLEASE.
PRACTICE WHAT IS IN THIS BOOK LINE BY LINE, ENGAGE YOUR OPPONENTS, AND GRADUALLY YOU WILL GRASP THE PRINCIPLE OF THE WAY.
LEARN THE HEART OF EACH STEP AND NO MATTER WHO YOU FIGHT, KNOW HIS MIND.
THE JOURNEY OF A THOUSAND RI PROCEEDS STEP BY STEP, SO THINK WITHOUT RUSHING.*

*A ri 里 equals 2.44 miles.

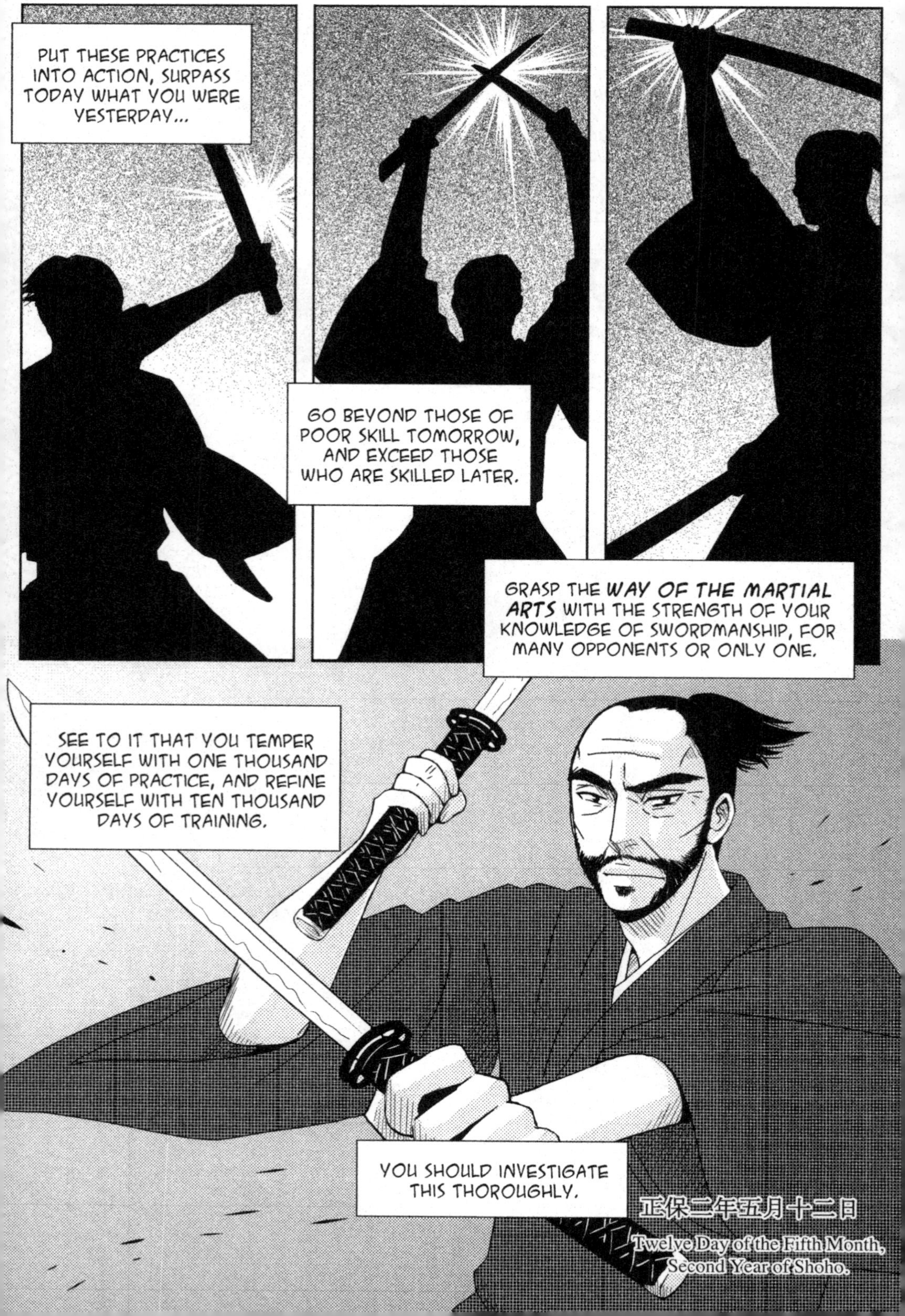
PUT THESE PRACTICES INTO ACTION, SURPASS TODAY WHAT YOU WERE YESTERDAY...
GO BEYOND THOSE OF POOR SKILL TOMORROW, AND EXCEED THOSE WHO ARE SKILLED LATER.
GRASP THE *WAY OF THE MARTIAL ARTS* WITH THE STRENGTH OF YOUR KNOWLEDGE OF SWORDMANSHIP, FOR MANY OPPONENTS OR ONLY ONE.
SEE TO IT THAT YOU TEMPER YOURSELF WITH ONE THOUSAND DAYS OF PRACTICE, AND REFINE YOURSELF WITH TEN THOUSAND DAYS OF TRAINING.
YOU SHOULD INVESTIGATE THIS THOROUGHLY.
正保二年五月十二日
Twelve Day of the Fifth Month, Second Year of Shoho.

3
FIRE

火

In the martial arts of the Two-Sword Style, I compare battle to fire. Many concern themselves with insignficant aspects, such as how to give the wrist a three- to five-inch advantage with the fingertips. In my martial art, you put your life on the line in battle, you distinguish the principles of life and death, you study the Way of the Sword, and practice how to strike and defeat your opponent. In doing this, you do not bother your thoughts with insignificant matters.

Who in the world can reach the goal set by my Way of the Martial Arts? Whoever would get to the heart of it, let him do so with conviction, practicing in the morning and training in the evening. After he has polished his techniques and powers, his free and easy strength will be wonderful. This is the spirit wherein, as a warrior, he will put these practices into action.

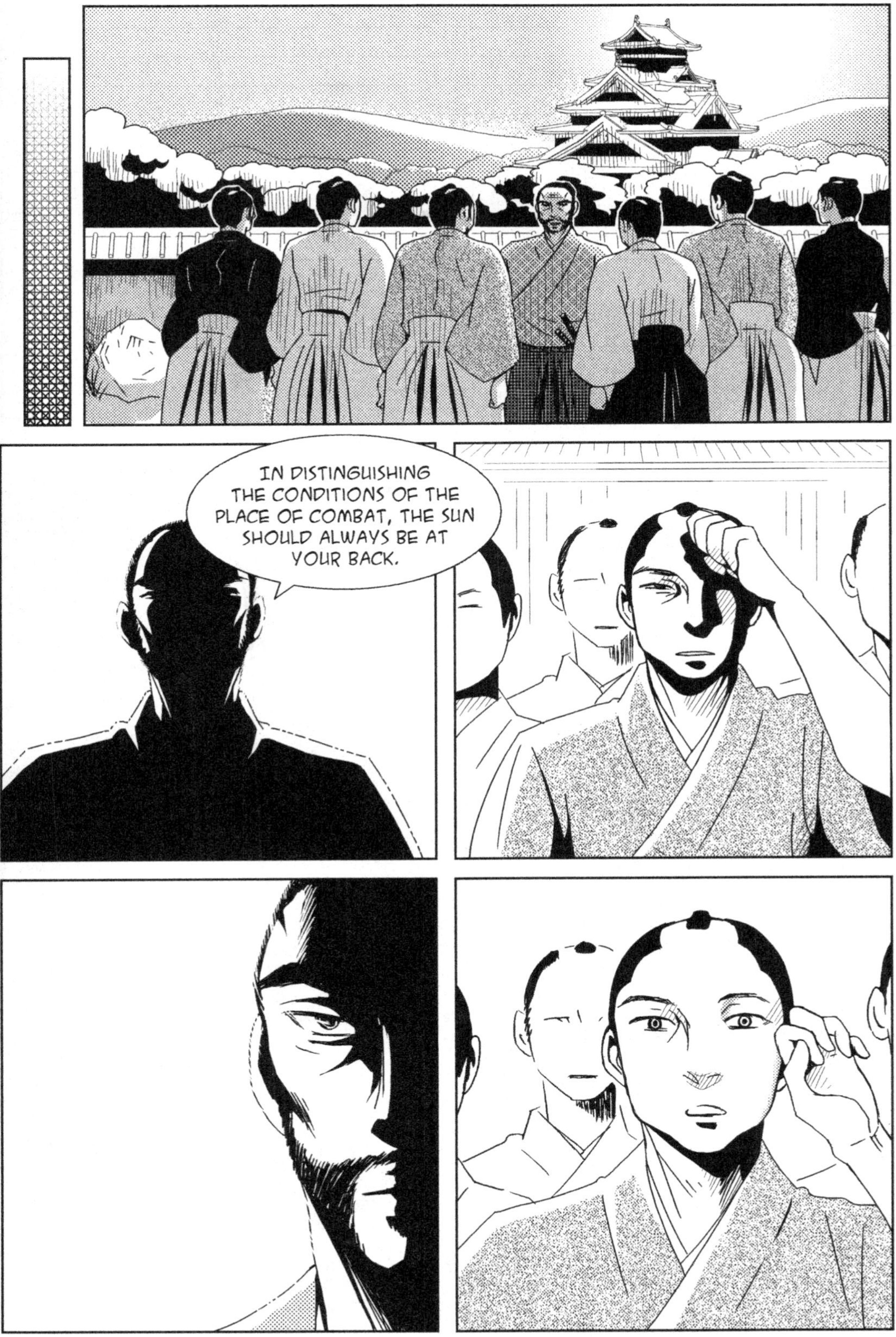
IN DISTINGUISHING THE CONDITIONS OF THE PLACE OF COMBAT, THE SUN SHOULD ALWAYS BE AT YOUR BACK.

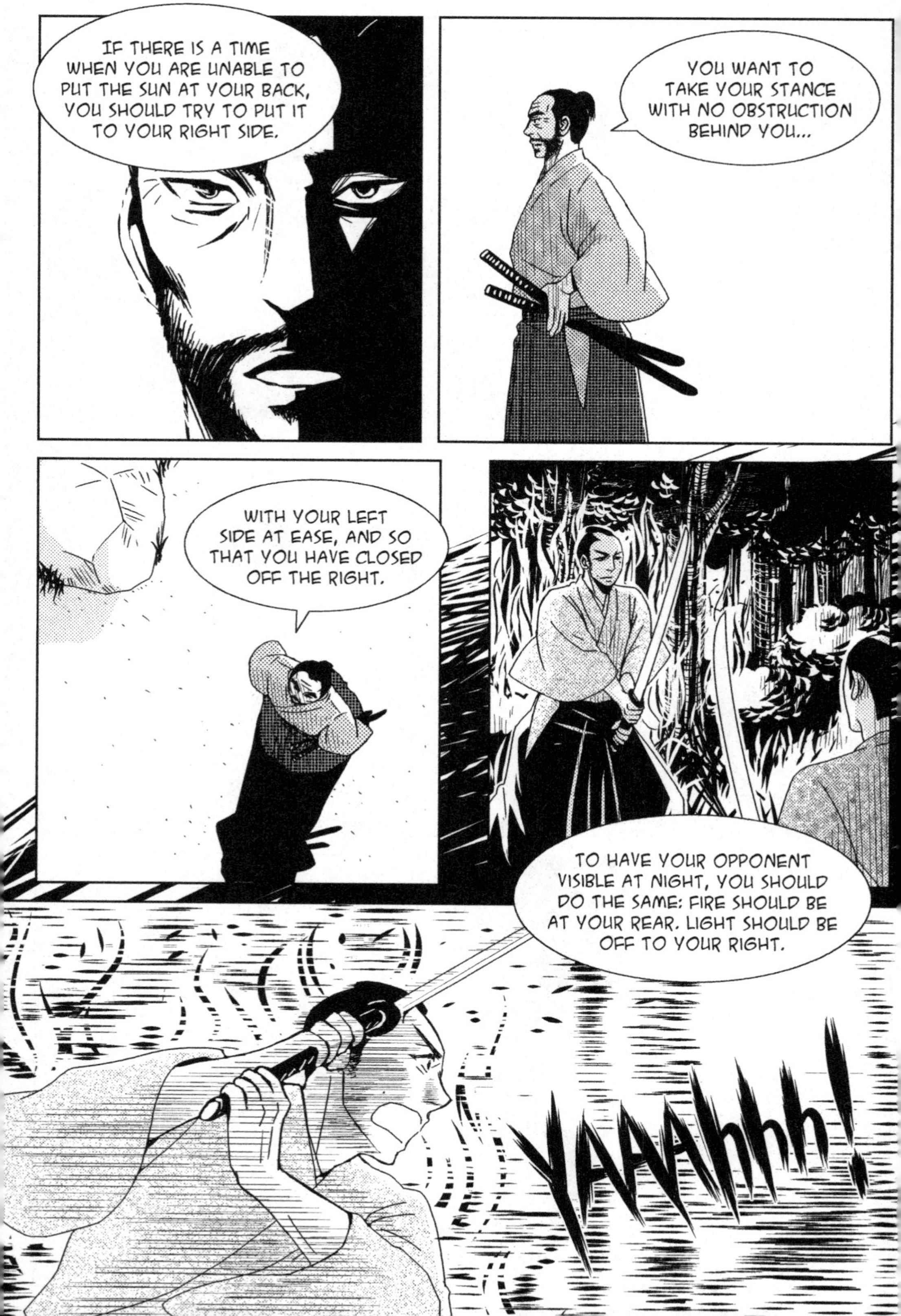
IF THERE IS A TIME WHEN YOU ARE UNABLE TO PUT THE SUN AT YOUR BACK, YOU SHOULD TRY TO PUT IT TO YOUR RIGHT SIDE.
YOU WANT TO TAKE YOUR STANCE WITH NO OBSTRUCTION BEHIND YOU...
WITH YOUR LEFT SIDE AT EASE, AND SO THAT YOU HAVE CLOSED OFF THE RIGHT.
TO HAVE YOUR OPPONENT VISIBLE AT NIGHT, YOU SHOULD DO THE SAME: FIRE SHOULD BE AT YOUR REAR. LIGHT SHOULD BE OFF TO YOUR RIGHT.
YAAAhhh!

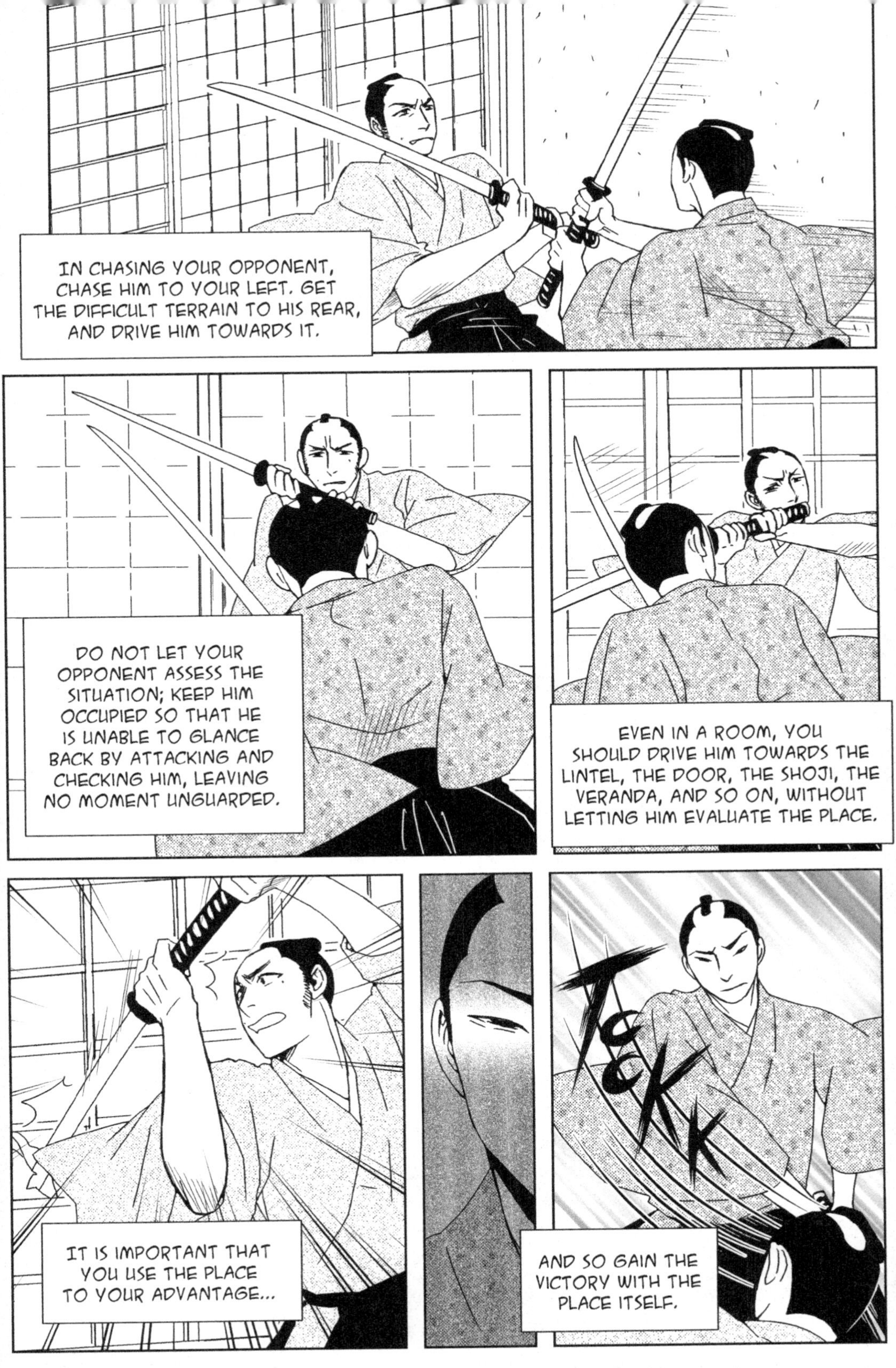
IN CHASING YOUR OPPONENT, CHASE HIM TO YOUR LEFT. GET THE DIFFICULT TERRAIN TO HIS REAR, AND DRIVE HIM TOWARDS IT.
DO NOT LET YOUR OPPONENT ASSESS THE SITUATION; KEEP HIM OCCUPIED SO THAT HE IS UNABLE TO GLANCE BACK BY ATTACKING AND CHECKING HIM, LEAVING NO MOMENT UNGUARDED.
EVEN IN A ROOM, YOU SHOULD DRIVE HIM TOWARDS THE LINTEL, THE DOOR, THE SHOJI, THE VERANDA, AND SO ON, WITHOUT LETTING HIM EVALUATE THE PLACE.
IT IS IMPORTANT THAT YOU USE THE PLACE TO YOUR ADVANTAGE...
AND SO GAIN THE VICTORY WITH THE PLACE ITSELF.
TSCKK

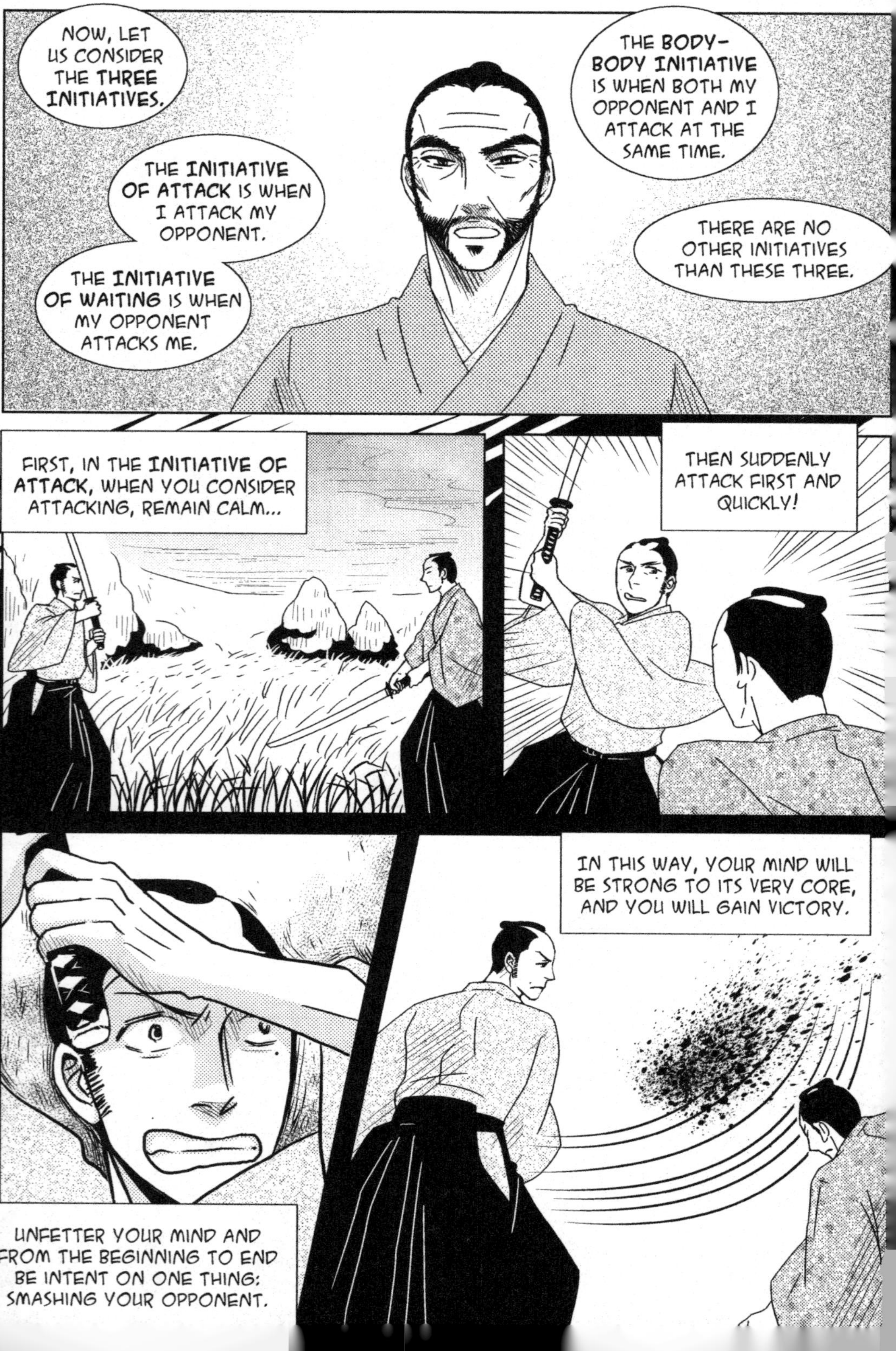
NOW, LET US CONSIDER THE THREE INITIATIVES.
THE INITIATIVE OF ATTACK IS WHEN I ATTACK MY OPPONENT.
THE INITIATIVE OF WAITING IS WHEN MY OPPONENT ATTACKS ME.
THE BODY-BODY INITIATIVE IS WHEN BOTH MY OPPONENT AND I ATTACK AT THE SAME TIME.
THERE ARE NO OTHER INITIATIVES THAN THESE THREE.
FIRST, IN THE INITIATIVE OF ATTACK, WHEN YOU CONSIDER ATTACKING, REMAIN CALM...
THEN SUDDENLY ATTACK FIRST AND QUICKLY!
UNFETTER YOUR MIND AND FROM THE BEGINNING TO END BE INTENT ON ONE THING: SMASHING YOUR OPPONENT.
IN THIS WAY, YOUR MIND WILL BE STRONG TO ITS VERY CORE, AND YOU WILL GAIN VICTORY.

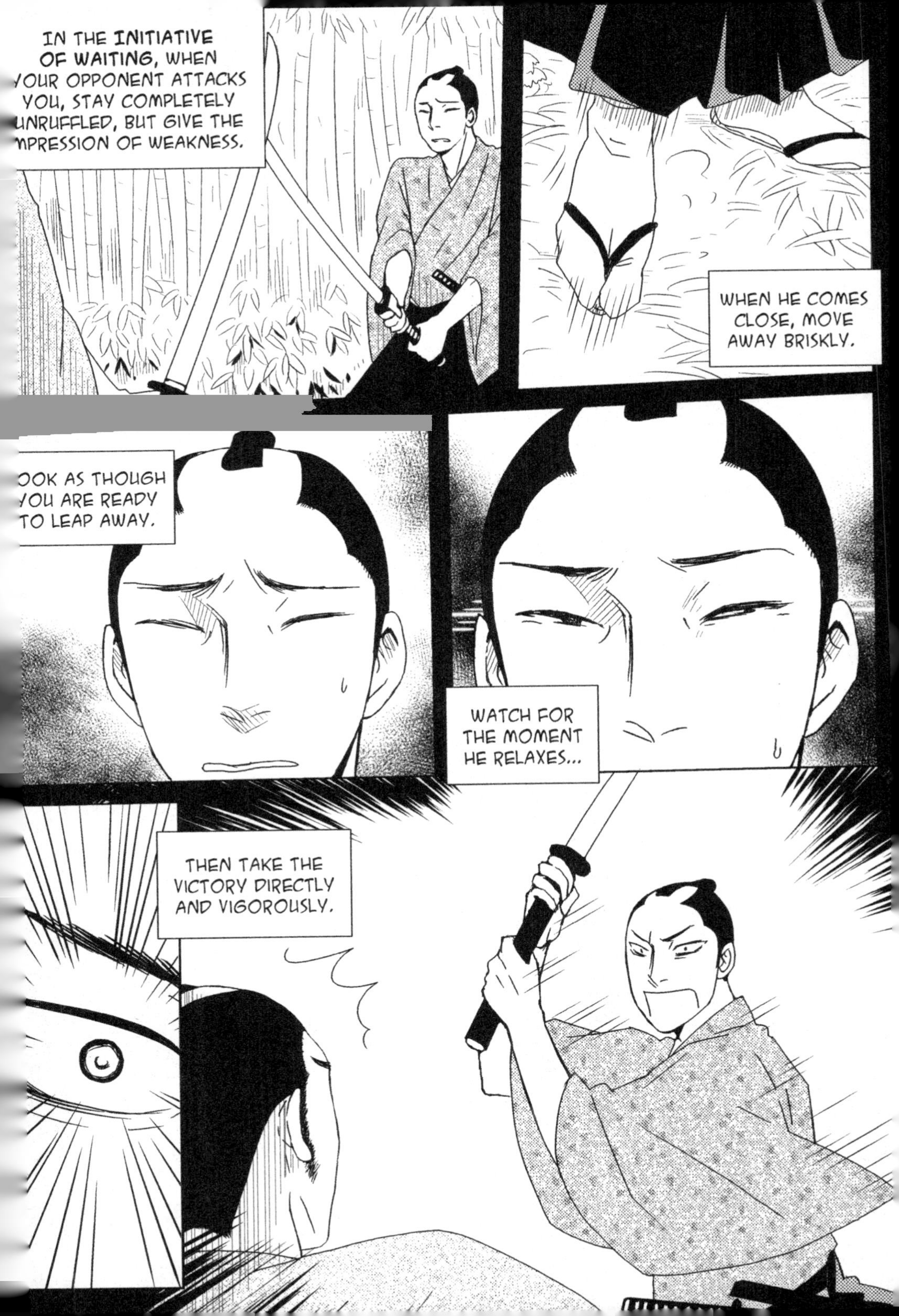

IN THE INITIATIVE OF WAITING, WHEN YOUR OPPONENT ATTACKS YOU, STAY COMPLETELY UNRUFFLED, BUT GIVE THE MPRESSION OF WEAKNESS.
WHEN HE COMES CLOSE, MOVE AWAY BRISKLY.
OOK AS THOUGH YOU ARE READY TO LEAP AWAY.
WATCH FOR THE MOMENT HE RELAXES...
THEN TAKE THE VICTORY DIRECTLY AND VIGOROUSLY.

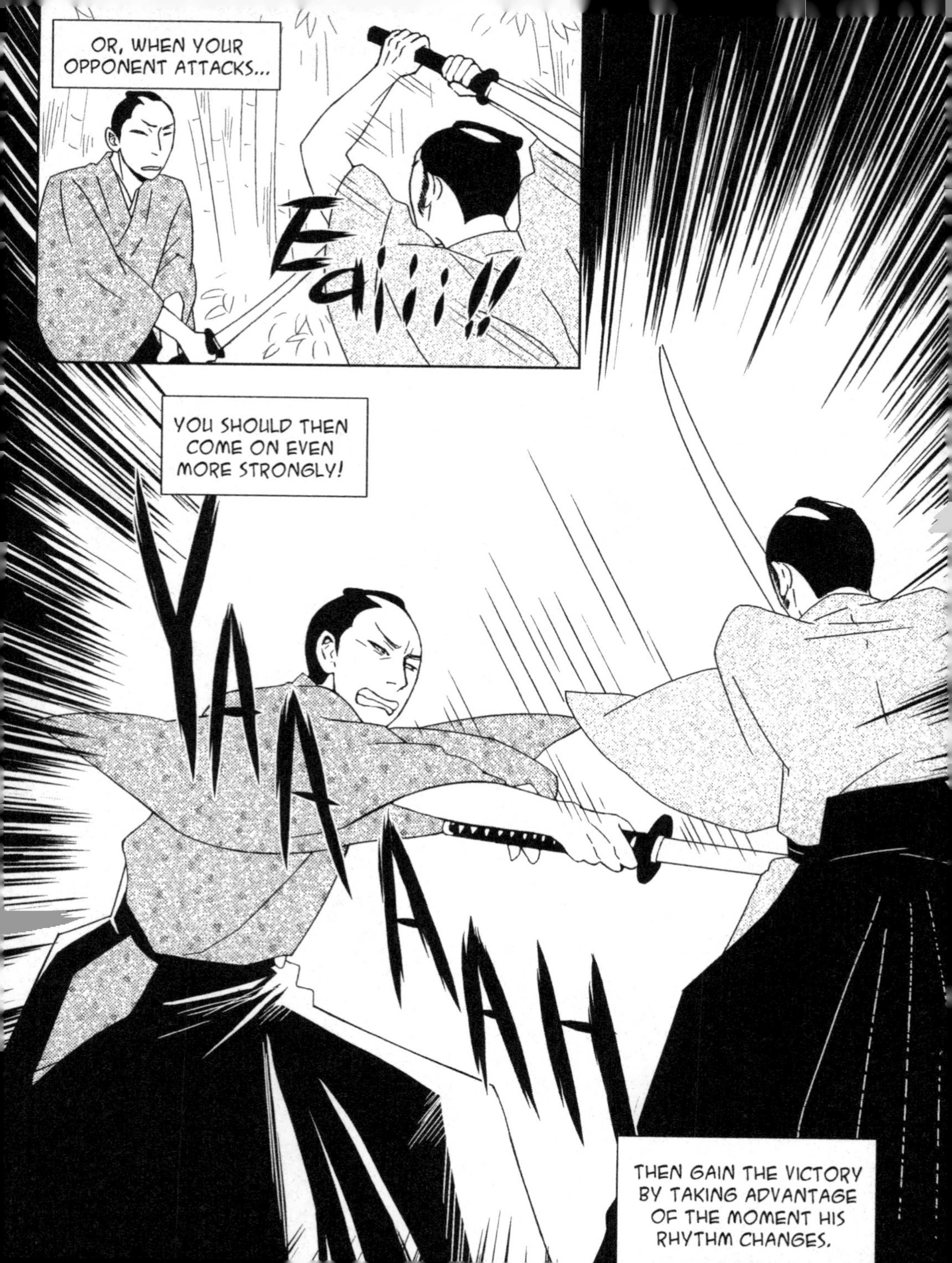

OR, WHEN YOUR OPPONENT ATTACKS...
Eaiii!!
YOU SHOULD THEN COME ON EVEN MORE STRONGLY!
YAAAAH
THEN GAIN THE VICTORY BY TAKING ADVANTAGE OF THE MOMENT HIS RHYTHM CHANGES.

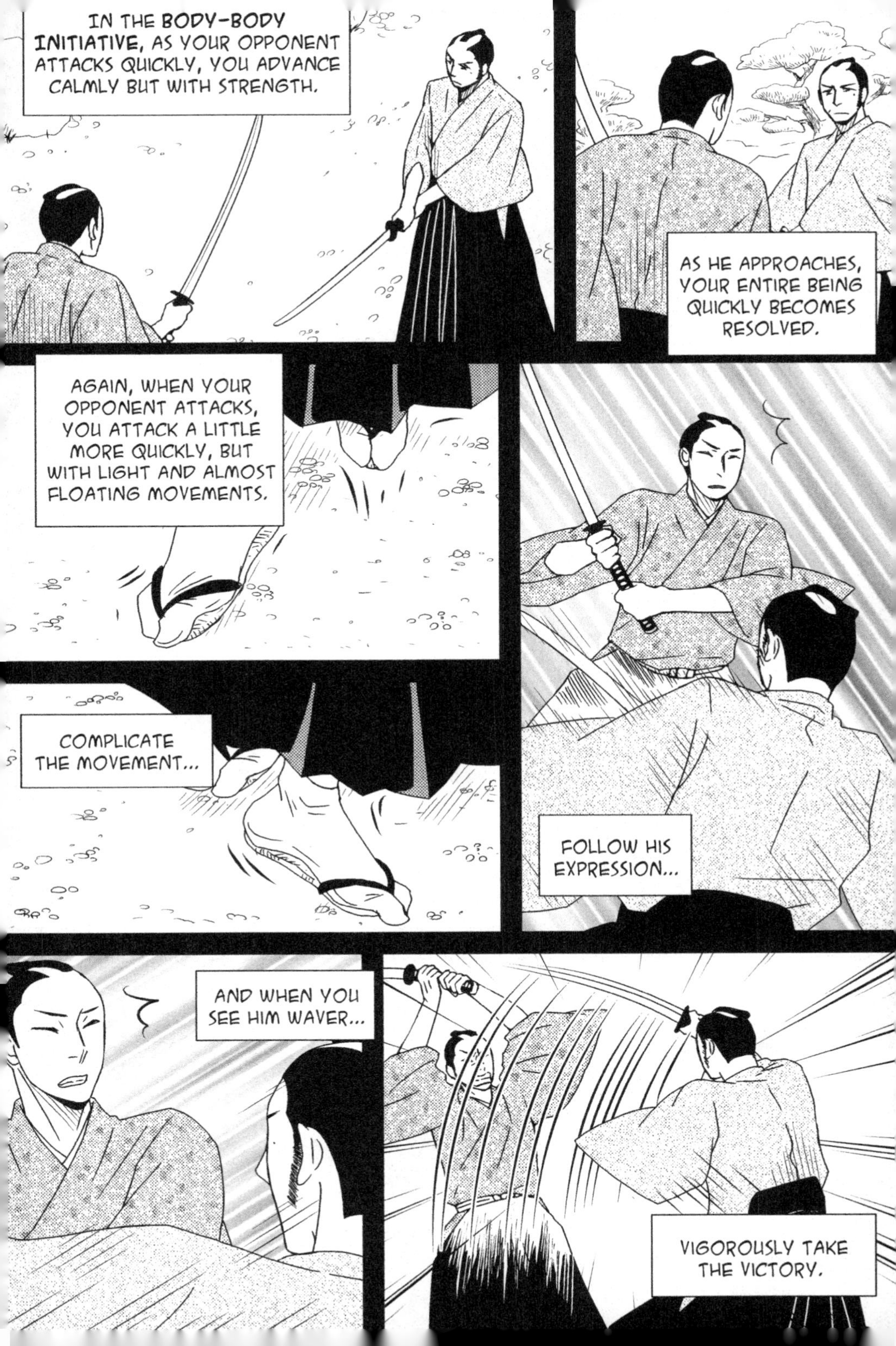
IN THE BODY-BODY INITIATIVE, AS YOUR OPPONENT ATTACKS QUICKLY, YOU ADVANCE CALMLY BUT WITH STRENGTH.
AS HE APPROACHES, YOUR ENTIRE BEING QUICKLY BECOMES RESOLVED.
AGAIN, WHEN YOUR OPPONENT ATTACKS, YOU ATTACK A LITTLE MORE QUICKLY, BUT WITH LIGHT AND ALMOST FLOATING MOVEMENTS.
COMPLICATE THE MOVEMENT...
FOLLOW HIS EXPRESSION...
AND WHEN YOU SEE HIM WAVER...
VIGOROUSLY TAKE THE VICTORY.

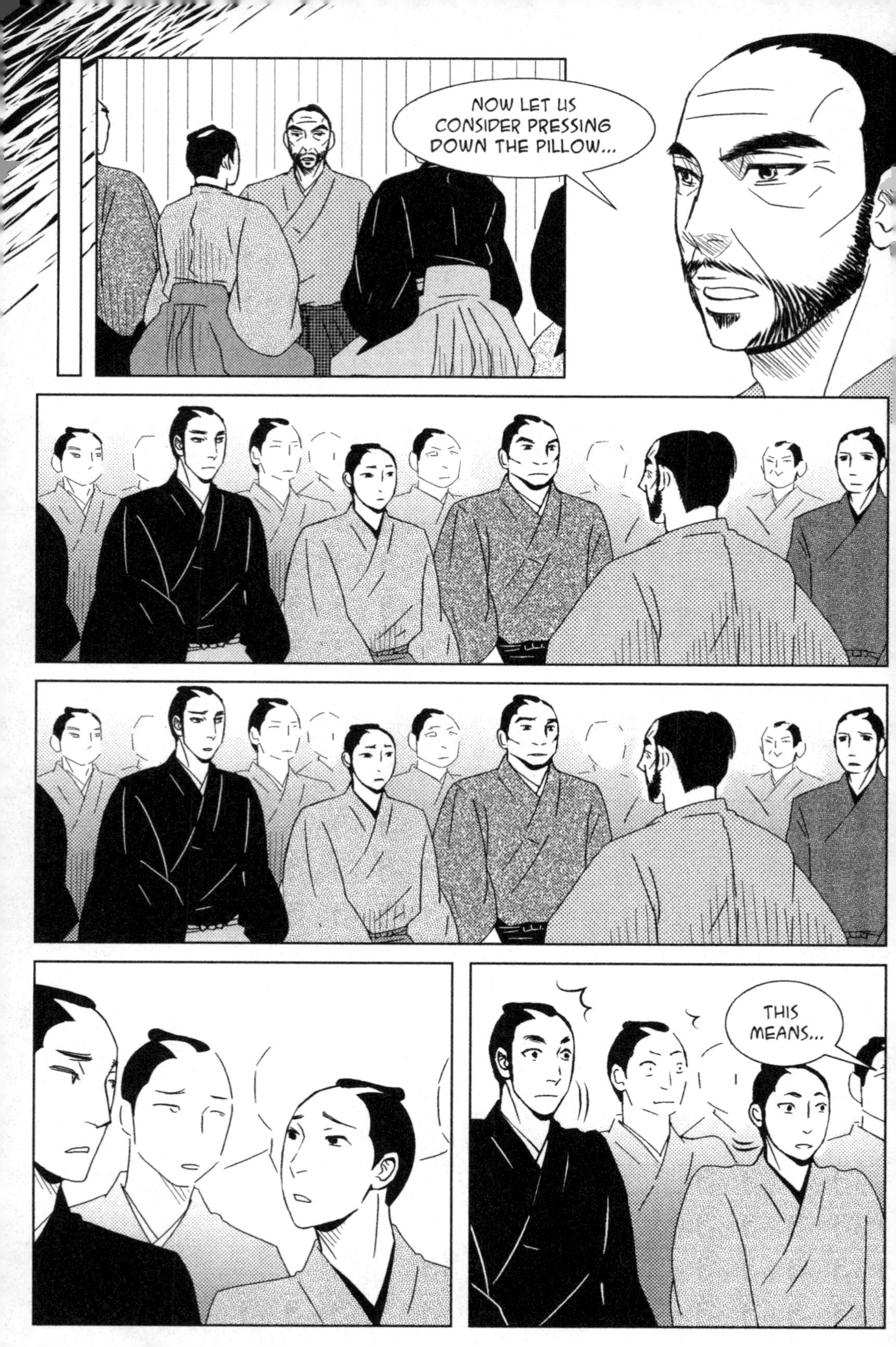
NOW LET US CONSIDER PRESSING DOWN THE PILLOW...
THIS MEANS...

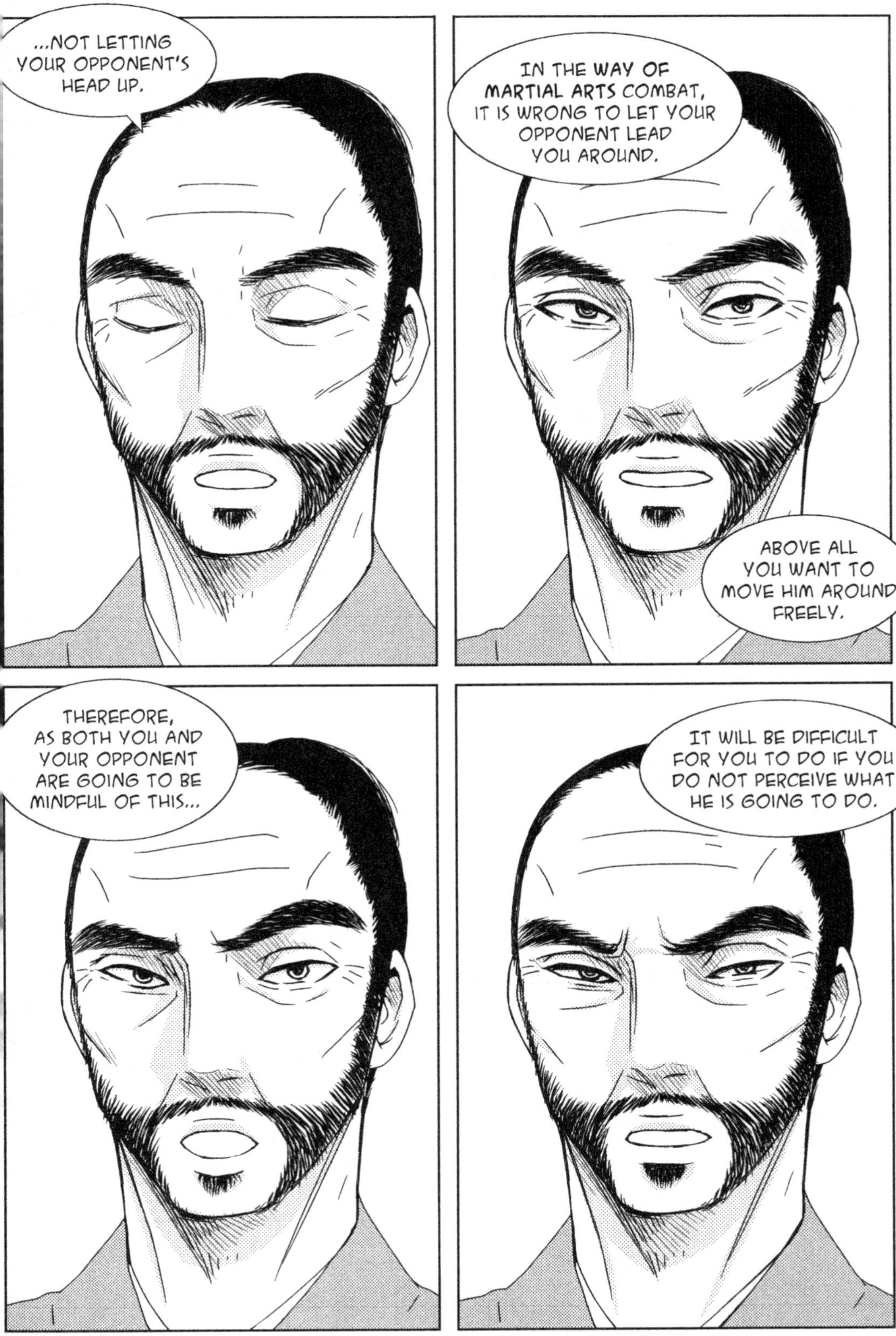
...NOT LETTING YOUR OPPONENT'S HEAD UP.
IN THE WAY OF MARTIAL ARTS COMBAT, IT IS WRONG TO LET YOUR OPPONENT LEAD YOU AROUND.
ABOVE ALL YOU WANT TO MOVE HIM AROUND FREELY.
THEREFORE, AS BOTH YOU AND YOUR OPPONENT ARE GOING TO BE MINDFUL OF THIS...
IT WILL BE DIFFICULT FOR YOU TO DO IF YOU DO NOT PERCEIVE WHAT HE IS GOING TO DO.

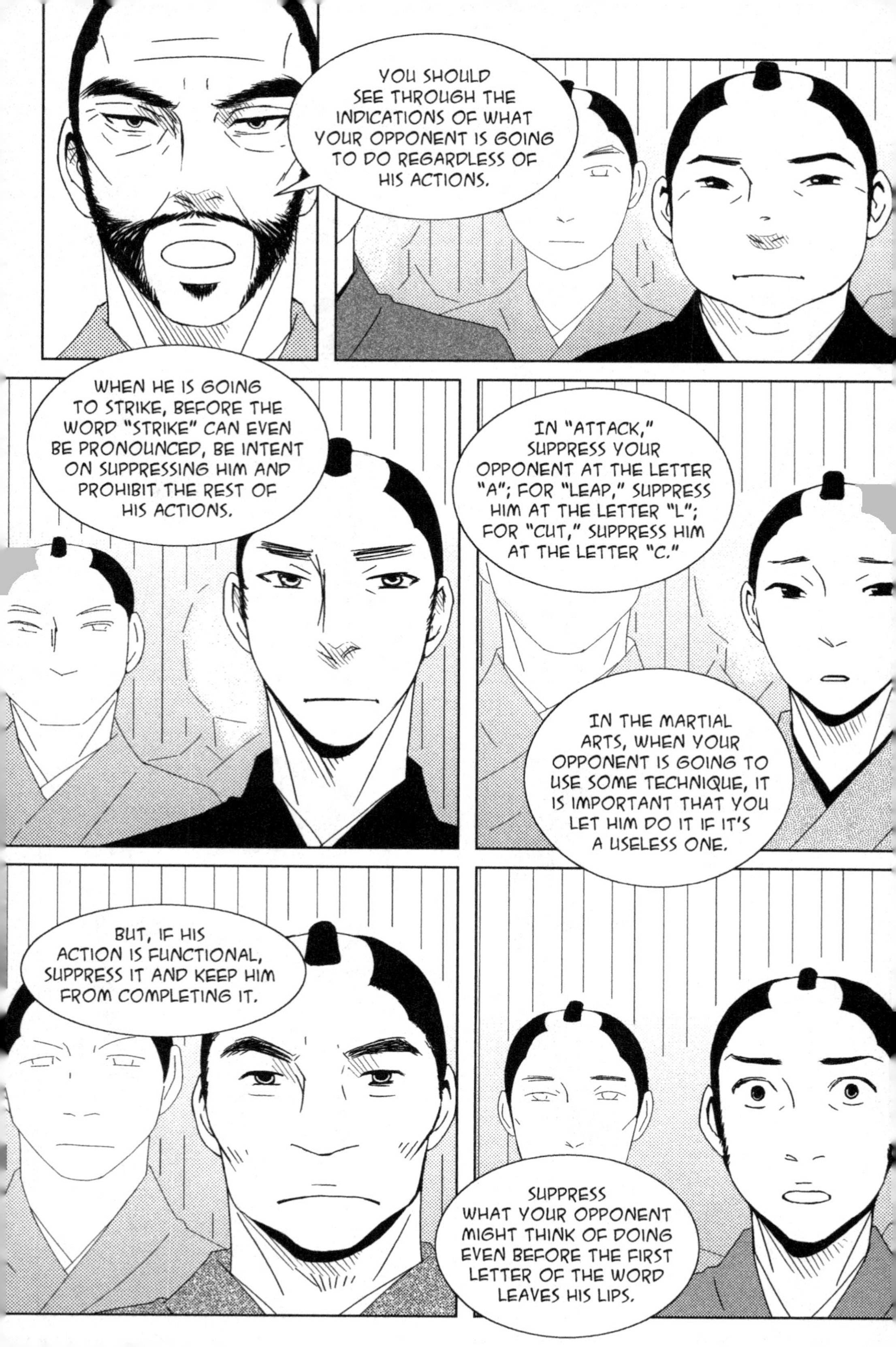
YOU SHOULD SEE THROUGH THE INDICATIONS OF WHAT YOUR OPPONENT IS GOING TO DO REGARDLESS OF HIS ACTIONS.
WHEN HE IS GOING TO STRIKE, BEFORE THE WORD "STRIKE" CAN EVEN BE PRONOUNCED, BE INTENT ON SUPPRESSING HIM AND PROHIBIT THE REST OF HIS ACTIONS.
IN "ATTACK," SUPPRESS YOUR OPPONENT AT THE LETTER "A"; FOR "LEAP," SUPPRESS HIM AT THE LETTER "L"; FOR "CUT," SUPPRESS HIM AT THE LETTER "C."
IN THE MARTIAL ARTS, WHEN YOUR OPPONENT IS GOING TO USE SOME TECHNIQUE, IT IS IMPORTANT THAT YOU LET HIM DO IT IF IT'S A USELESS ONE.
BUT, IF HIS ACTION IS FUNCTIONAL, SUPPRESS IT AND KEEP HIM FROM COMPLETING IT.
SUPPRESS WHAT YOUR OPPONENT MIGHT THINK OF DOING EVEN BEFORE THE FIRST LETTER OF THE WORD LEAVES HIS LIPS.

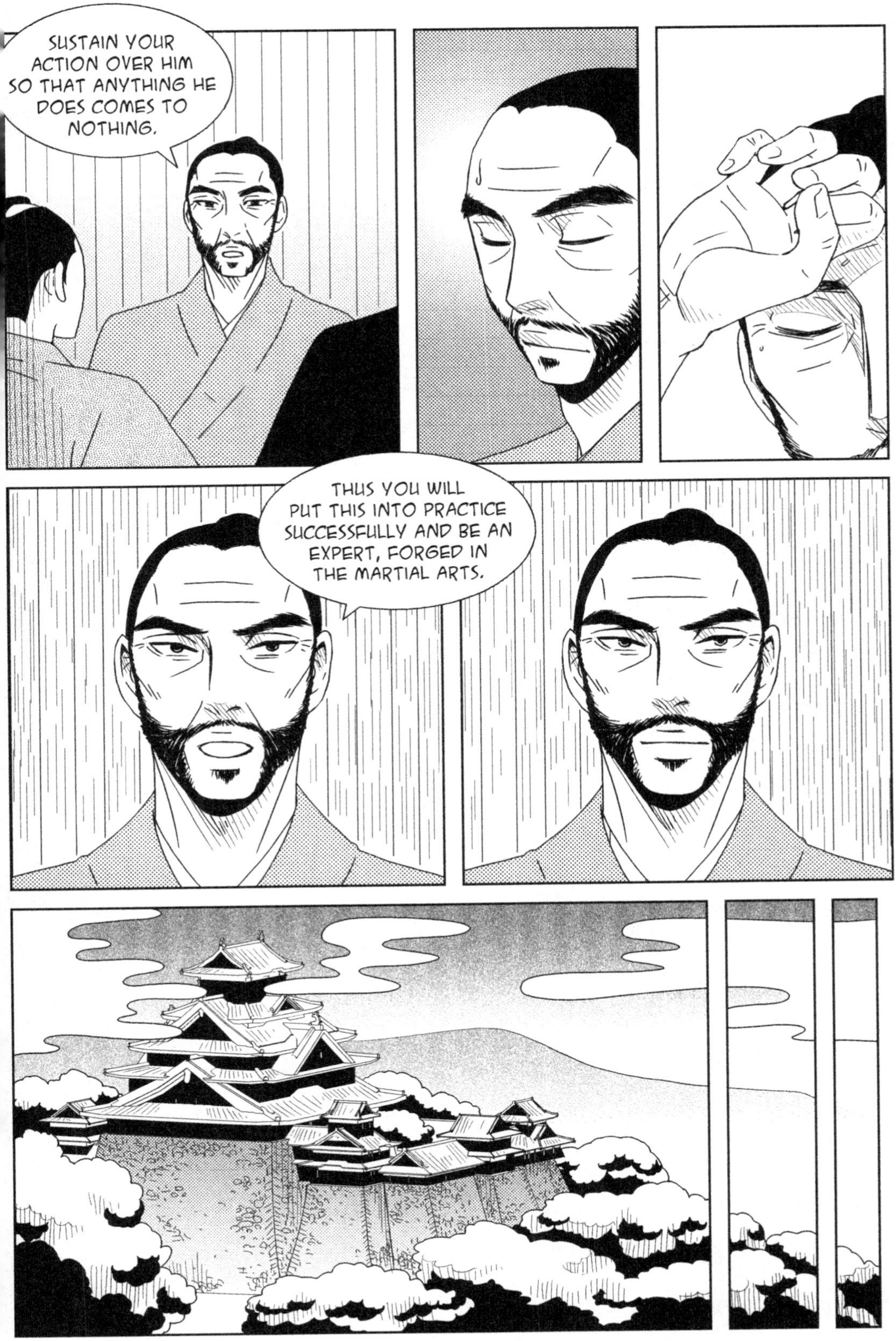
SUSTAIN YOUR ACTION OVER HIM SO THAT ANYTHING HE DOES COMES TO NOTHING.
THUS YOU WILL PUT THIS INTO PRACTICE SUCCESSFULLY AND BE AN EXPERT, FORGED IN THE MARTIAL ARTS.

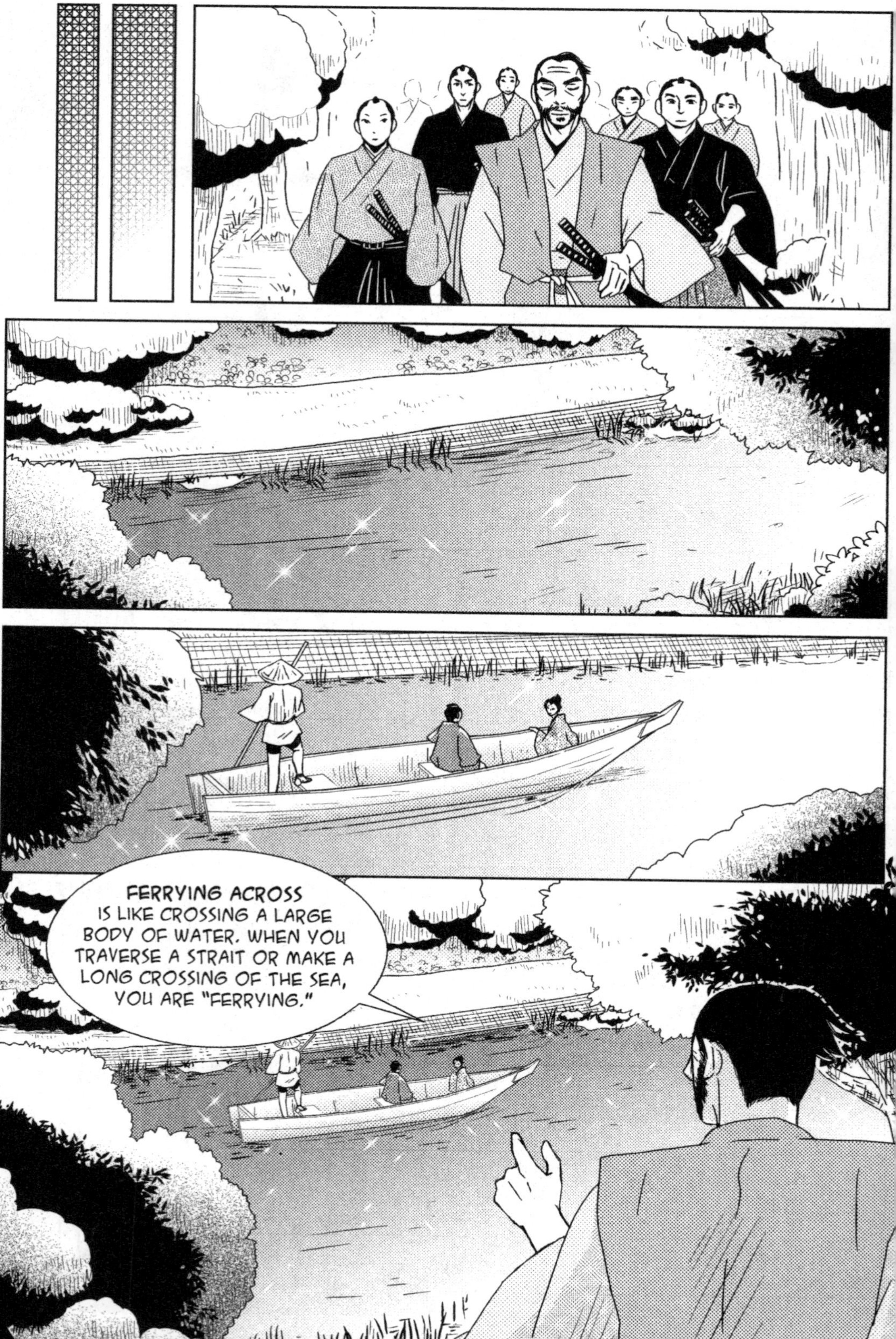
FERRYING ACROSS IS LIKE CROSSING A LARGE BODY OF WATER. WHEN YOU TRAVERSE A STRAIT OR MAKE A LONG CROSSING OF THE SEA, YOU ARE "FERRYING."

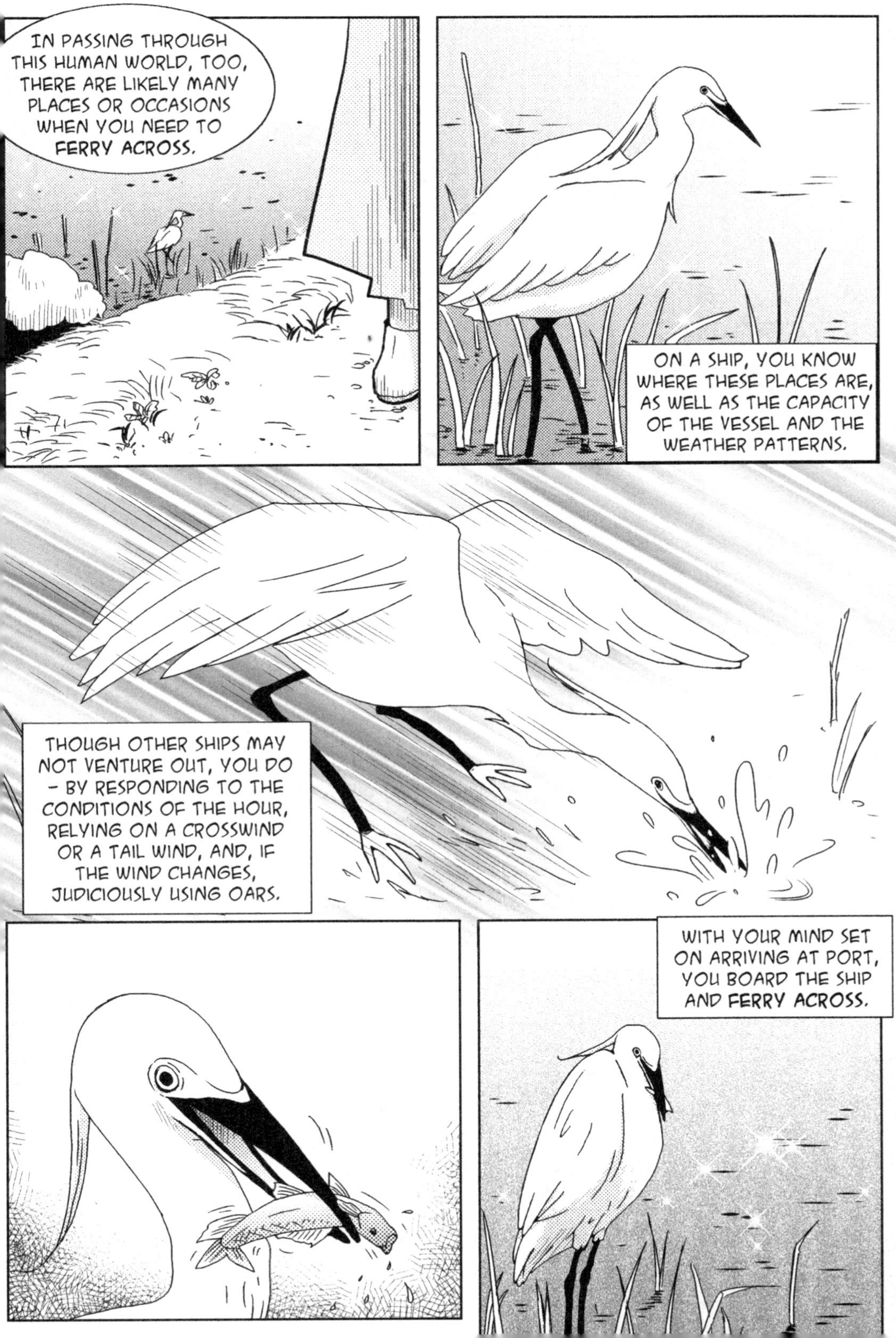
IN PASSING THROUGH THIS HUMAN WORLD, TOO, THERE ARE LIKELY MANY PLACES OR OCCASIONS WHEN YOU NEED TO FERRY ACROSS.
ON A SHIP, YOU KNOW WHERE THESE PLACES ARE, AS WELL AS THE CAPACITY OF THE VESSEL AND THE WEATHER PATTERNS.
THOUGH OTHER SHIPS MAY NOT VENTURE OUT, YOU DO – BY RESPONDING TO THE CONDITIONS OF THE HOUR, RELYING ON A CROSSWIND OR A TAIL WIND, AND, IF THE WIND CHANGES, JUDICIOUSLY USING OARS.
WITH YOUR MIND SET ON ARRIVING AT PORT, YOU BOARD THE SHIP AND FERRY ACROSS.

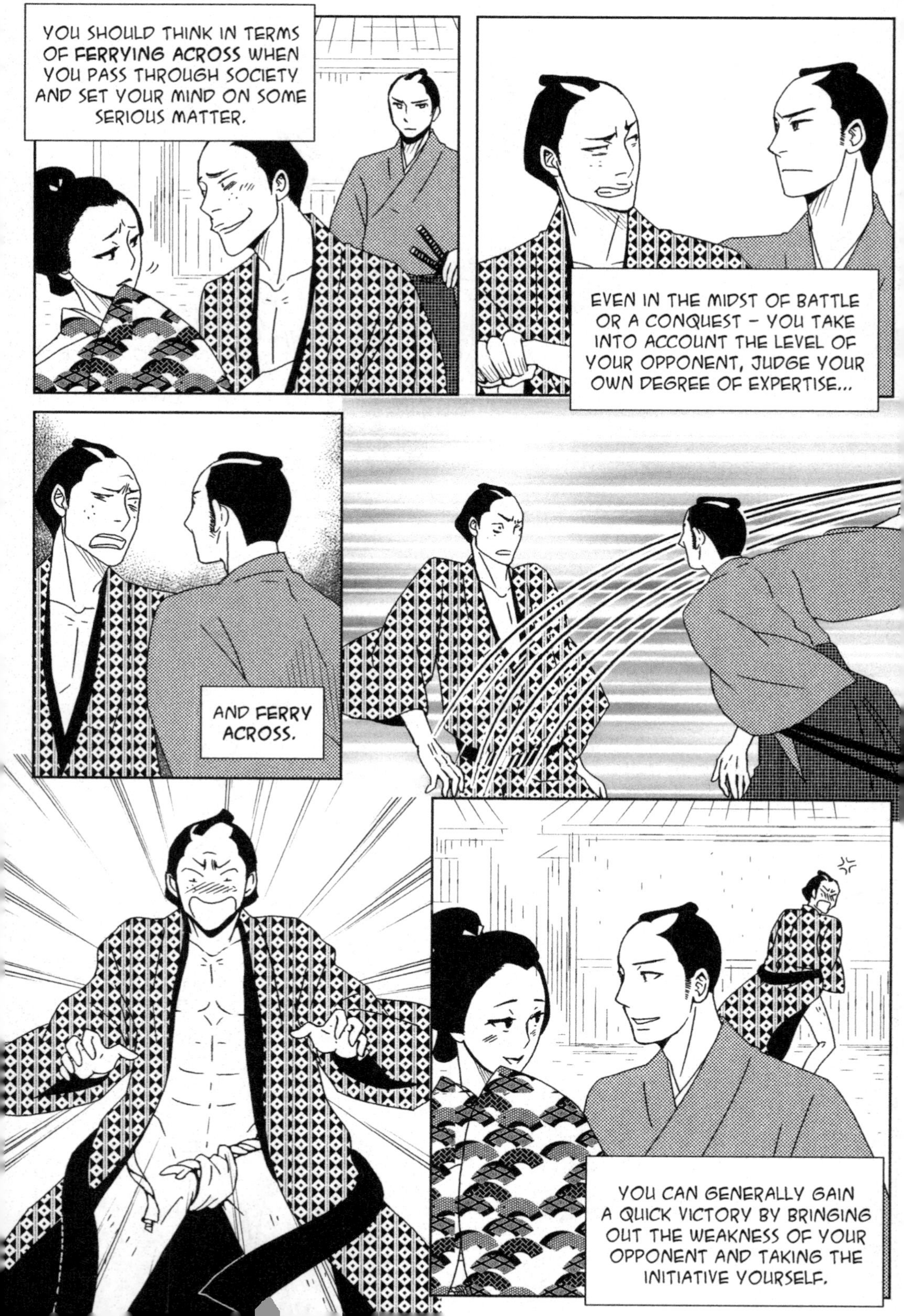

YOU SHOULD THINK IN TERMS OF FERRYING ACROSS WHEN YOU PASS THROUGH SOCIETY AND SET YOUR MIND ON SOME SERIOUS MATTER.
EVEN IN THE MIDST OF BATTLE OR A CONQUEST - YOU TAKE INTO ACCOUNT THE LEVEL OF YOUR OPPONENT, JUDGE YOUR OWN DEGREE OF EXPERTISE...
AND FERRY ACROSS.
YOU CAN GENERALLY GAIN A QUICK VICTORY BY BRINGING OUT THE WEAKNESS OF YOUR OPPONENT AND TAKING THE INITIATIVE YOURSELF.

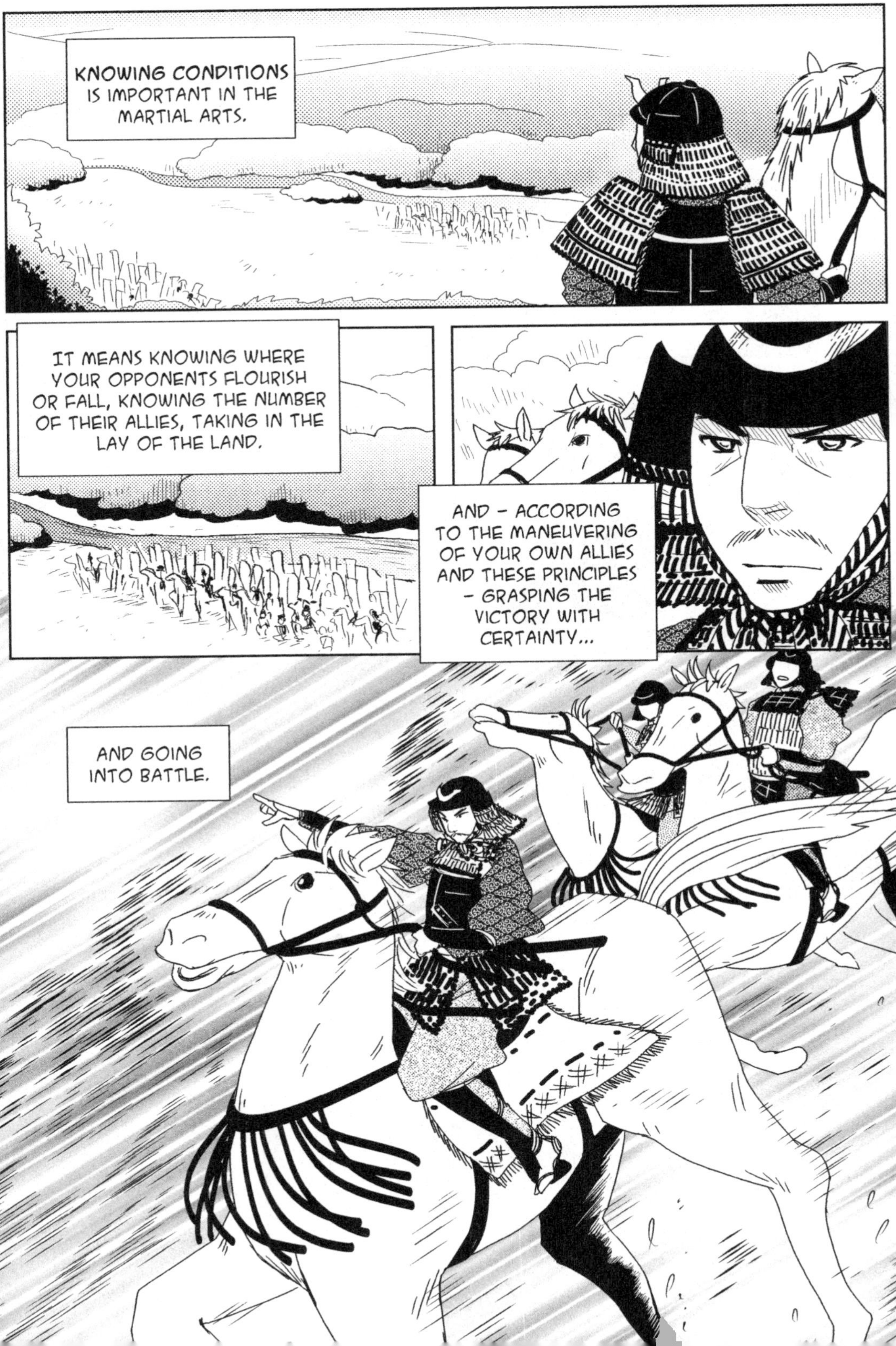
KNOWING CONDITIONS IS IMPORTANT IN THE MARTIAL ARTS.
IT MEANS KNOWING WHERE YOUR OPPONENTS FLOURISH OR FALL, KNOWING THE NUMBER OF THEIR ALLIES, TAKING IN THE LAY OF THE LAND.
AND – ACCORDING TO THE MANEUVERING OF YOUR OWN ALLIES AND THESE PRINCIPLES – GRASPING THE VICTORY WITH CERTAINTY...
AND GOING INTO BATTLE.

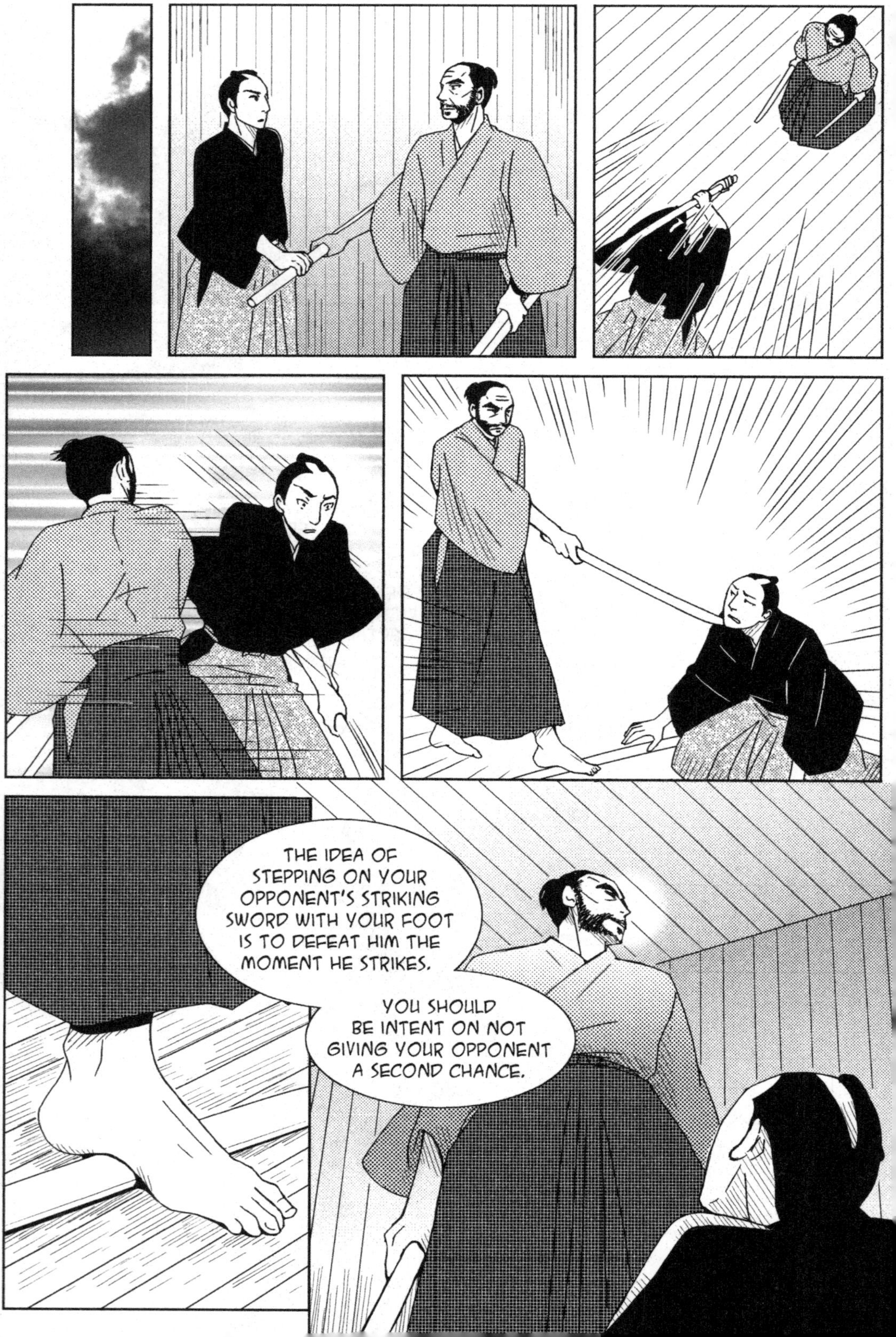
THE IDEA OF STEPPING ON YOUR OPPONENT'S STRIKING SWORD WITH YOUR FOOT IS TO DEFEAT HIM THE MOMENT HE STRIKES.
YOU SHOULD BE INTENT ON NOT GIVING YOUR OPPONENT A SECOND CHANCE.

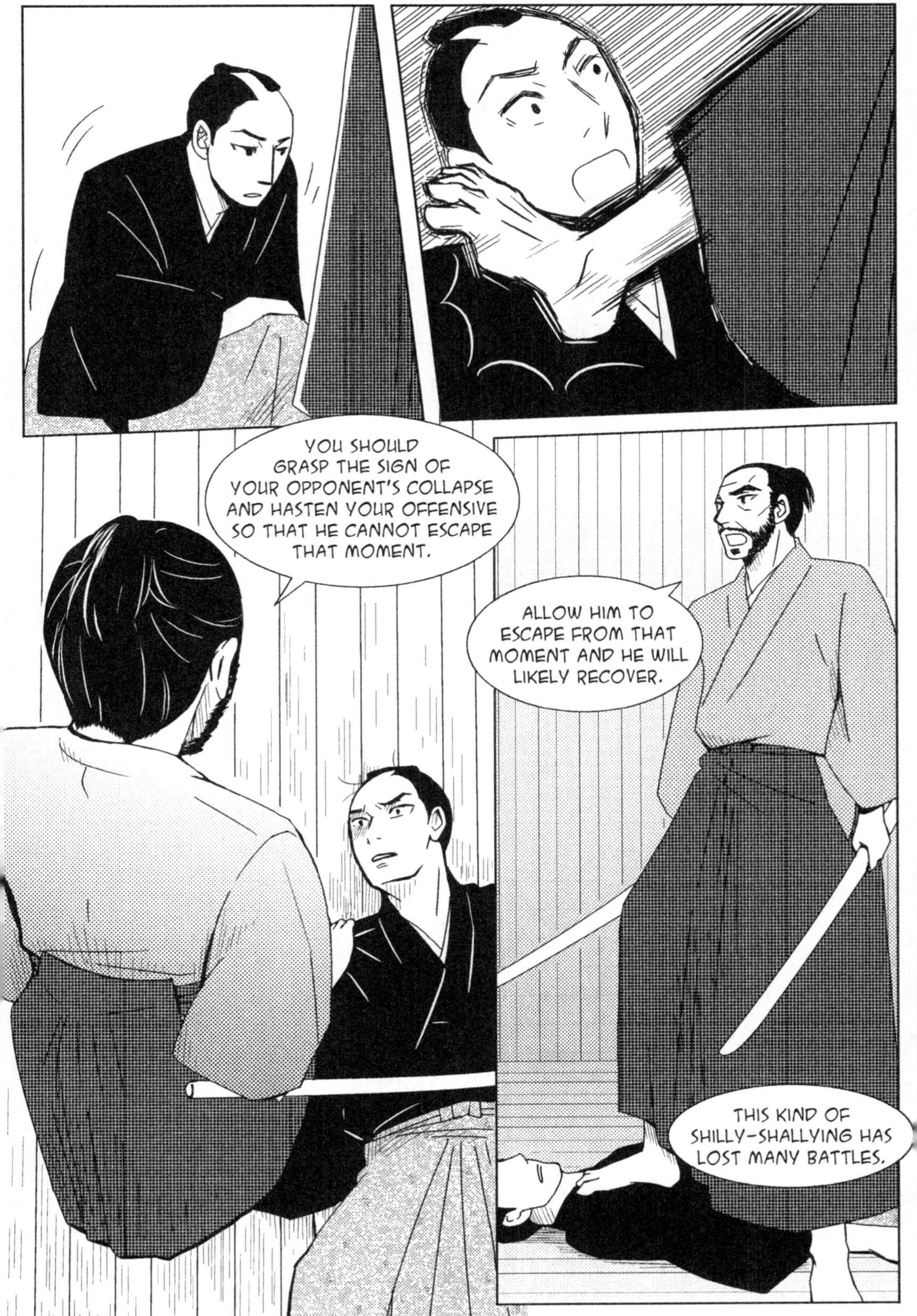
YOU SHOULD GRASP THE SIGN OF YOUR OPPONENT'S COLLAPSE AND HASTEN YOUR OFFENSIVE SO THAT HE CANNOT ESCAPE THAT MOMENT.
ALLOW HIM TO ESCAPE FROM THAT MOMENT AND HE WILL LIKELY RECOVER.
THIS KIND OF SHILLY-SHALLYING HAS LOST MANY BATTLES.

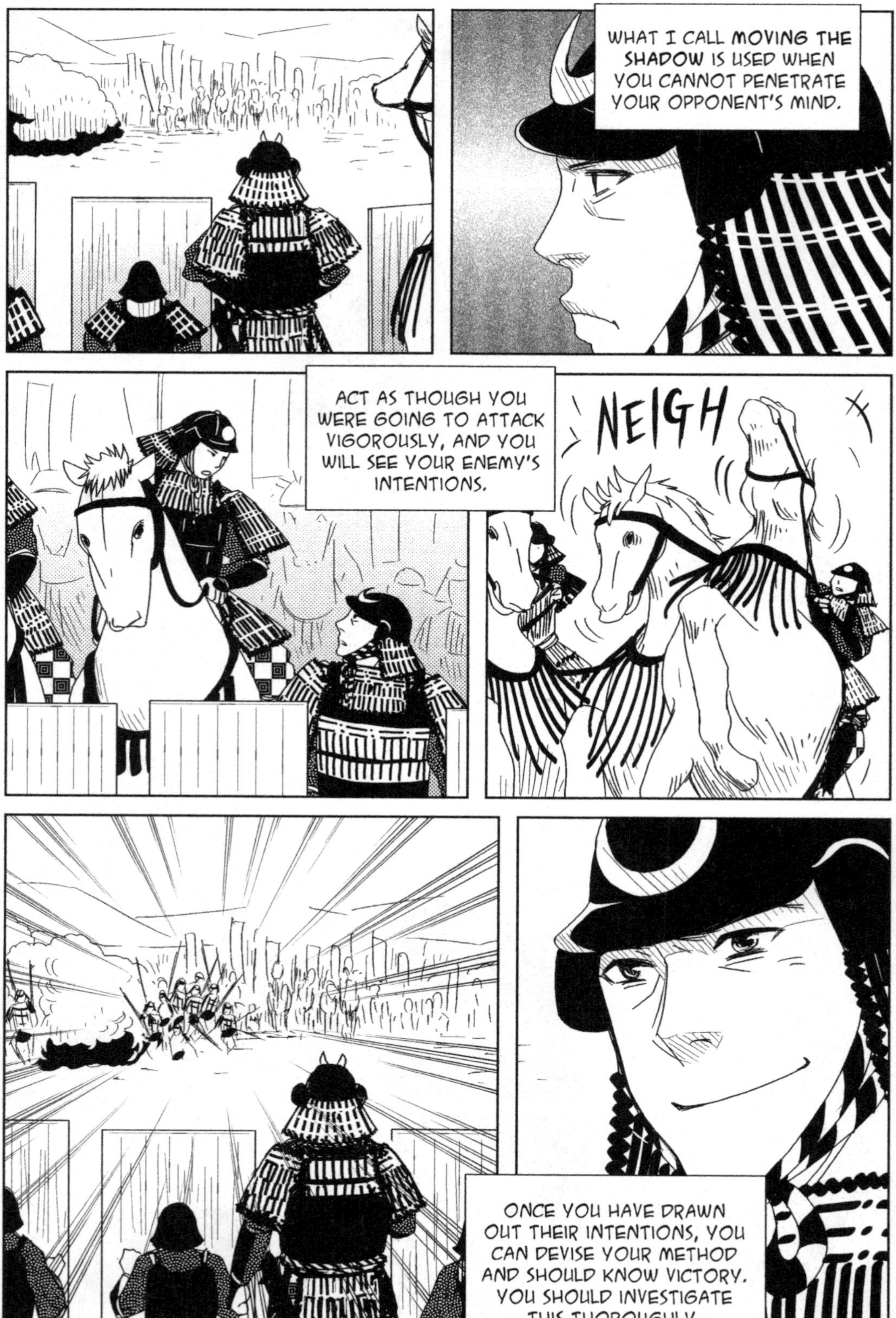
WHAT I CALL MOVING THE SHADOW IS USED WHEN YOU CANNOT PENETRATE YOUR OPPONENT'S MIND.
ACT AS THOUGH YOU WERE GOING TO ATTACK VIGOROUSLY, AND YOU WILL SEE YOUR ENEMY'S INTENTIONS.
NEIGH
ONCE YOU HAVE DRAWN OUT THEIR INTENTIONS, YOU CAN DEVISE YOUR METHOD AND SHOULD KNOW VICTORY. YOU SHOULD INVESTIGATE THIS THOROUGHLY.

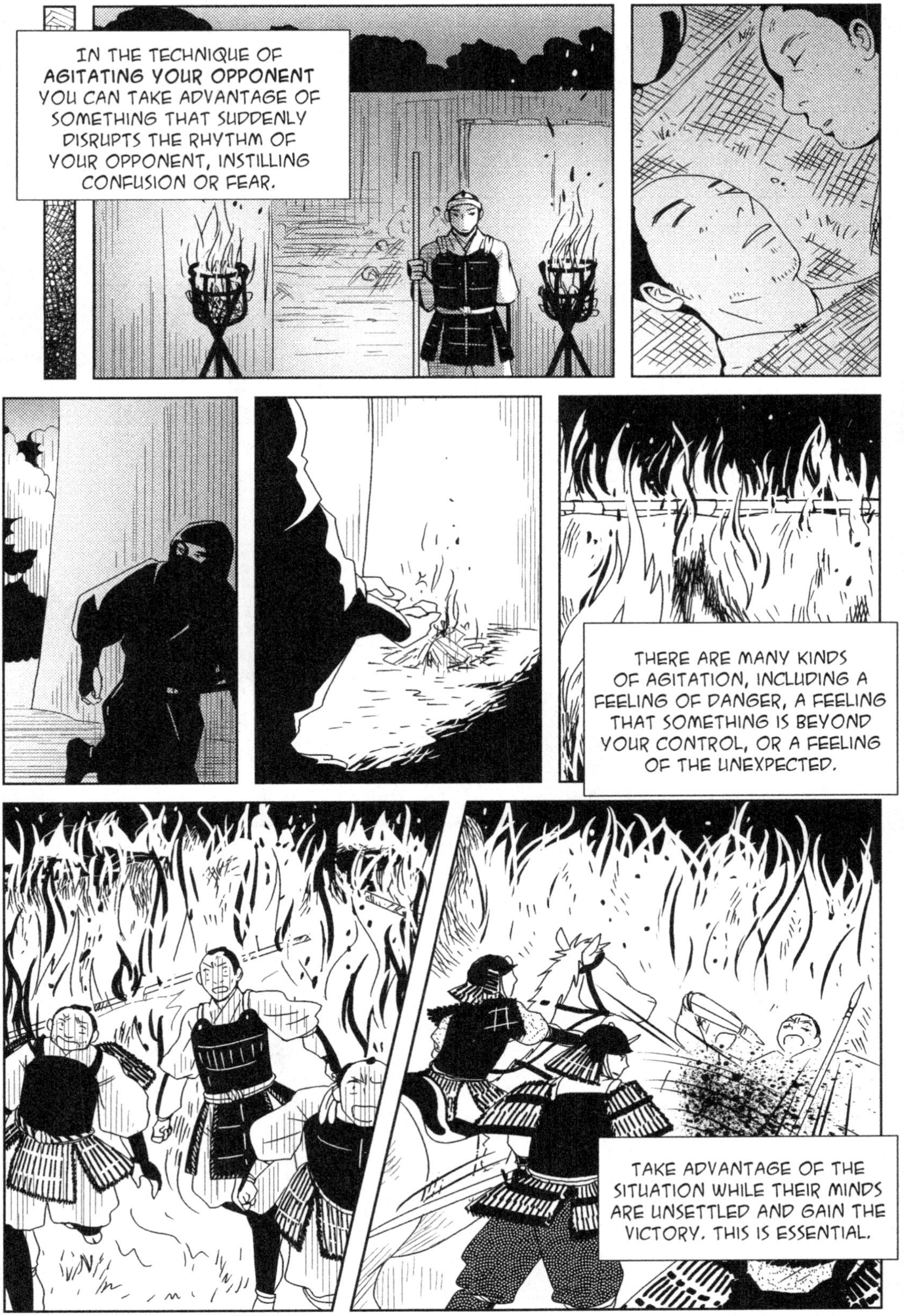
IN THE TECHNIQUE OF AGITATING YOUR OPPONENT YOU CAN TAKE ADVANTAGE OF SOMETHING THAT SUDDENLY DISRUPTS THE RHYTHM OF YOUR OPPONENT, INSTILLING CONFUSION OR FEAR.
THERE ARE MANY KINDS OF AGITATION, INCLUDING A FEELING OF DANGER, A FEELING THAT SOMETHING IS BEYOND YOUR CONTROL, OR A FEELING OF THE UNEXPECTED.
TAKE ADVANTAGE OF THE SITUATION WHILE THEIR MINDS ARE UNSETTLED AND GAIN THE VICTORY. THIS IS ESSENTIAL.

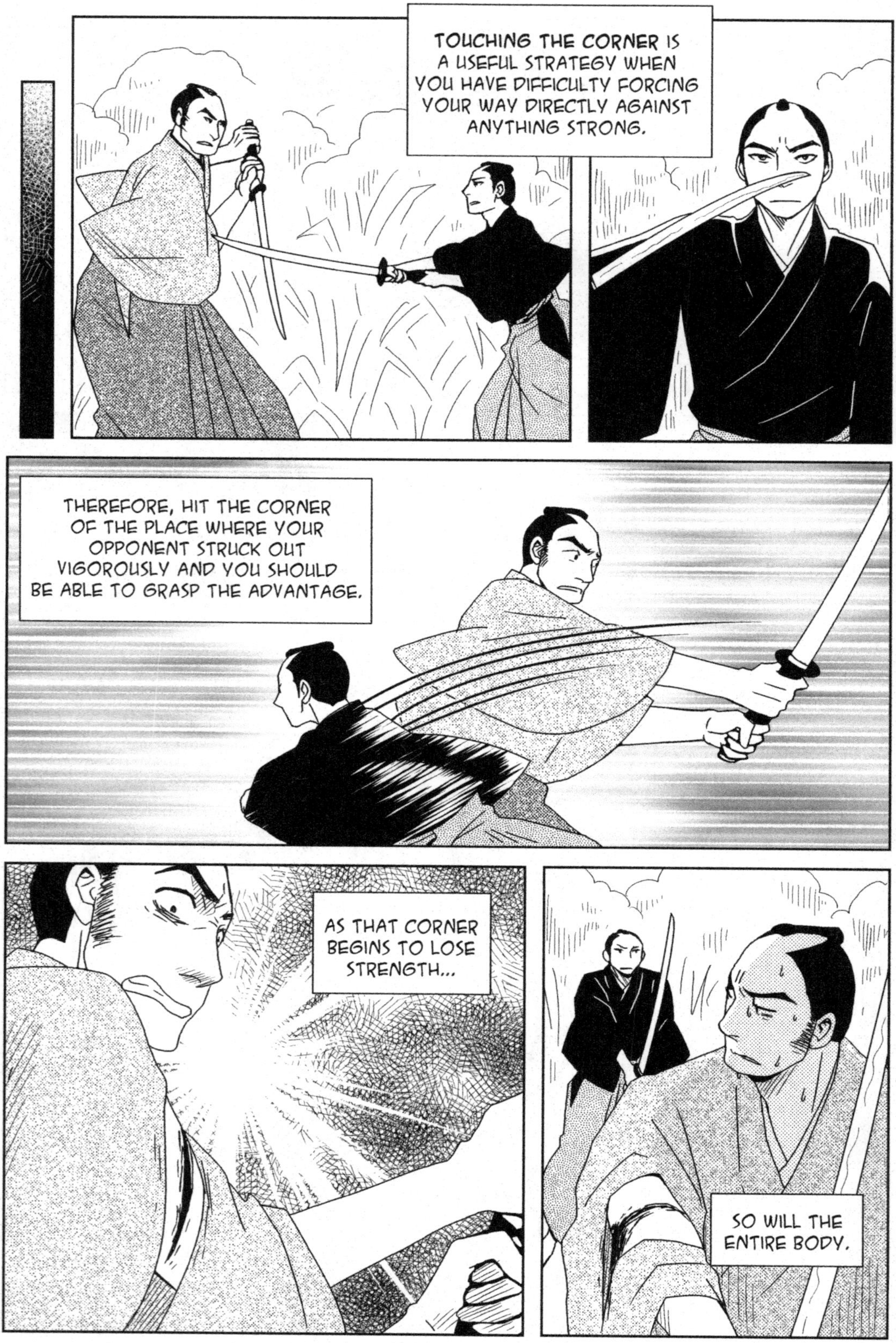
TOUCHING THE CORNER IS A USEFUL STRATEGY WHEN YOU HAVE DIFFICULTY FORCING YOUR WAY DIRECTLY AGAINST ANYTHING STRONG.
THEREFORE, HIT THE CORNER OF THE PLACE WHERE YOUR OPPONENT STRUCK OUT VIGOROUSLY AND YOU SHOULD BE ABLE TO GRASP THE ADVANTAGE.
AS THAT CORNER BEGINS TO LOSE STRENGTH...
SO WILL THE ENTIRE BODY.

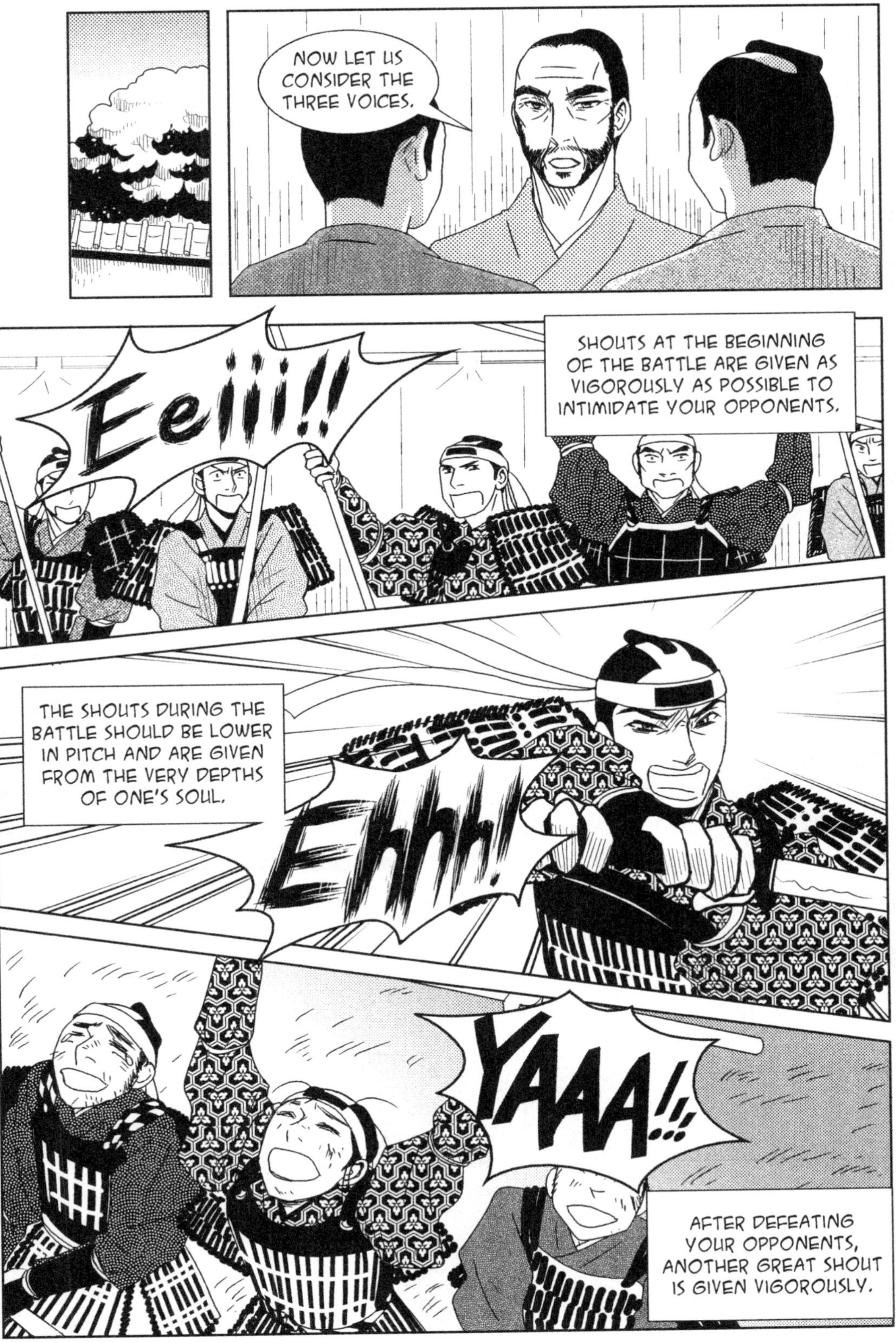
NOW LET US CONSIDER THE THREE VOICES.
SHOUTS AT THE BEGINNING OF THE BATTLE ARE GIVEN AS VIGOROUSLY AS POSSIBLE TO INTIMIDATE YOUR OPPONENTS.
Eeiii!!
THE SHOUTS DURING THE BATTLE SHOULD BE LOWER IN PITCH AND ARE GIVEN FROM THE VERY DEPTHS OF ONE'S SOUL.
Ehhh!
YAAA!!!
AFTER DEFEATING YOUR OPPONENTS, ANOTHER GREAT SHOUT IS GIVEN VIGOROUSLY.

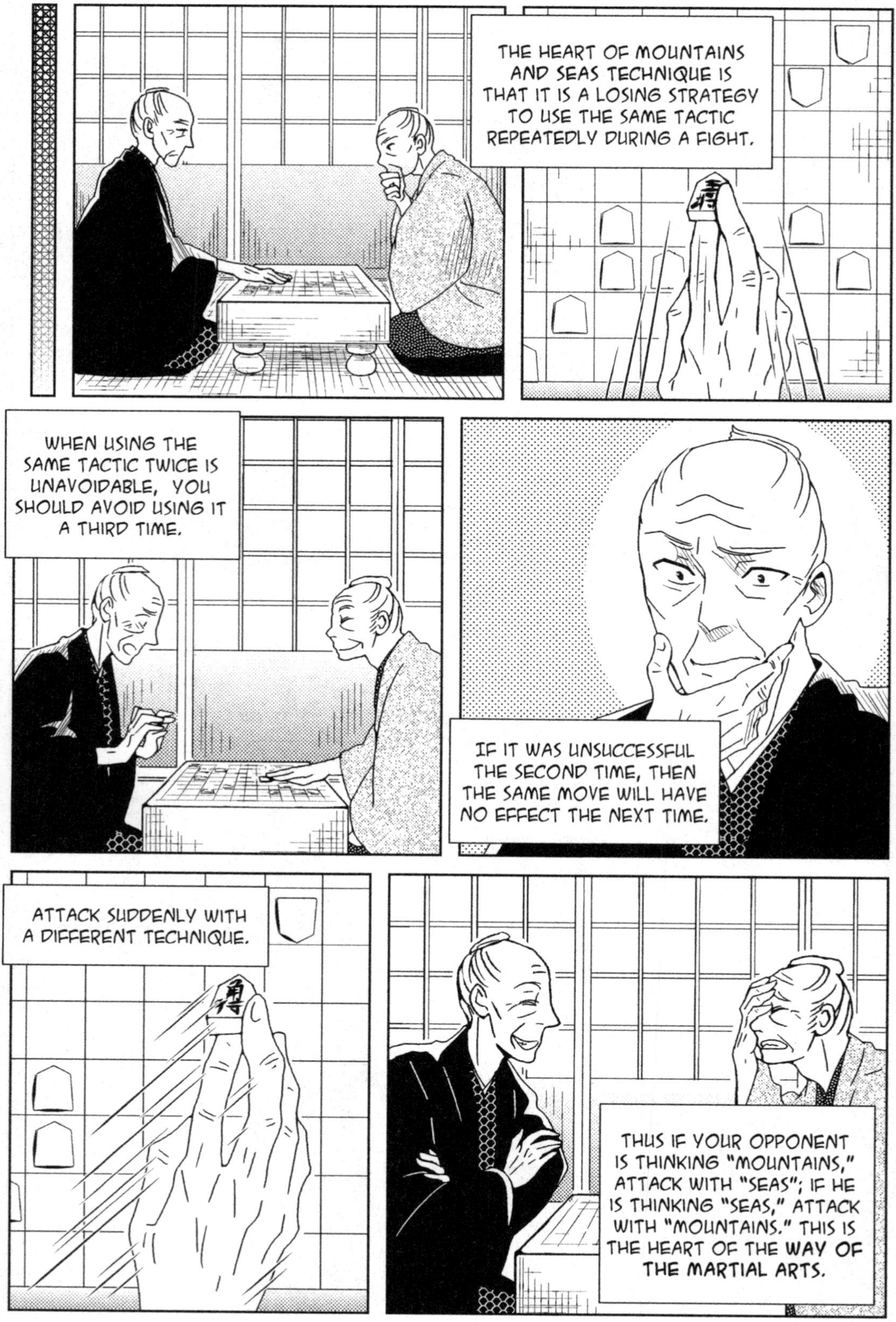
THE HEART OF MOUNTAINS AND SEAS TECHNIQUE IS THAT IT IS A LOSING STRATEGY TO USE THE SAME TACTIC REPEATEDLY DURING A FIGHT.
WHEN USING THE SAME TACTIC TWICE IS UNAVOIDABLE, YOU SHOULD AVOID USING IT A THIRD TIME.
IF IT WAS UNSUCCESSFUL THE SECOND TIME, THEN THE SAME MOVE WILL HAVE NO EFFECT THE NEXT TIME.
ATTACK SUDDENLY WITH A DIFFERENT TECHNIQUE.
THUS IF YOUR OPPONENT IS THINKING "MOUNTAINS," ATTACK WITH "SEAS"; IF HE IS THINKING "SEAS," ATTACK WITH "MOUNTAINS." THIS IS THE HEART OF THE WAY OF THE MARTIAL ARTS.

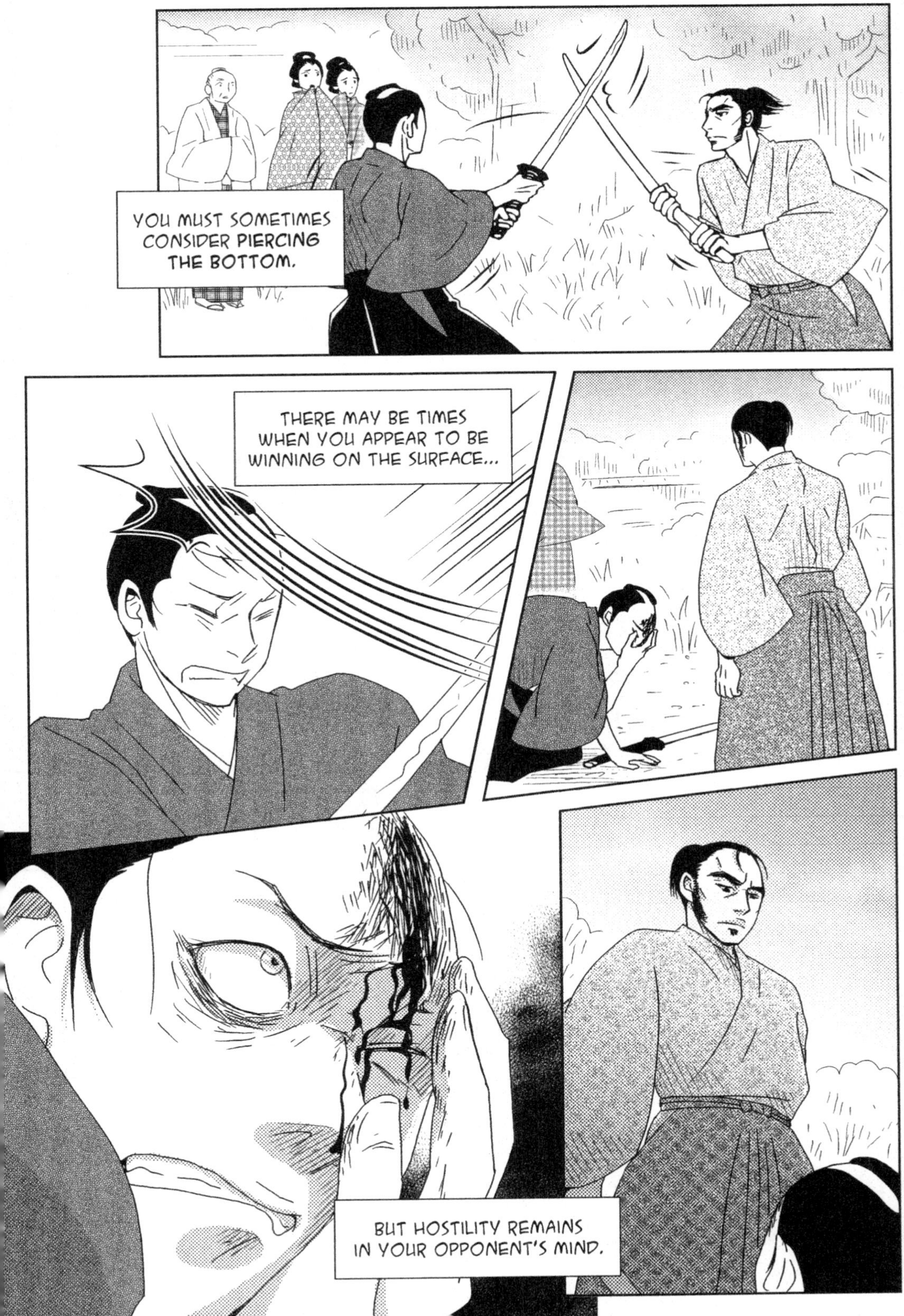
YOU MUST SOMETIMES CONSIDER PIERCING THE BOTTOM.
THERE MAY BE TIMES WHEN YOU APPEAR TO BE WINNING ON THE SURFACE...
BUT HOSTILITY REMAINS IN YOUR OPPONENT'S MIND.

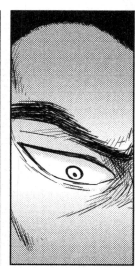

IN SUCH SITUATIONS,
IT IS IMPORTANT THAT
YOU DESTROY YOUR
OPPONENT'S SPIRIT.

AND MAKE SURE
THAT HE HAS BEEN
DEFEATED TO THE VERY
BOTTOM OF HIS HEART.

THIS CAN BE DONE
WITH THE SWORD, THE
BODY, OR THE MIND.

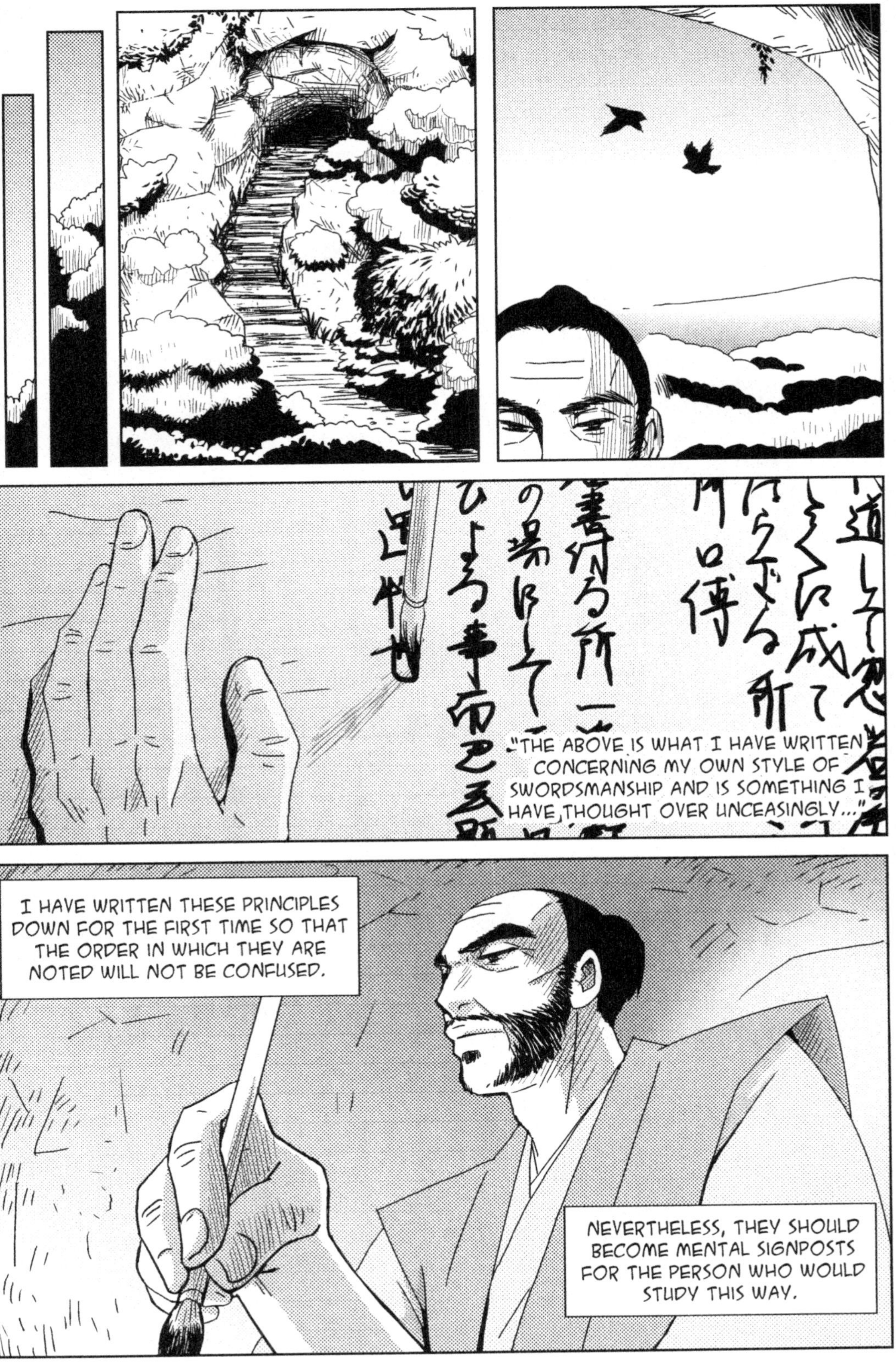
"THE ABOVE IS WHAT I HAVE WRITTEN CONCERNING MY OWN STYLE OF SWORDSMANSHIP AND IS SOMETHING I HAVE THOUGHT OVER UNCEASINGLY..."
I HAVE WRITTEN THESE PRINCIPLES DOWN FOR THE FIRST TIME SO THAT THE ORDER IN WHICH THEY ARE NOTED WILL NOT BE CONFUSED.
NEVERTHELESS, THEY SHOULD BECOME MENTAL SIGNPOSTS FOR THE PERSON WHO WOULD STUDY THIS WAY.

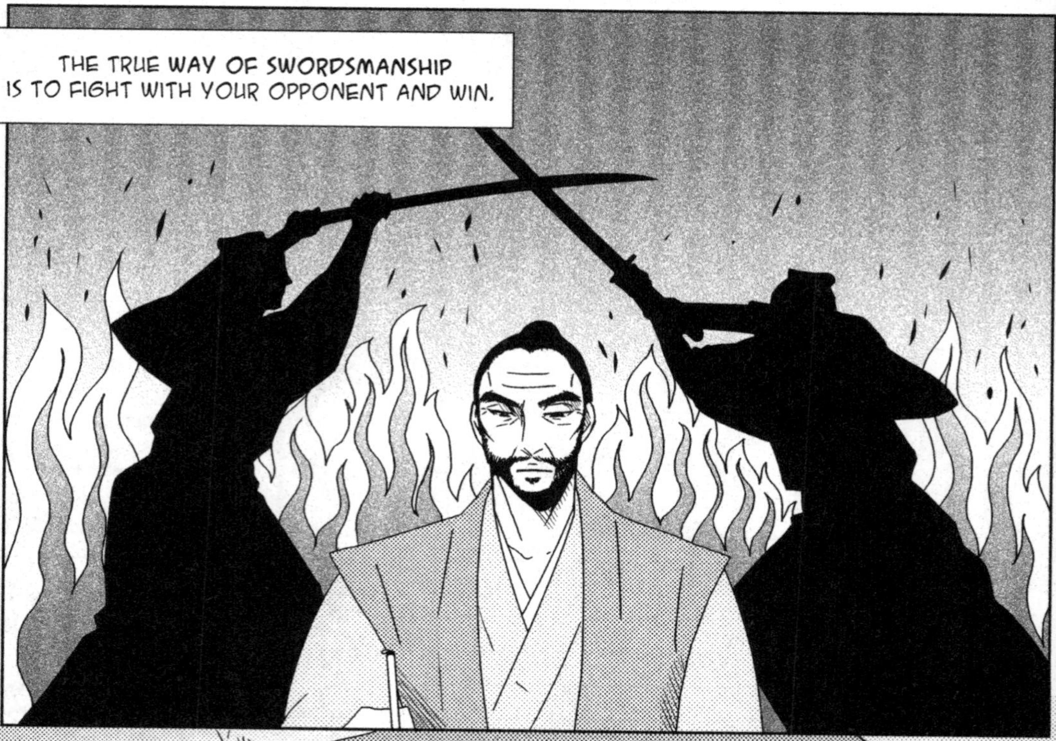
THE TRUE WAY OF SWORDSMANSHIP IS TO FIGHT WITH YOUR OPPONENT AND WIN.

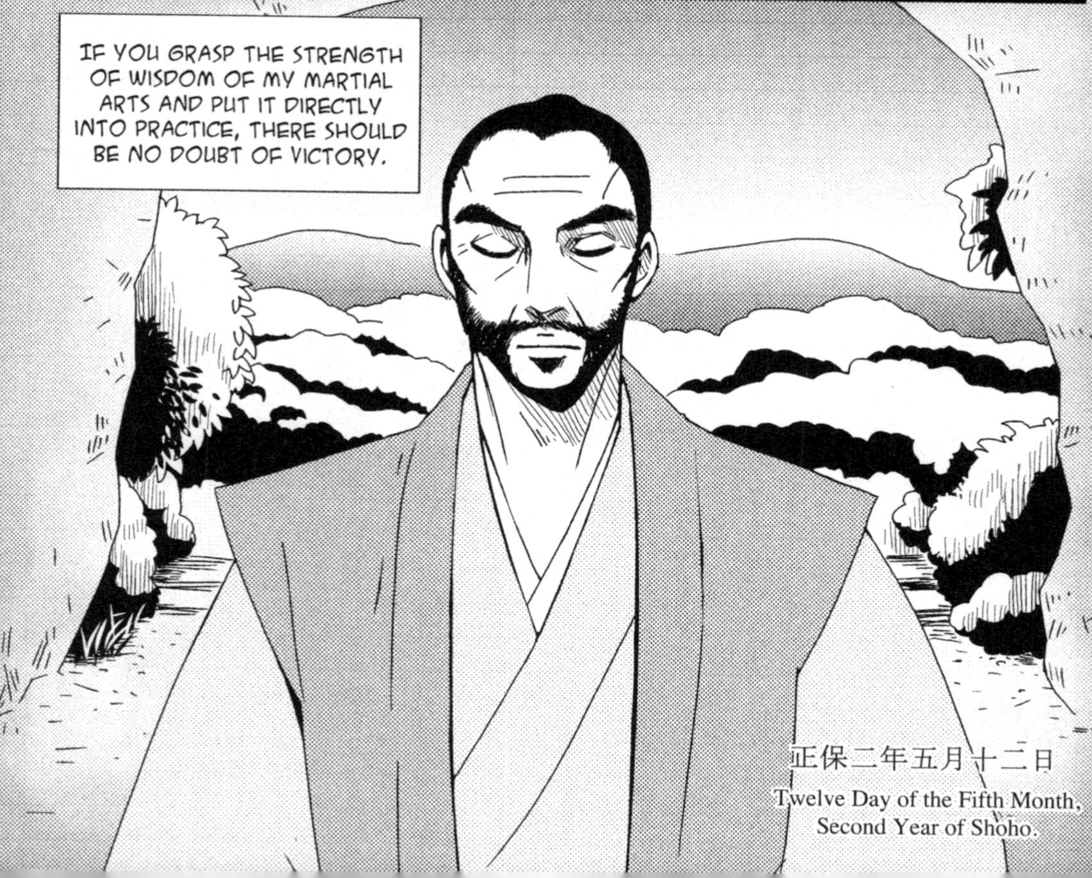
IF YOU GRASP THE STRENGTH OF WISDOM OF MY MARTIAL ARTS AND PUT IT DIRECTLY INTO PRACTICE, THERE SHOULD BE NO DOUBT OF VICTORY.
正保二年五月十二日
Twelve Day of the Fifth Month, Second Year of Shoho.

4

WIND

風

In the martial arts, you know the Way of other styles. As I write about these other styles of martial arts here, I have designated this as "The Wind Chapter." It would be quite difficult to understand the Way of my style without knowing the Way of others.

The other schools get along with this as a performance art, as a method of making a living, as a colorful decoration, or as a means of forcing flowers to bloom. Yet, can it be the True Way if it has been made into a salable item?

Moreover, the other martial arts in the world only give fine attention to swordsmanship: teaching ways of handling the sword, body, posture, or hand positions. Can you understand how to win by these things? In this chapter, I will express with certainty that none of these are the True Way.

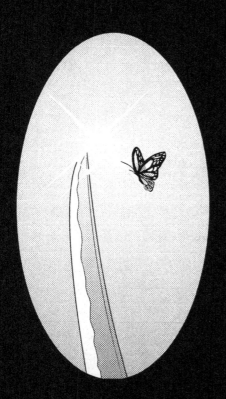

HEY, COME ON! QUICKLY!

WHAT? WHAT'S HAPPENED?

SENSEI IS GOING TO FIGHT!

REALLY?

EHH???

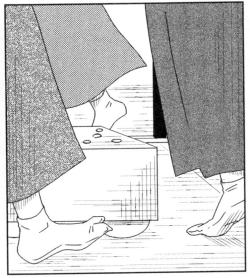

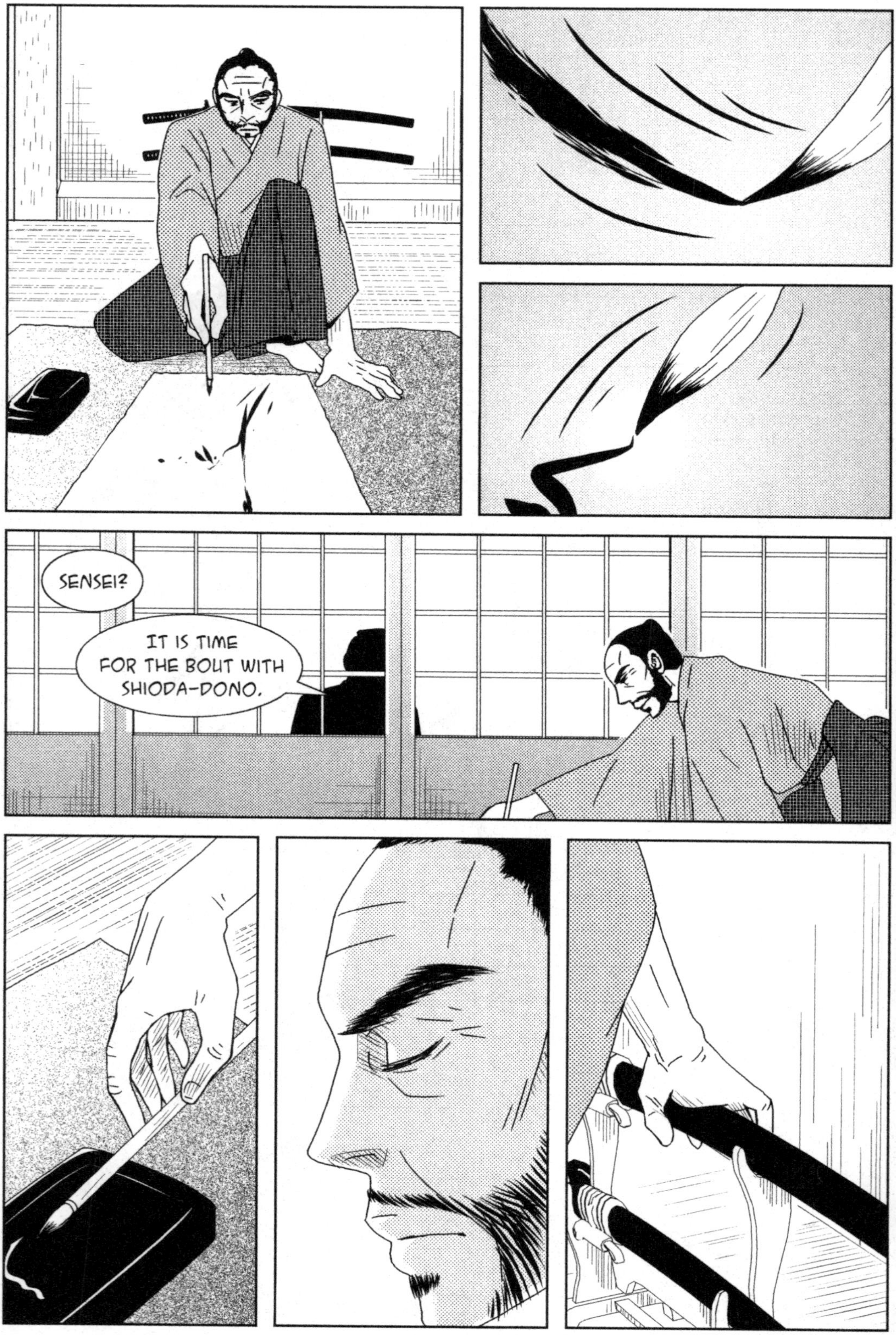
SENSEI?
IT IS TIME FOR THE BOUT WITH SHIODA-DONO.

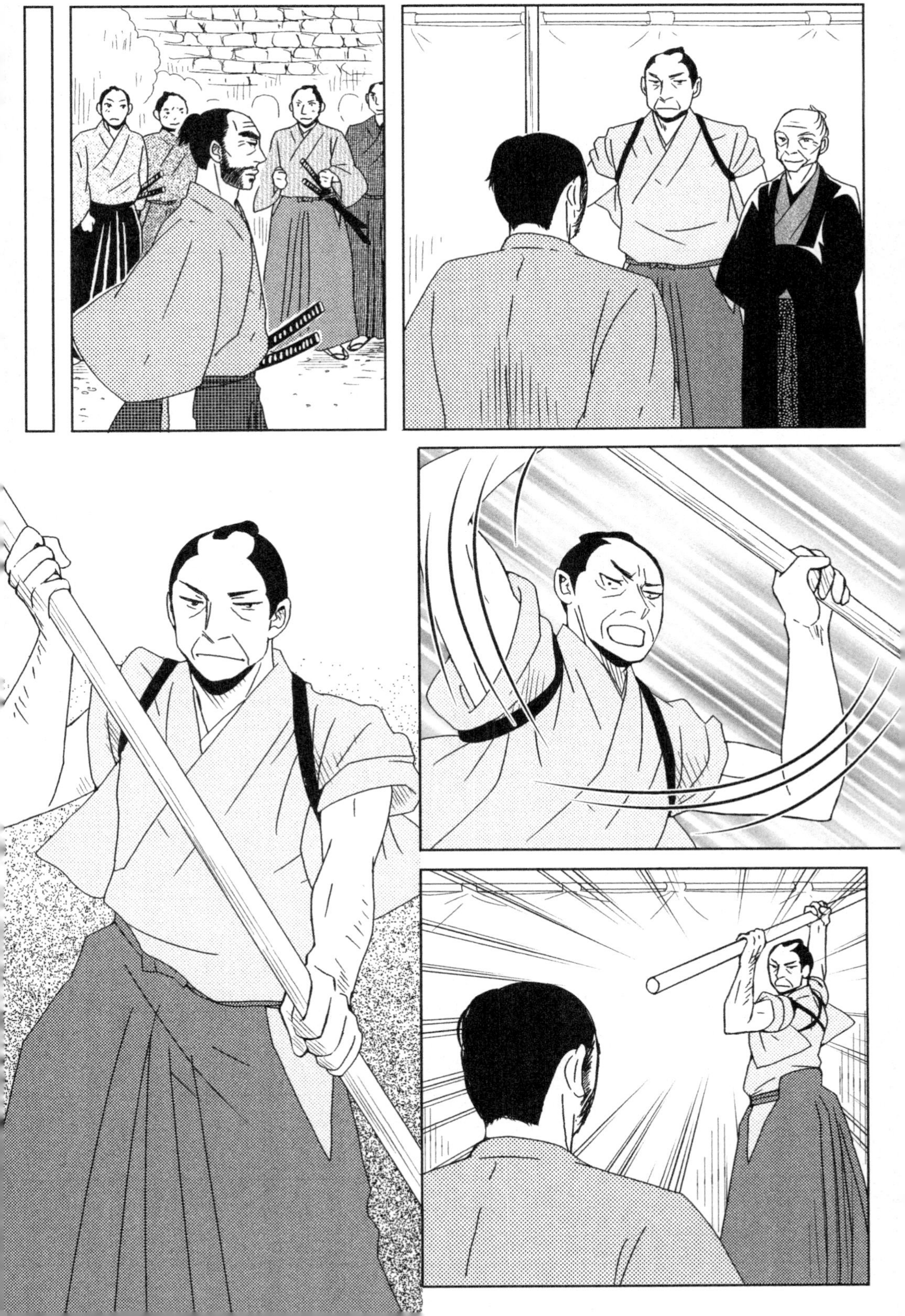

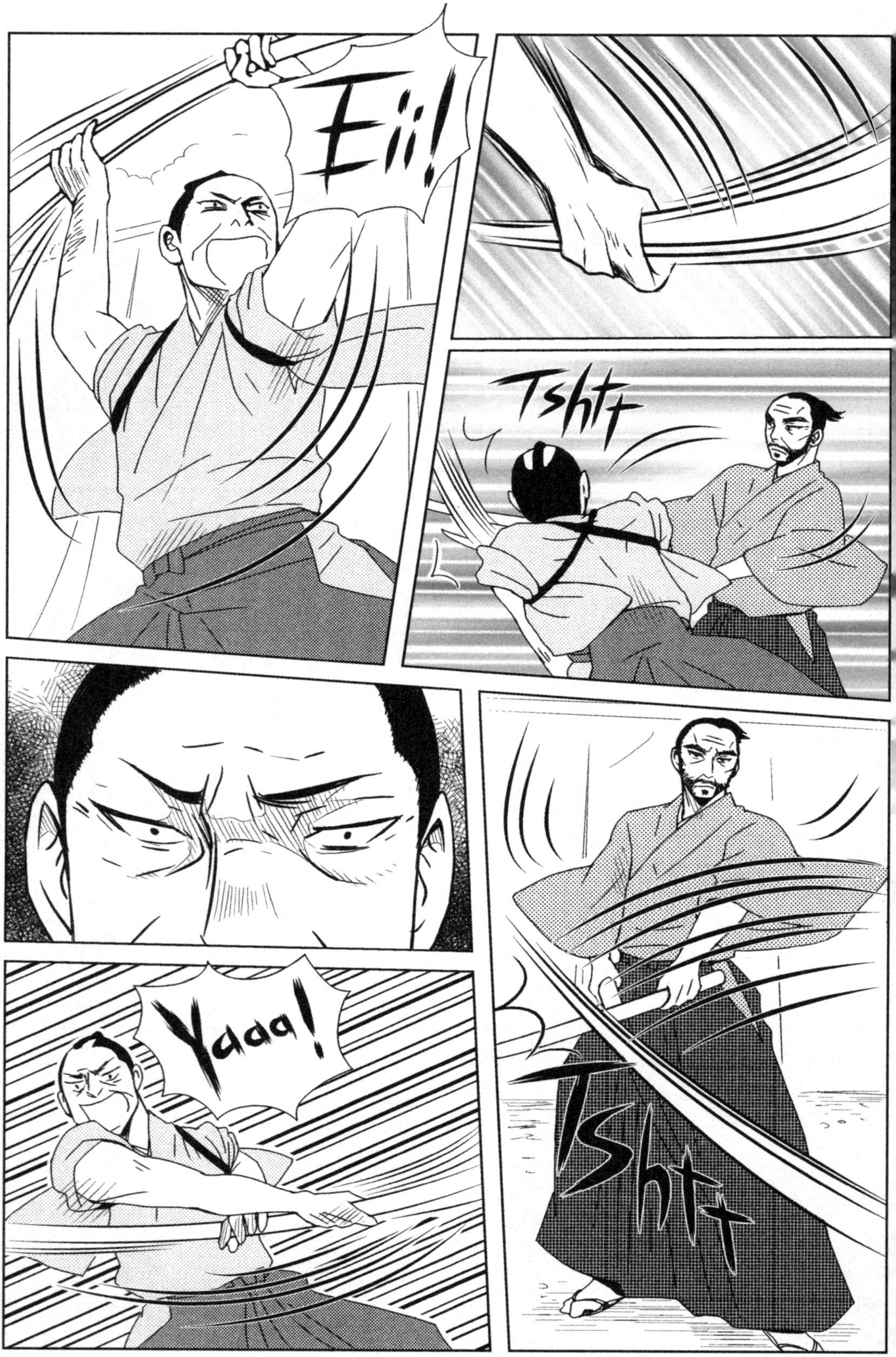
Eii!
Tshtt
Yaaa!
Tshtt

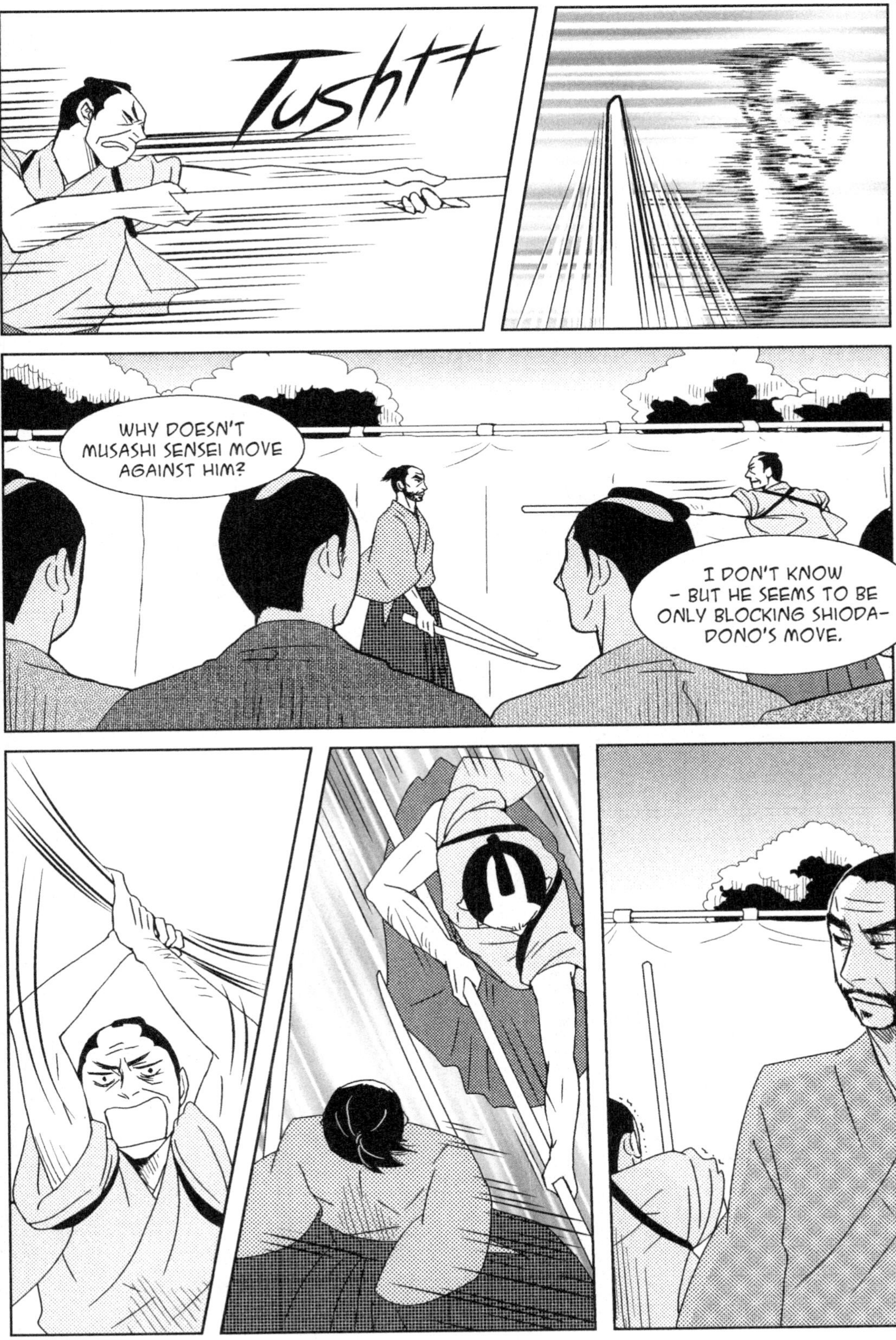
Tusht+
WHY DOESN'T MUSASHI SENSEI MOVE AGAINST HIM?
I DON'T KNOW - BUT HE SEEMS TO BE ONLY BLOCKING SHIODA-DONO'S MOVE.

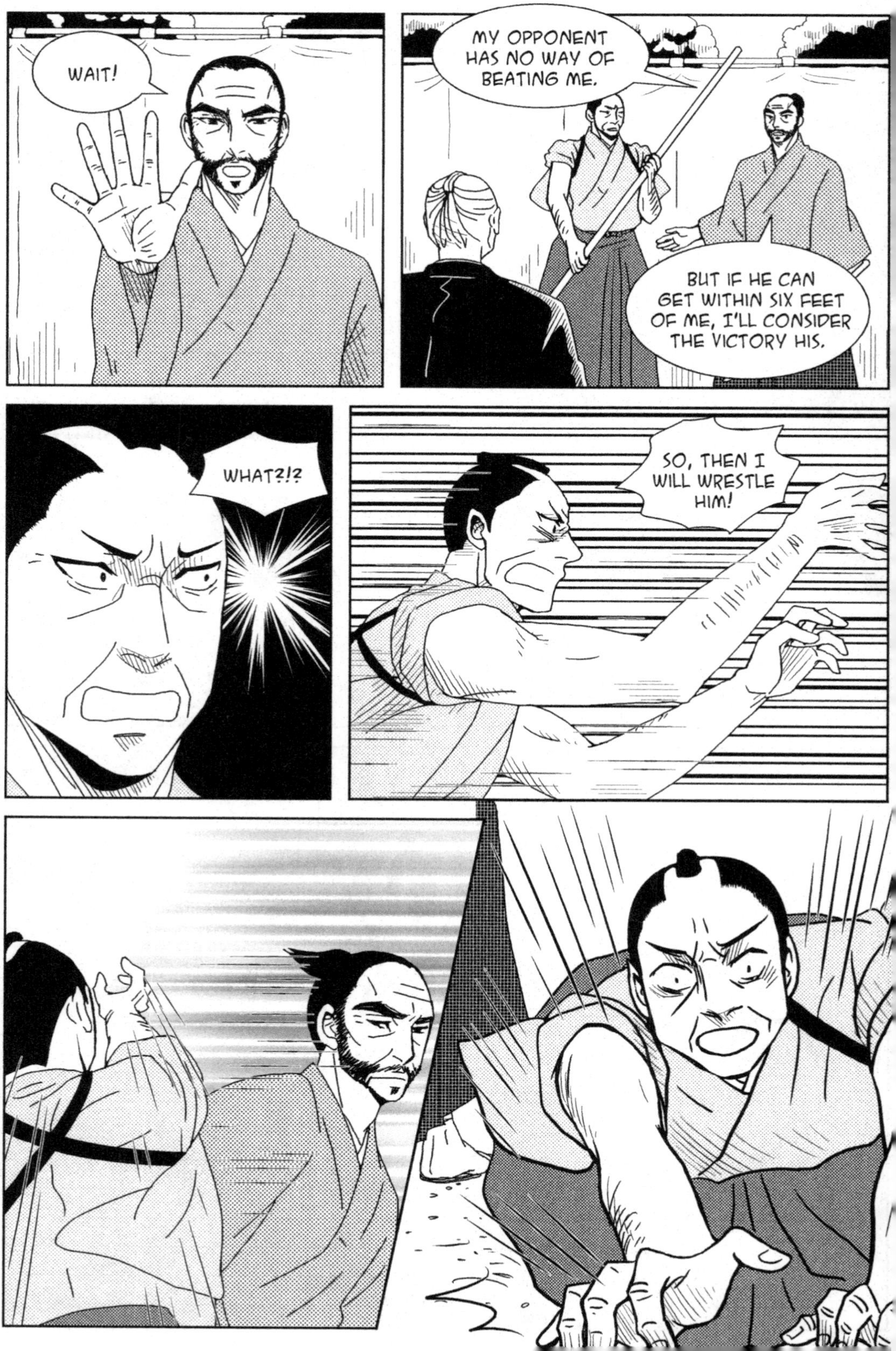
WAIT!
MY OPPONENT HAS NO WAY OF BEATING ME.
BUT IF HE CAN GET WITHIN SIX FEET OF ME, I'LL CONSIDER THE VICTORY HIS.
WHAT?!?
SO, THEN I WILL WRESTLE HIM!

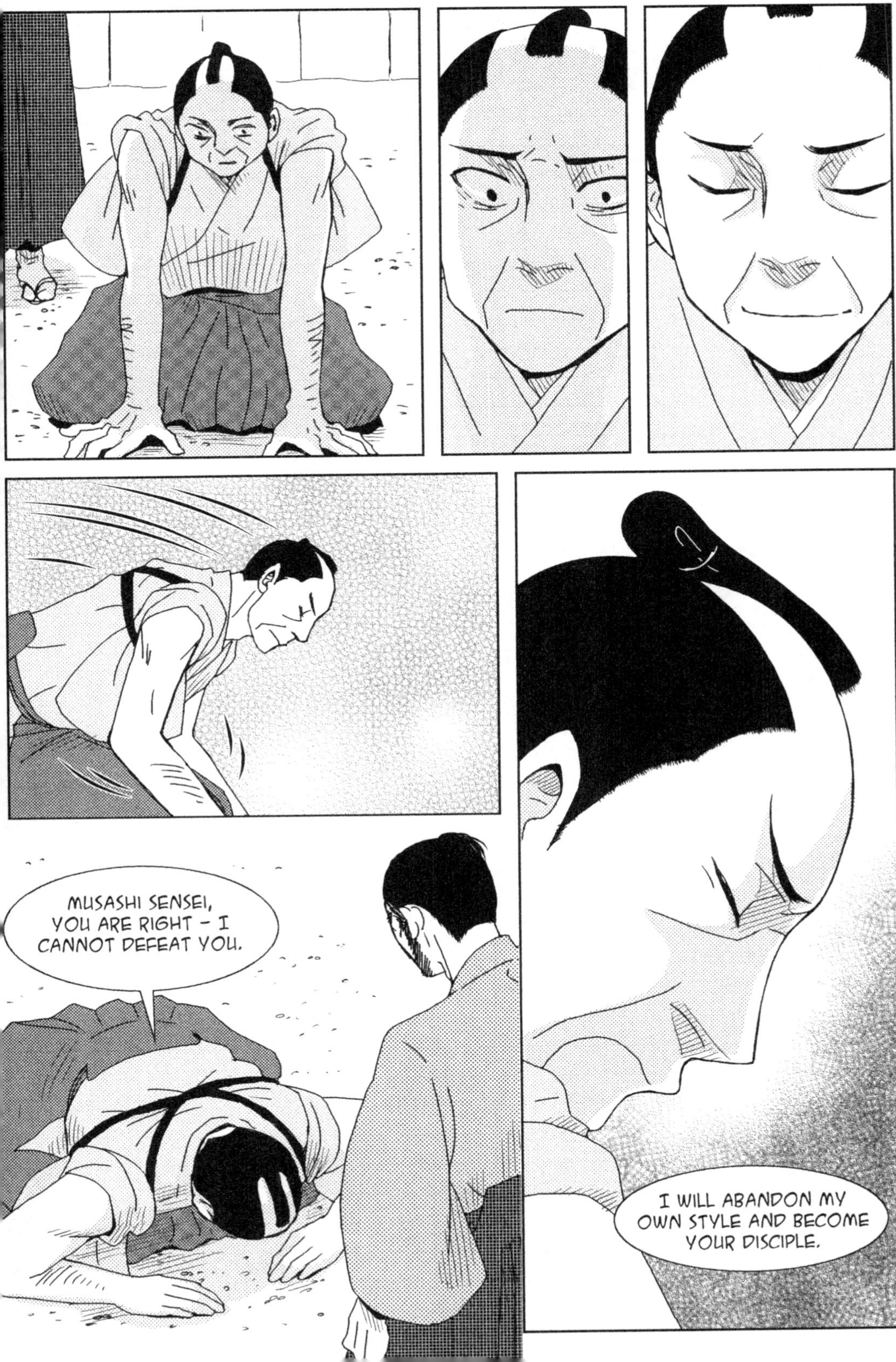
MUSASHI SENSEI, YOU ARE RIGHT – I CANNOT DEFEAT YOU.
I WILL ABANDON MY OWN STYLE AND BECOME YOUR DISCIPLE.

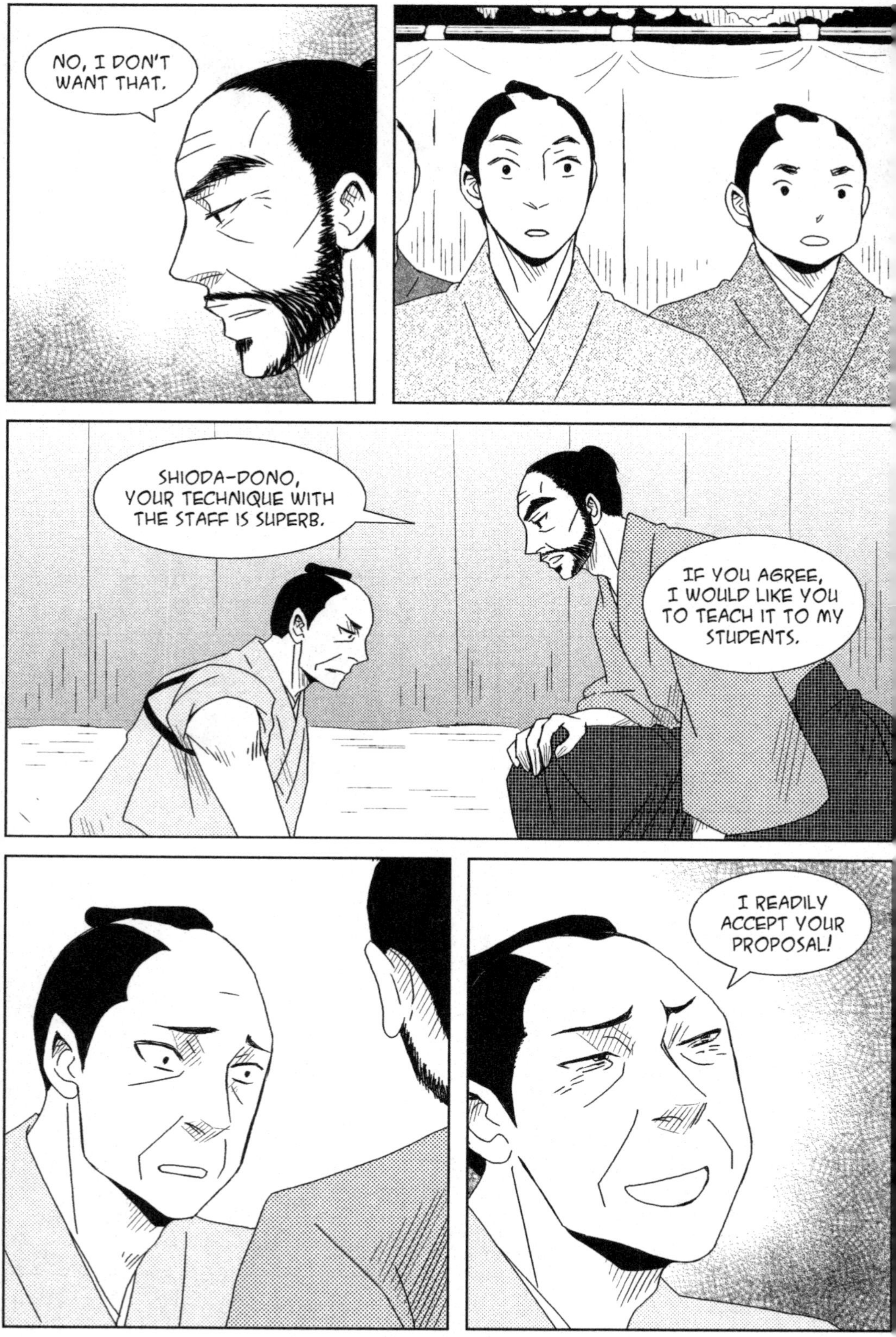
NO, I DON'T WANT THAT.
SHIODA-DONO, YOUR TECHNIQUE WITH THE STAFF IS SUPERB.
IF YOU AGREE, I WOULD LIKE YOU TO TEACH IT TO MY STUDENTS.
I READILY ACCEPT YOUR PROPOSAL!

THIS WAS MUSASHI'S LAST BOUT.

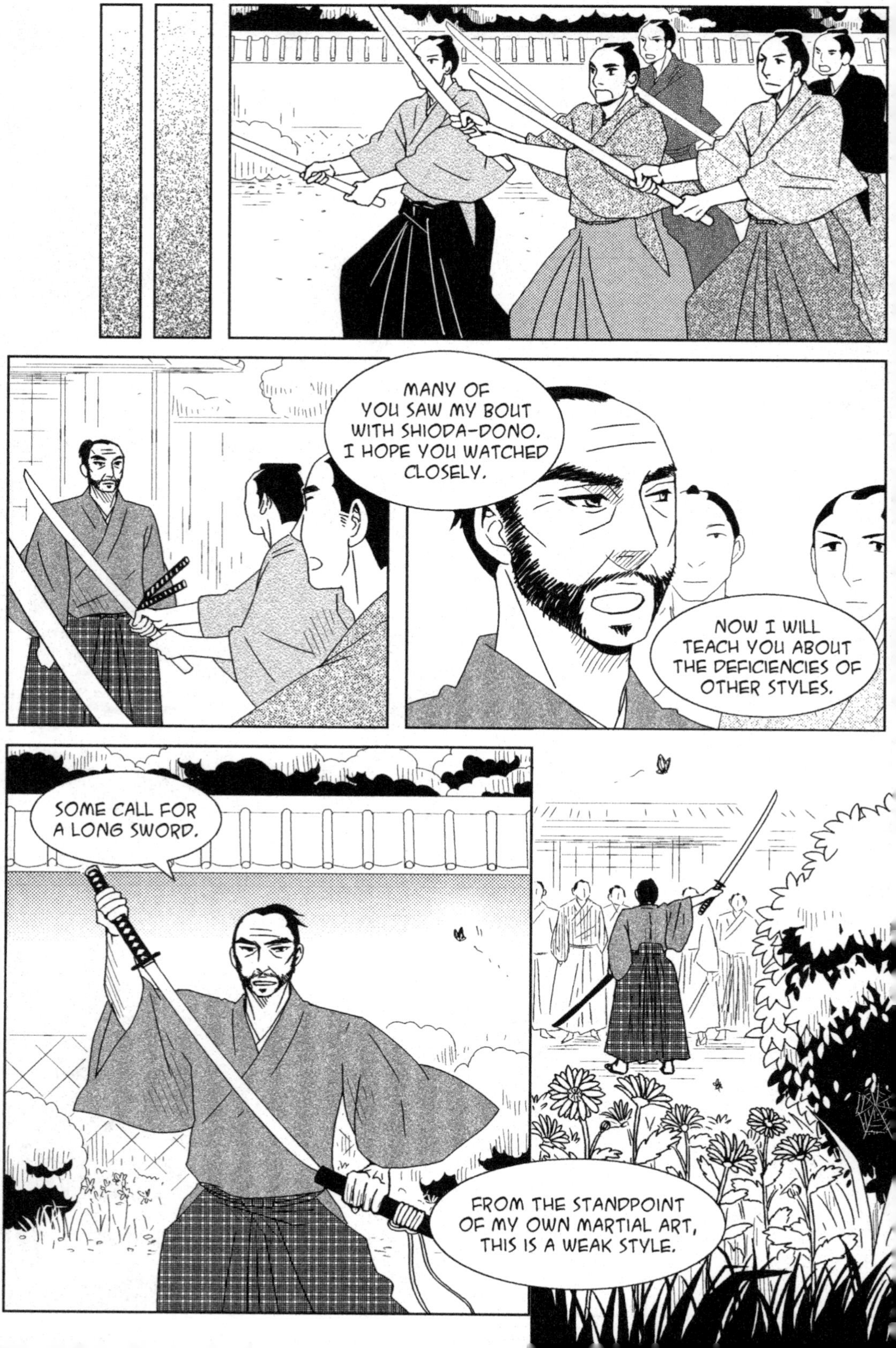
MANY OF YOU SAW MY BOUT WITH SHIODA-DONO. I HOPE YOU WATCHED CLOSELY.
NOW I WILL TEACH YOU ABOUT THE DEFICIENCIES OF OTHER STYLES.
SOME CALL FOR A LONG SWORD.
FROM THE STANDPOINT OF MY OWN MARTIAL ART, THIS IS A WEAK STYLE.

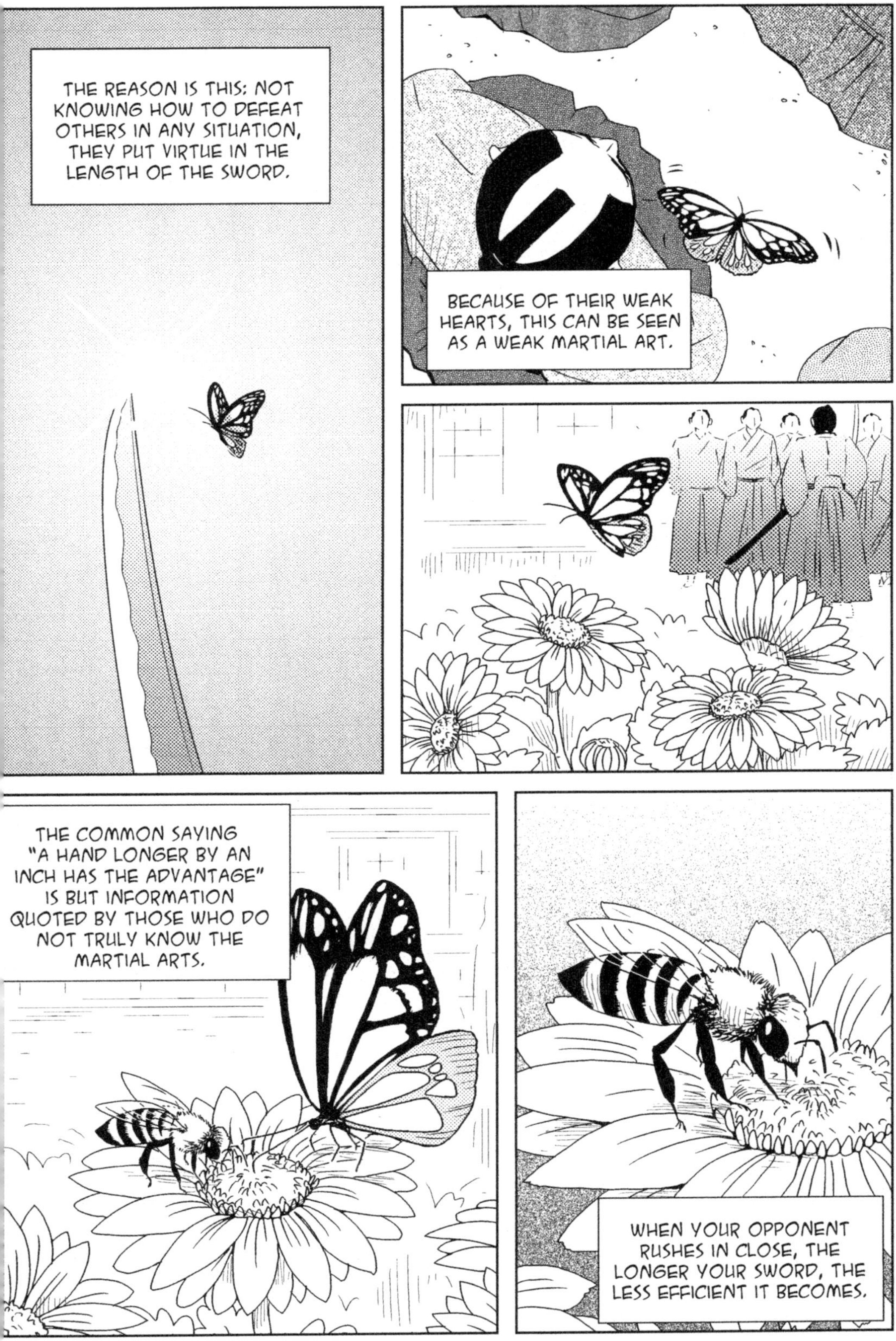
THE REASON IS THIS: NOT KNOWING HOW TO DEFEAT OTHERS IN ANY SITUATION, THEY PUT VIRTUE IN THE LENGTH OF THE SWORD.
BECAUSE OF THEIR WEAK HEARTS, THIS CAN BE SEEN AS A WEAK MARTIAL ART.
THE COMMON SAYING "A HAND LONGER BY AN INCH HAS THE ADVANTAGE" IS BUT INFORMATION QUOTED BY THOSE WHO DO NOT TRULY KNOW THE MARTIAL ARTS.
WHEN YOUR OPPONENT RUSHES IN CLOSE, THE LONGER YOUR SWORD, THE LESS EFFICIENT IT BECOMES.

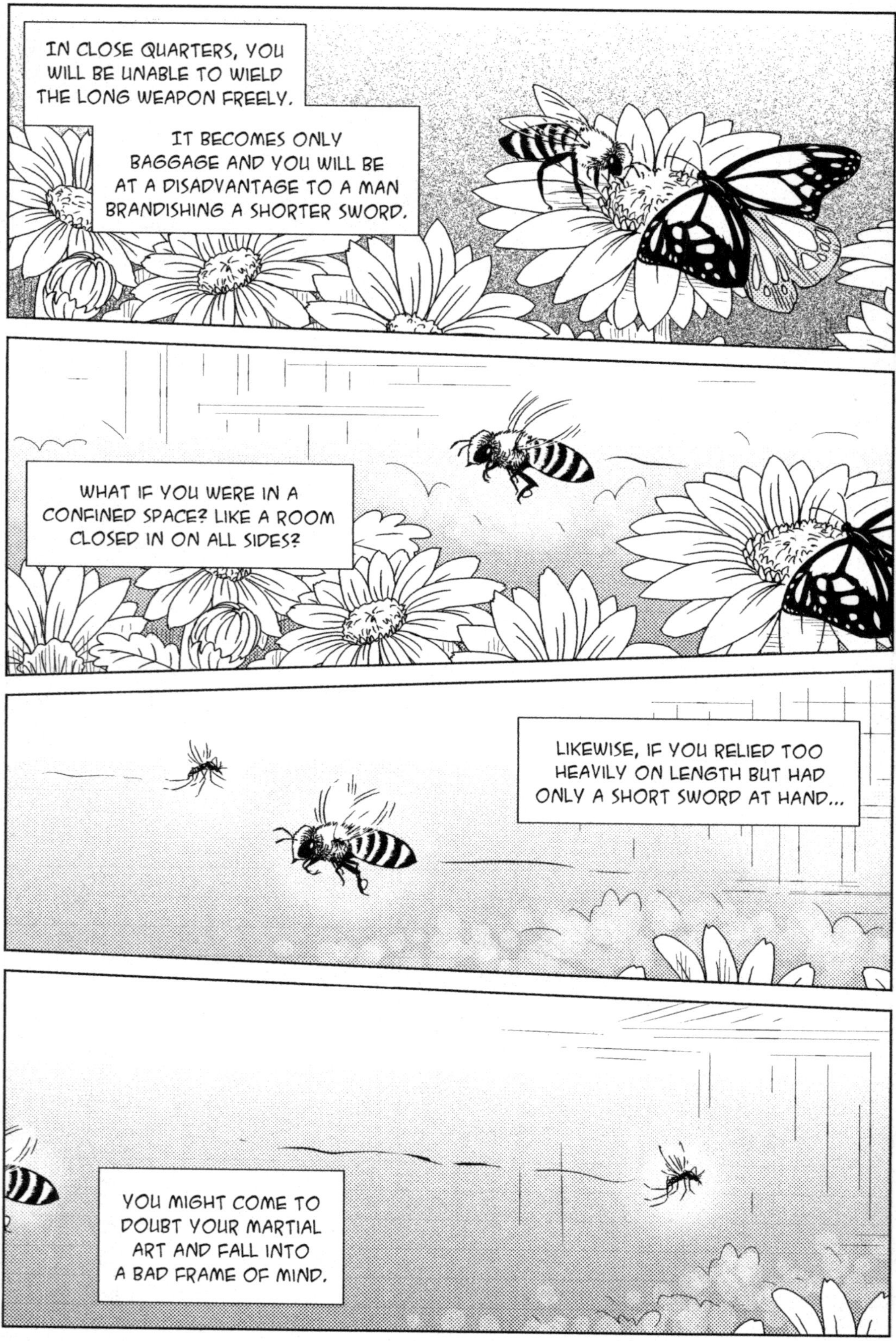

IN CLOSE QUARTERS, YOU WILL BE UNABLE TO WIELD THE LONG WEAPON FREELY.
IT BECOMES ONLY BAGGAGE AND YOU WILL BE AT A DISADVANTAGE TO A MAN BRANDISHING A SHORTER SWORD.
WHAT IF YOU WERE IN A CONFINED SPACE? LIKE A ROOM CLOSED IN ON ALL SIDES?
LIKEWISE, IF YOU RELIED TOO HEAVILY ON LENGTH BUT HAD ONLY A SHORT SWORD AT HAND...
YOU MIGHT COME TO DOUBT YOUR MARTIAL ART AND FALL INTO A BAD FRAME OF MIND.

A LONG SWORD IS LIKE HAVING MANY MEN IN A FACE-OFF, WHILE A SHORT SWORD IS LIKE HAVING ONLY A FEW.

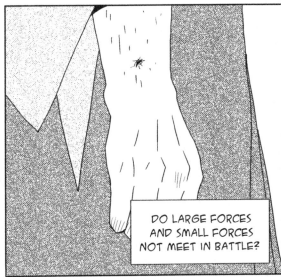

DO LARGE FORCES AND SMALL FORCES NOT MEET IN BATTLE?

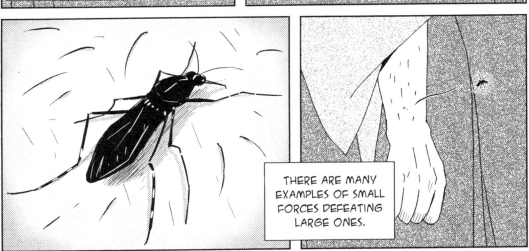

THERE ARE MANY EXAMPLES OF SMALL FORCES DEFEATING LARGE ONES.

IN MY MARTIAL ART, WE DISLIKE SUCH ONE-SIDEDNESS AND NARROWNESS OF MIND.

YOU SHOULD INVESTIGATE THIS THOROUGHLY.

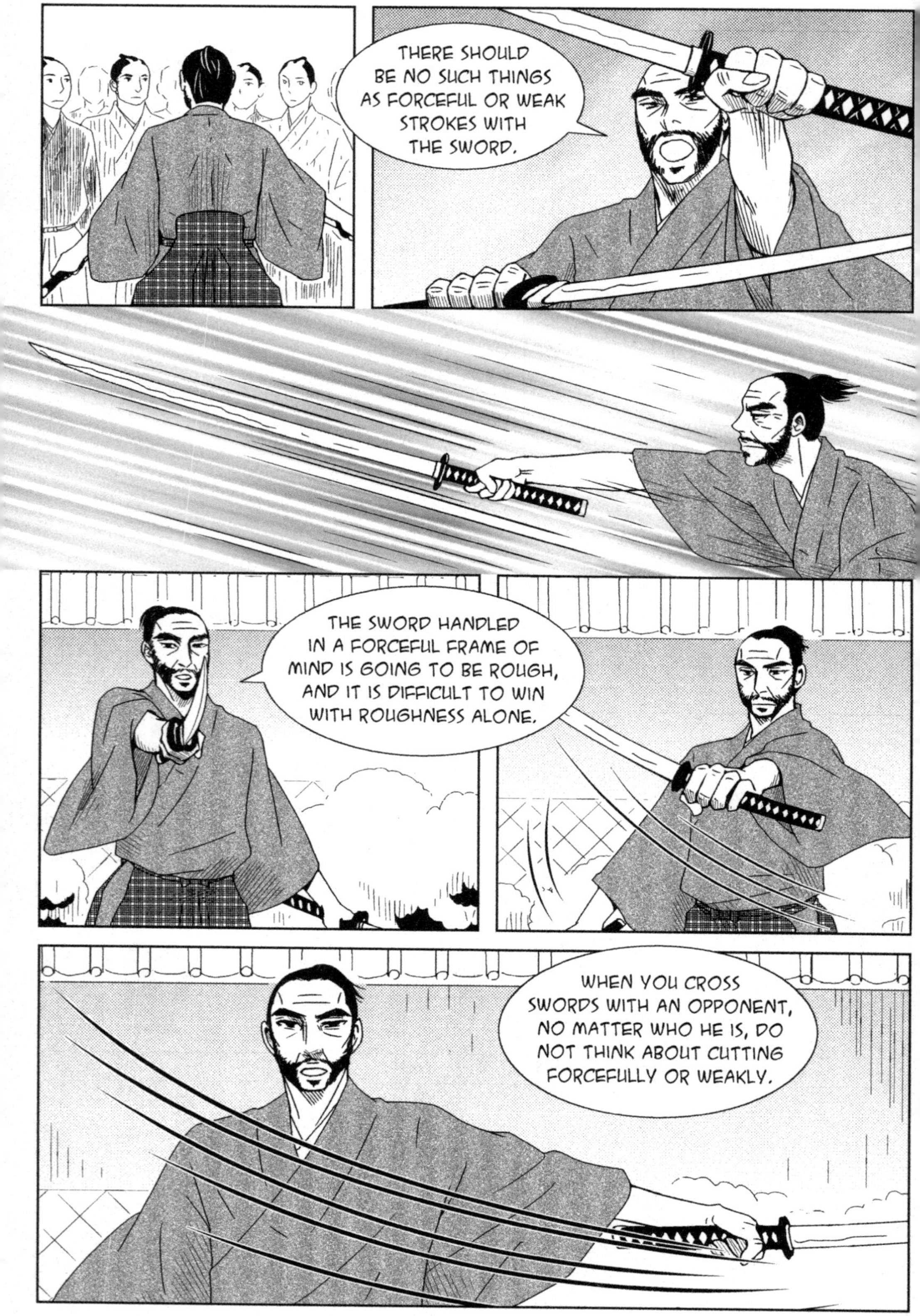

THERE SHOULD BE NO SUCH THINGS AS FORCEFUL OR WEAK STROKES WITH THE SWORD.
THE SWORD HANDLED IN A FORCEFUL FRAME OF MIND IS GOING TO BE ROUGH, AND IT IS DIFFICULT TO WIN WITH ROUGHNESS ALONE.
WHEN YOU CROSS SWORDS WITH AN OPPONENT, NO MATTER WHO HE IS, DO NOT THINK ABOUT CUTTING FORCEFULLY OR WEAKLY.

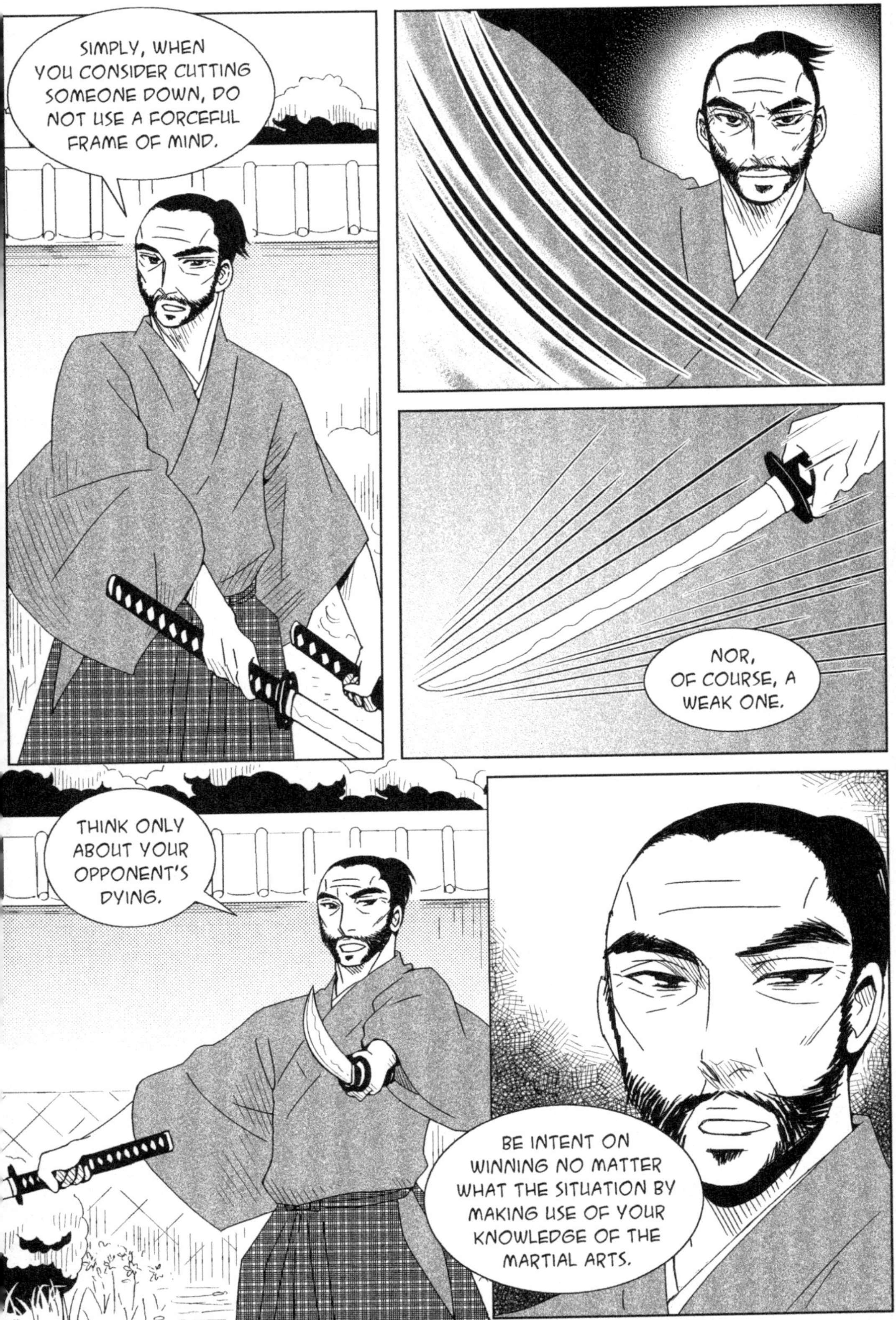
SIMPLY, WHEN YOU CONSIDER CUTTING SOMEONE DOWN, DO NOT USE A FORCEFUL FRAME OF MIND.
NOR, OF COURSE, A WEAK ONE.
THINK ONLY ABOUT YOUR OPPONENT'S DYING.
BE INTENT ON WINNING NO MATTER WHAT THE SITUATION BY MAKING USE OF YOUR KNOWLEDGE OF THE MARTIAL ARTS.

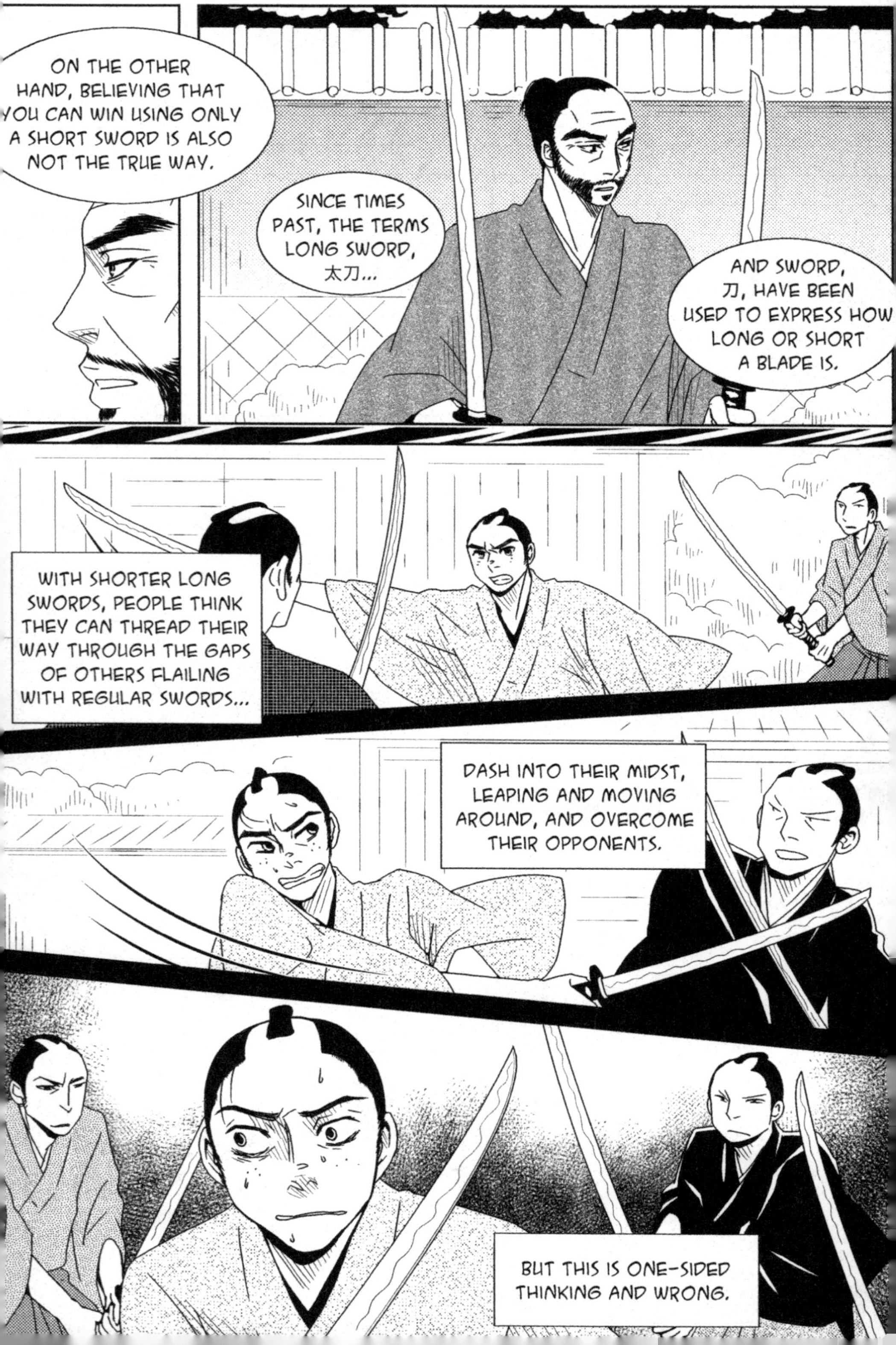
ON THE OTHER HAND, BELIEVING THAT YOU CAN WIN USING ONLY A SHORT SWORD IS ALSO NOT THE TRUE WAY.
SINCE TIMES PAST, THE TERMS LONG SWORD, 太刀...
AND SWORD, 刀, HAVE BEEN USED TO EXPRESS HOW LONG OR SHORT A BLADE IS.
WITH SHORTER LONG SWORDS, PEOPLE THINK THEY CAN THREAD THEIR WAY THROUGH THE GAPS OF OTHERS FLAILING WITH REGULAR SWORDS...
DASH INTO THEIR MIDST, LEAPING AND MOVING AROUND, AND OVERCOME THEIR OPPONENTS.
BUT THIS IS ONE-SIDED THINKING AND WRONG.

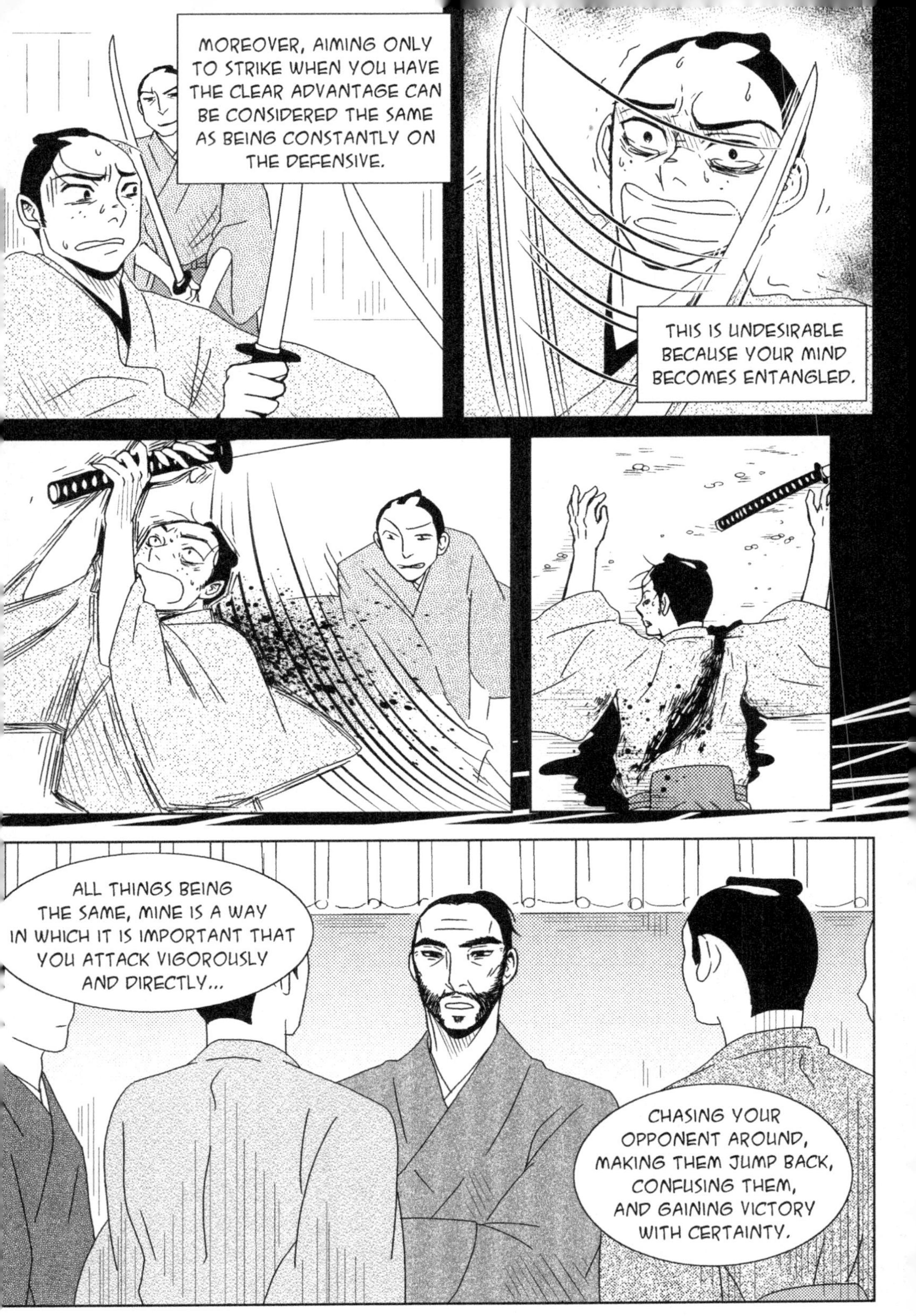
MOREOVER, AIMING ONLY TO STRIKE WHEN YOU HAVE THE CLEAR ADVANTAGE CAN BE CONSIDERED THE SAME AS BEING CONSTANTLY ON THE DEFENSIVE.
THIS IS UNDESIRABLE BECAUSE YOUR MIND BECOMES ENTANGLED.
ALL THINGS BEING THE SAME, MINE IS A WAY IN WHICH IT IS IMPORTANT THAT YOU ATTACK VIGOROUSLY AND DIRECTLY...
CHASING YOUR OPPONENT AROUND, MAKING THEM JUMP BACK, CONFUSING THEM, AND GAINING VICTORY WITH CERTAINTY.

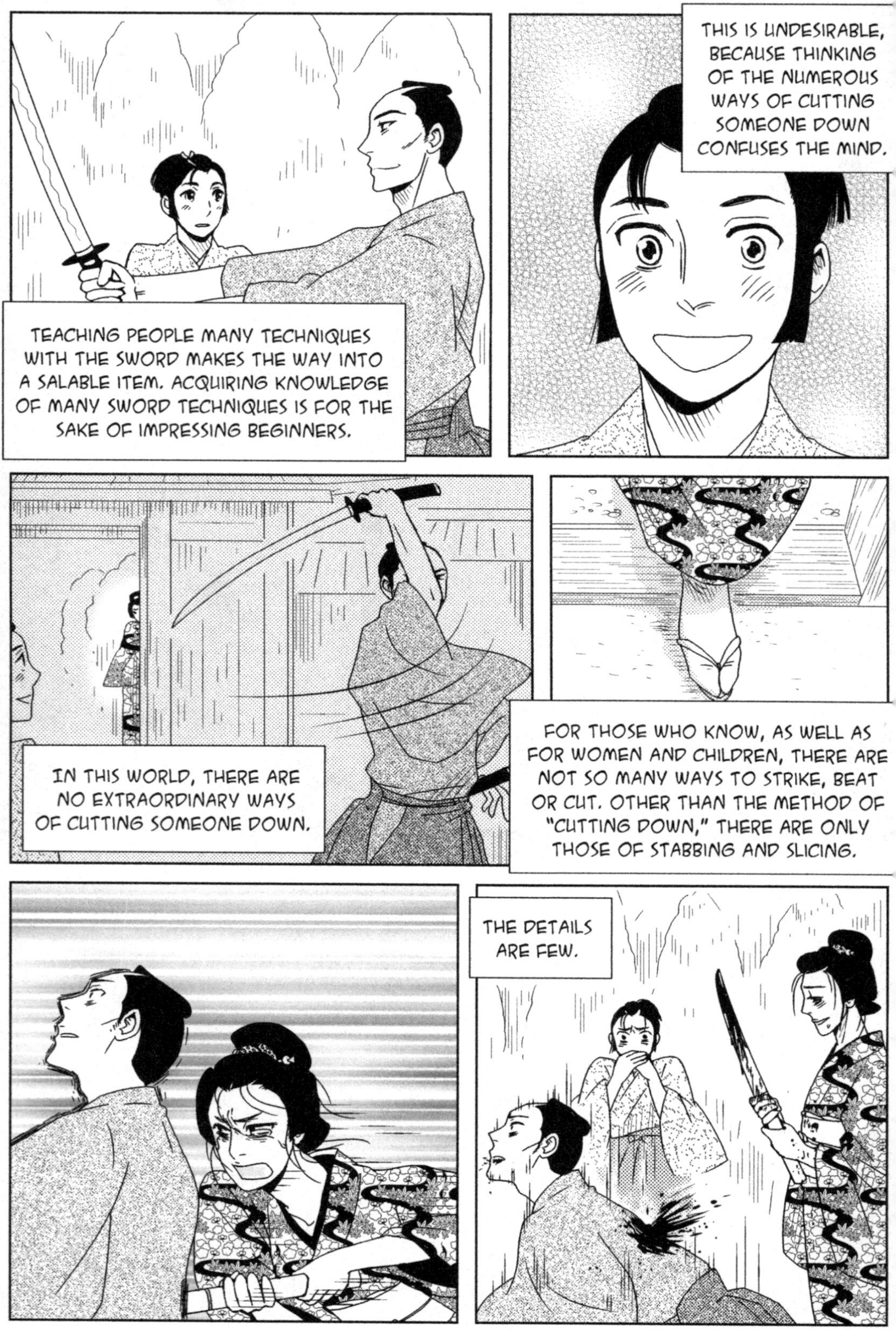
TEACHING PEOPLE MANY TECHNIQUES WITH THE SWORD MAKES THE WAY INTO A SALABLE ITEM. ACQUIRING KNOWLEDGE OF MANY SWORD TECHNIQUES IS FOR THE SAKE OF IMPRESSING BEGINNERS.
THIS IS UNDESIRABLE, BECAUSE THINKING OF THE NUMEROUS WAYS OF CUTTING SOMEONE DOWN CONFUSES THE MIND.
IN THIS WORLD, THERE ARE NO EXTRAORDINARY WAYS OF CUTTING SOMEONE DOWN.
FOR THOSE WHO KNOW, AS WELL AS FOR WOMEN AND CHILDREN, THERE ARE NOT SO MANY WAYS TO STRIKE, BEAT OR CUT. OTHER THAN THE METHOD OF "CUTTING DOWN," THERE ARE ONLY THOSE OF STABBING AND SLICING.
THE DETAILS ARE FEW.

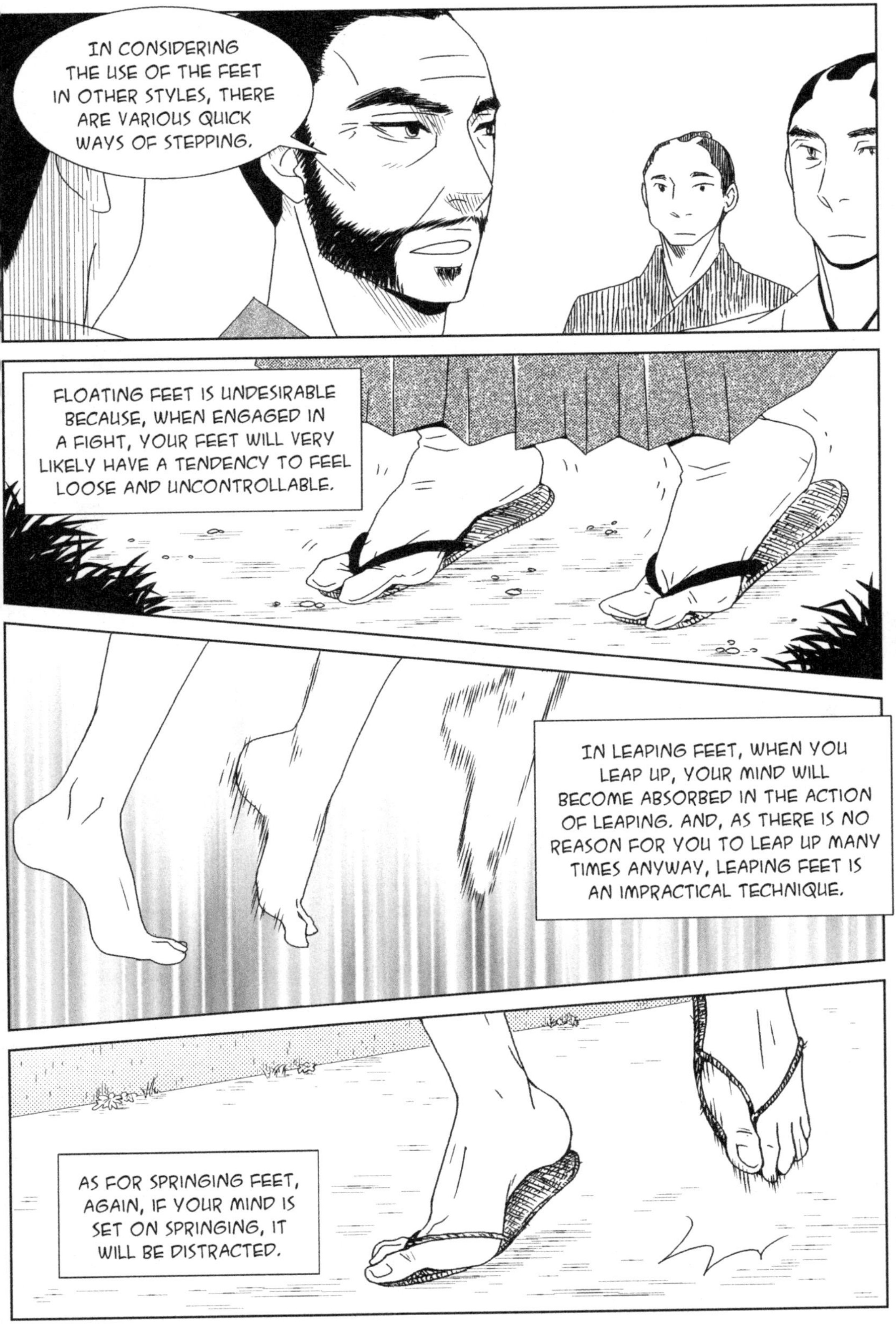
IN CONSIDERING THE USE OF THE FEET IN OTHER STYLES, THERE ARE VARIOUS QUICK WAYS OF STEPPING.
FLOATING FEET IS UNDESIRABLE BECAUSE, WHEN ENGAGED IN A FIGHT, YOUR FEET WILL VERY LIKELY HAVE A TENDENCY TO FEEL LOOSE AND UNCONTROLLABLE.
IN LEAPING FEET, WHEN YOU LEAP UP, YOUR MIND WILL BECOME ABSORBED IN THE ACTION OF LEAPING. AND, AS THERE IS NO REASON FOR YOU TO LEAP UP MANY TIMES ANYWAY, LEAPING FEET IS AN IMPRACTICAL TECHNIQUE.
AS FOR SPRINGING FEET, AGAIN, IF YOUR MIND IS SET ON SPRINGING, IT WILL BE DISTRACTED.

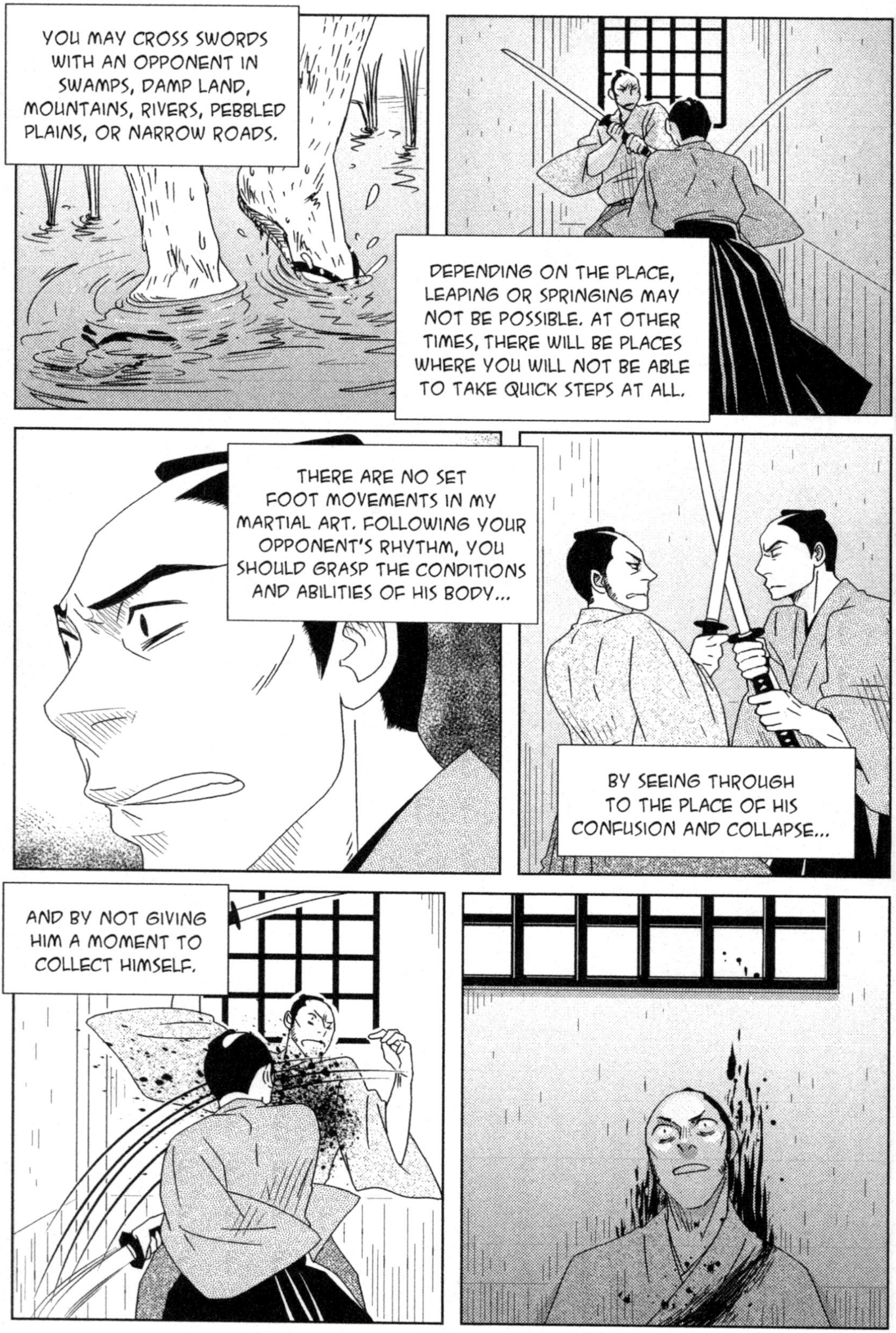
YOU MAY CROSS SWORDS WITH AN OPPONENT IN SWAMPS, DAMP LAND, MOUNTAINS, RIVERS, PEBBLED PLAINS, OR NARROW ROADS.
DEPENDING ON THE PLACE, LEAPING OR SPRINGING MAY NOT BE POSSIBLE. AT OTHER TIMES, THERE WILL BE PLACES WHERE YOU WILL NOT BE ABLE TO TAKE QUICK STEPS AT ALL.
THERE ARE NO SET FOOT MOVEMENTS IN MY MARTIAL ART. FOLLOWING YOUR OPPONENT'S RHYTHM, YOU SHOULD GRASP THE CONDITIONS AND ABILITIES OF HIS BODY...
BY SEEING THROUGH TO THE PLACE OF HIS CONFUSION AND COLLAPSE...
AND BY NOT GIVING HIM A MOMENT TO COLLECT HIMSELF.

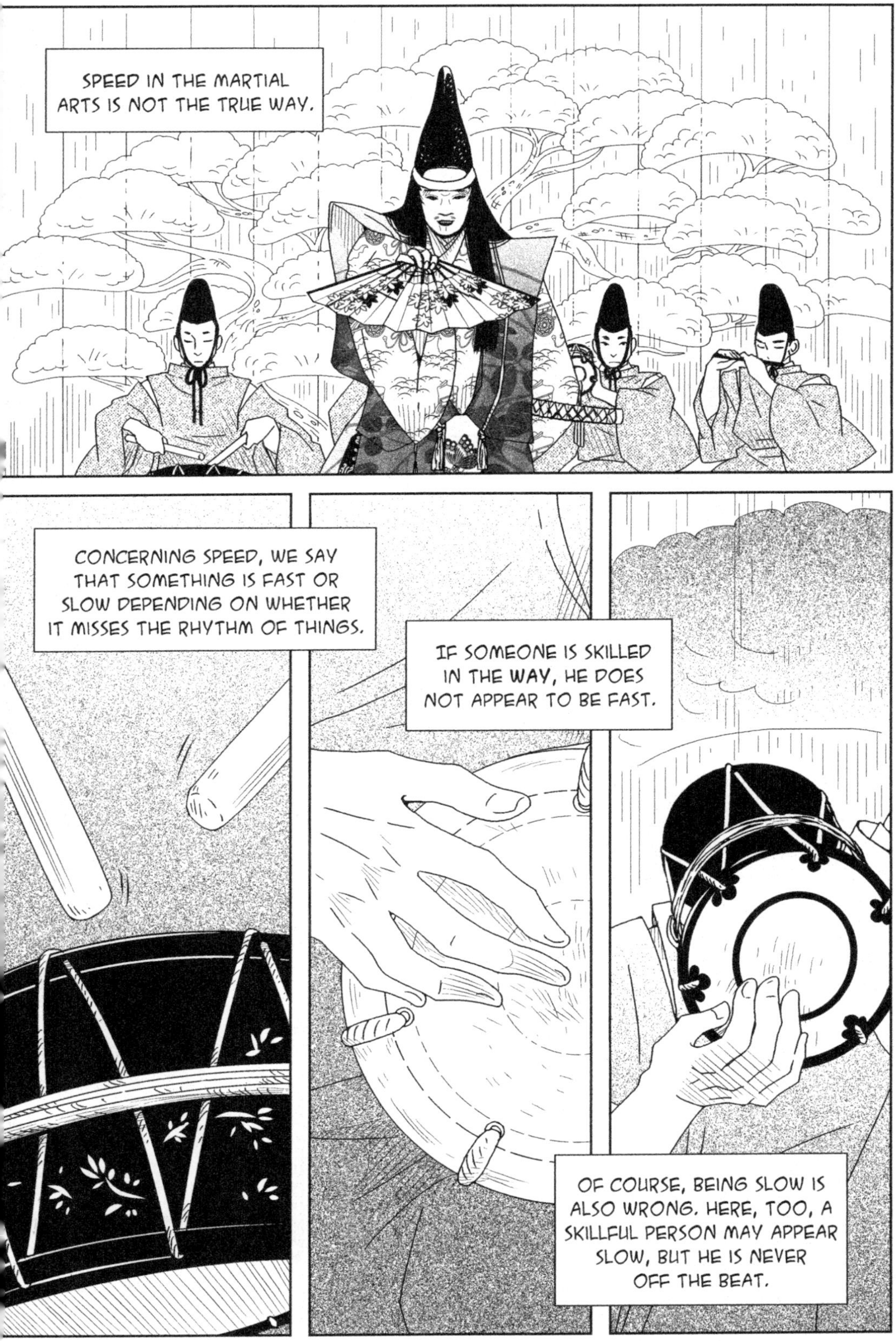
SPEED IN THE MARTIAL ARTS IS NOT THE TRUE WAY.
CONCERNING SPEED, WE SAY THAT SOMETHING IS FAST OR SLOW DEPENDING ON WHETHER IT MISSES THE RHYTHM OF THINGS.
IF SOMEONE IS SKILLED IN THE WAY, HE DOES NOT APPEAR TO BE FAST.
OF COURSE, BEING SLOW IS ALSO WRONG. HERE, TOO, A SKILLFUL PERSON MAY APPEAR SLOW, BUT HE IS NEVER OFF THE BEAT.

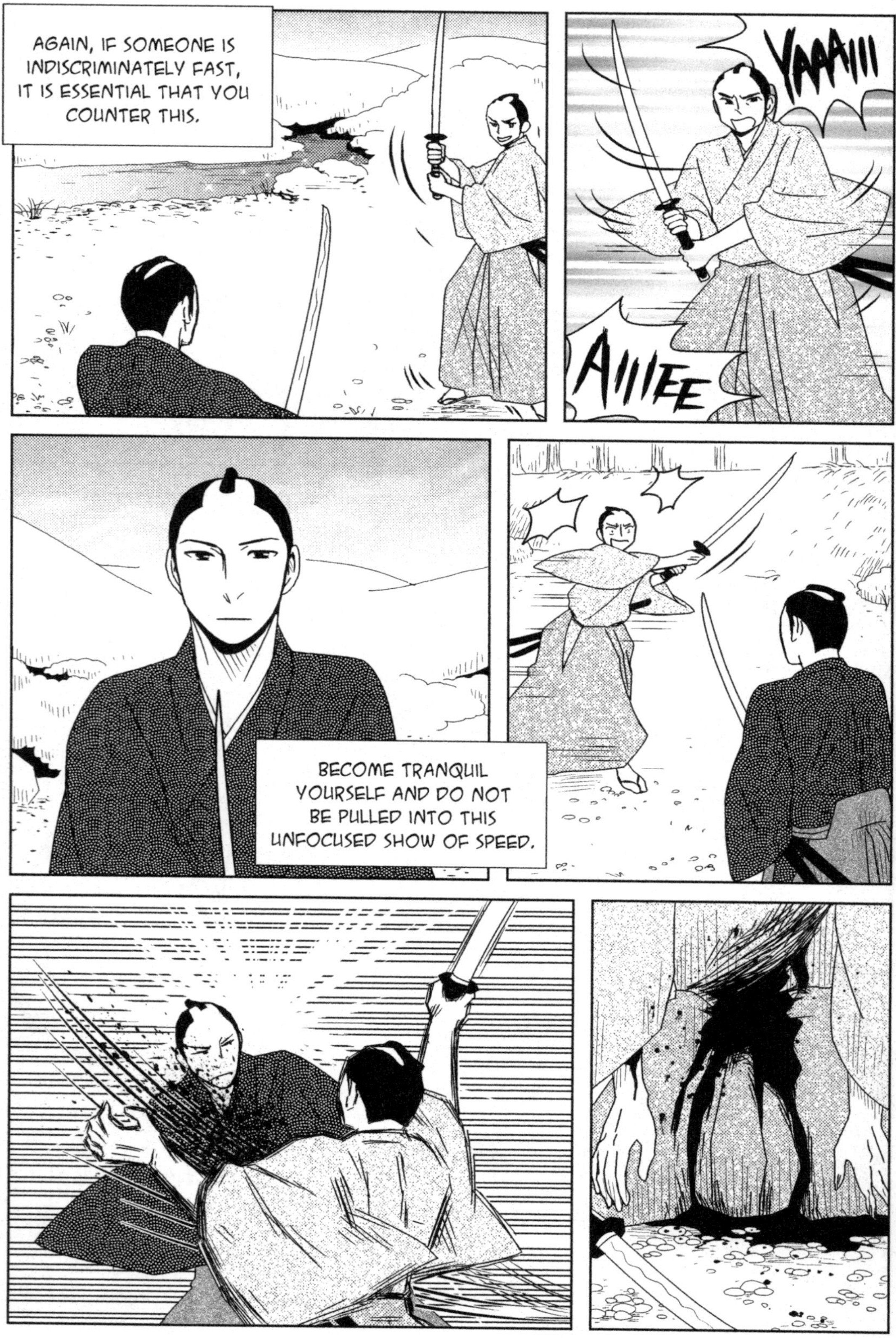

AGAIN, IF SOMEONE IS INDISCRIMINATELY FAST, IT IS ESSENTIAL THAT YOU COUNTER THIS.
YAAAIII
AIIIEE
BECOME TRANQUIL YOURSELF AND DO NOT BE PULLED INTO THIS UNFOCUSED SHOW OF SPEED.

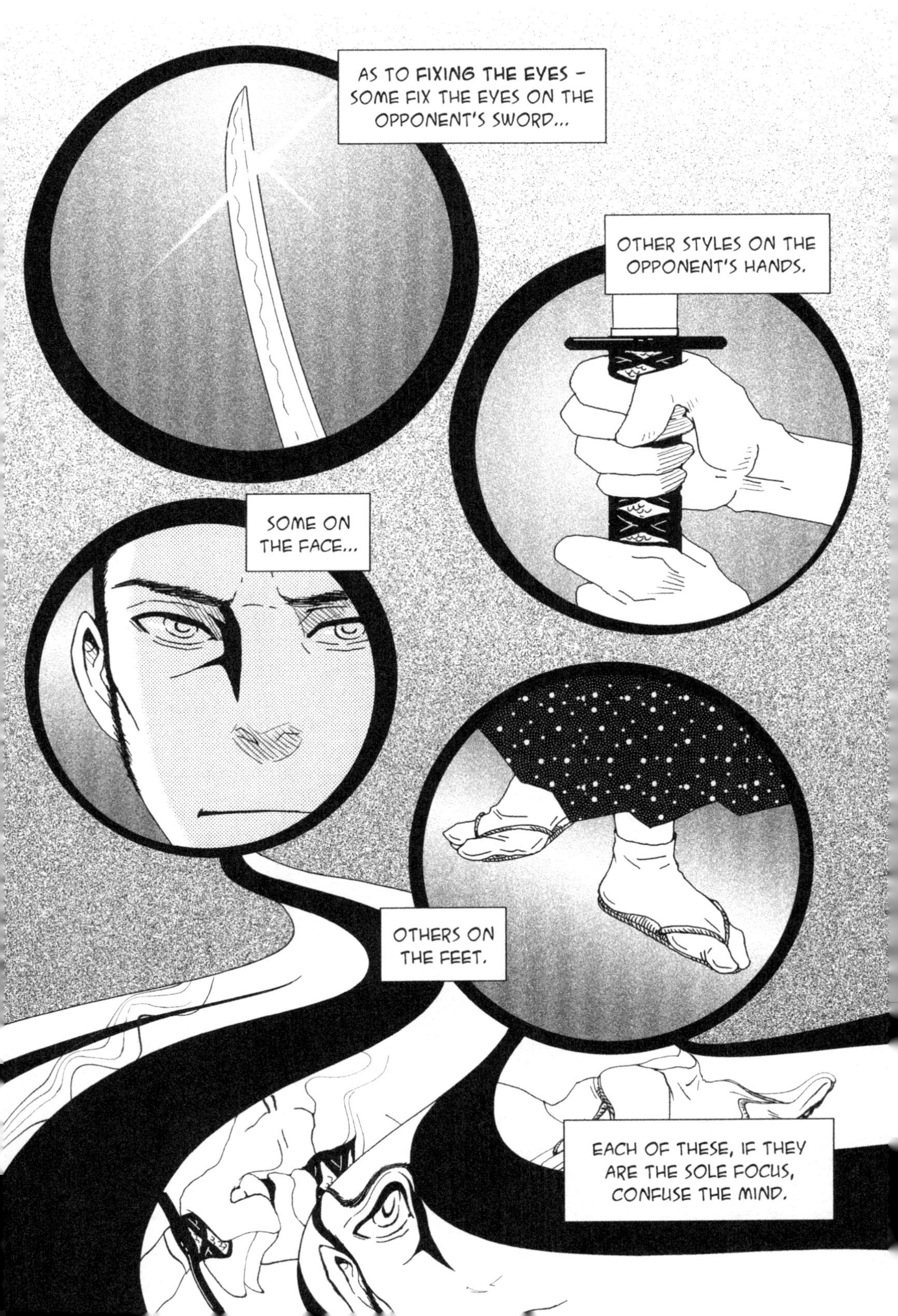
AS TO FIXING THE EYES – SOME FIX THE EYES ON THE OPPONENT'S SWORD...
OTHER STYLES ON THE OPPONENT'S HANDS.
SOME ON THE FACE...
OTHERS ON THE FEET.
EACH OF THESE, IF THEY ARE THE SOLE FOCUS, CONFUSE THE MIND.

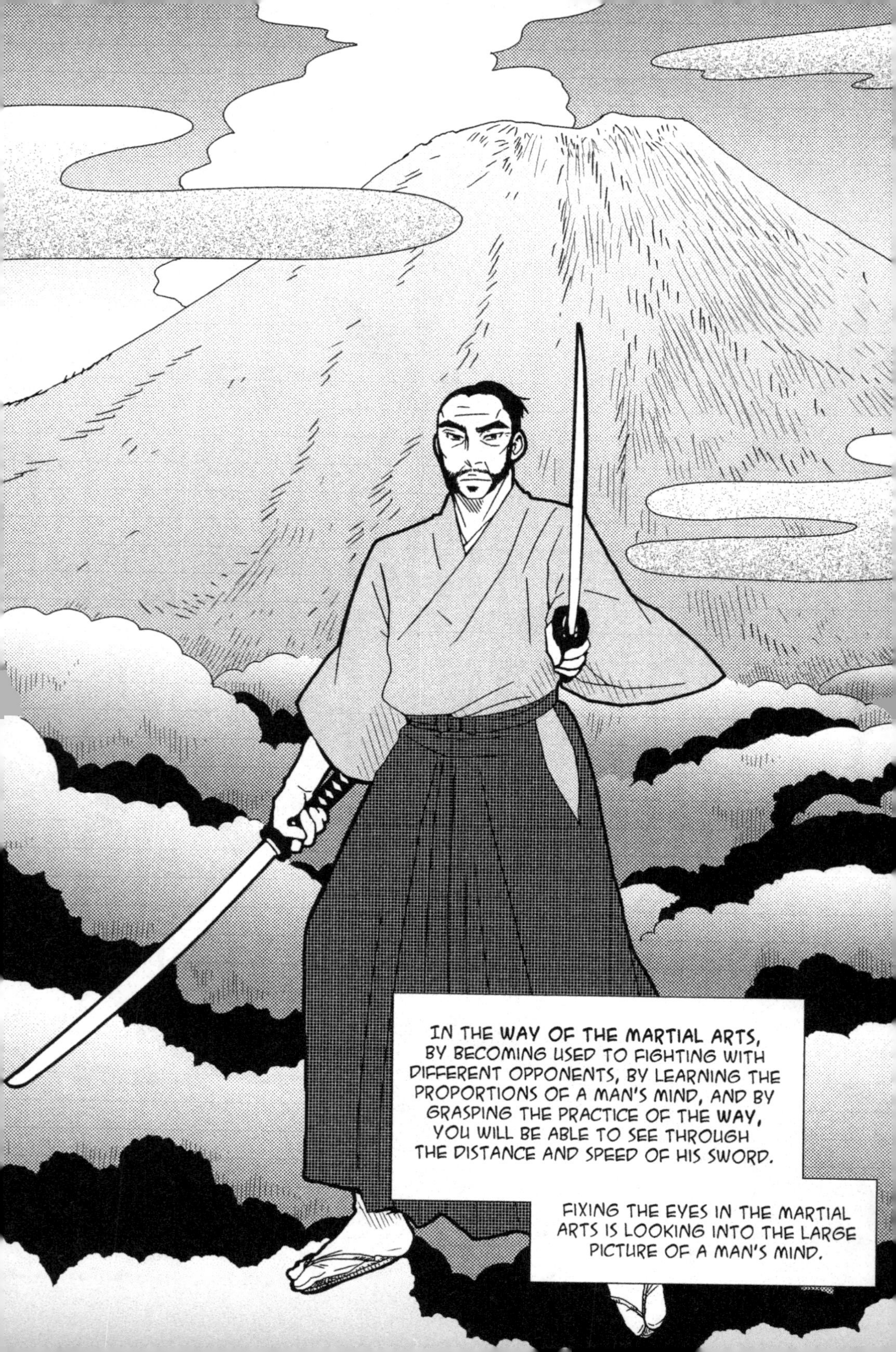
IN THE WAY OF THE MARTIAL ARTS, BY BECOMING USED TO FIGHTING WITH DIFFERENT OPPONENTS, BY LEARNING THE PROPORTIONS OF A MAN'S MIND, AND BY GRASPING THE PRACTICE OF THE WAY, YOU WILL BE ABLE TO SEE THROUGH THE DISTANCE AND SPEED OF HIS SWORD.
FIXING THE EYES IN THE MARTIAL ARTS IS LOOKING INTO THE LARGE PICTURE OF A MAN'S MIND.

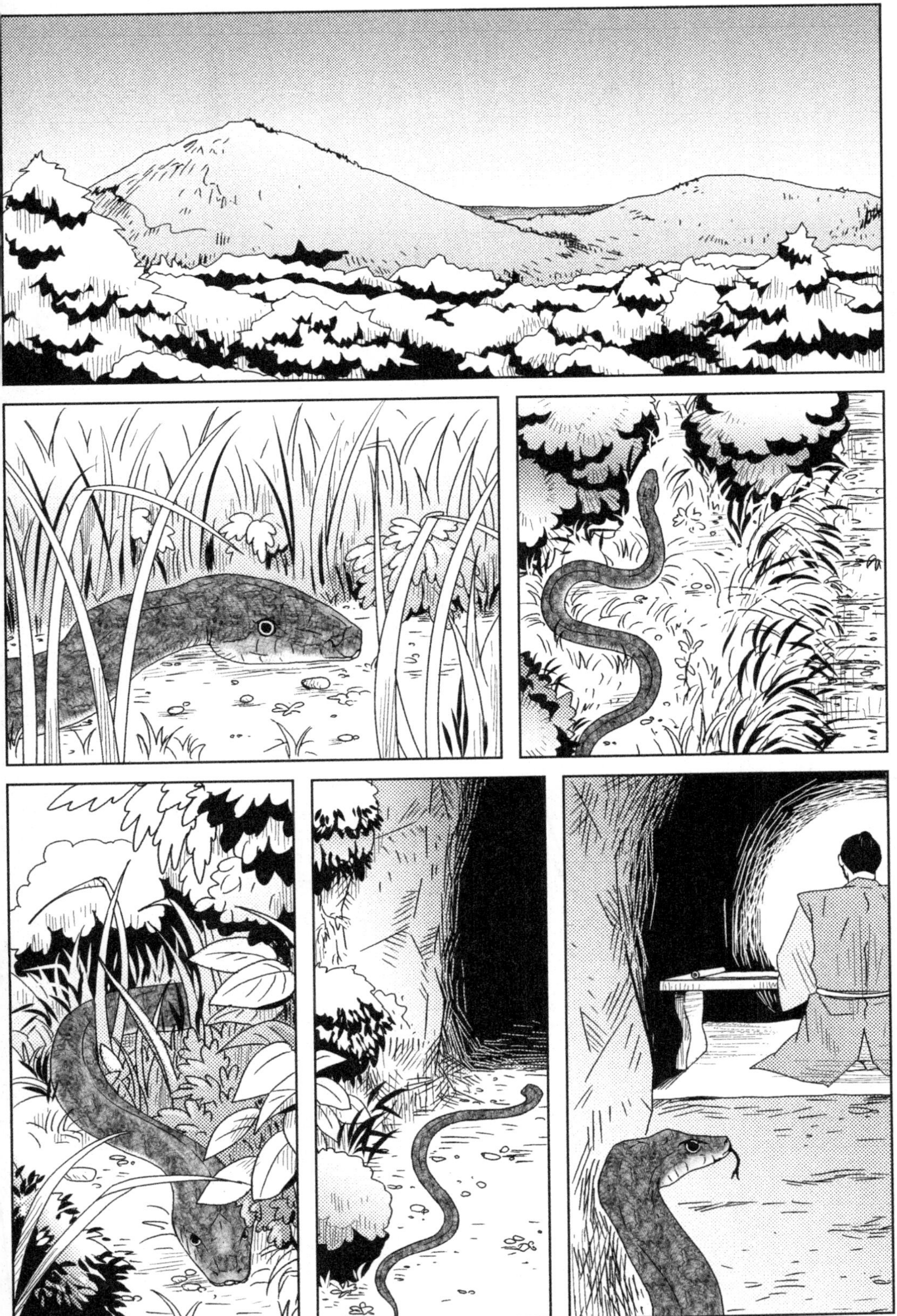

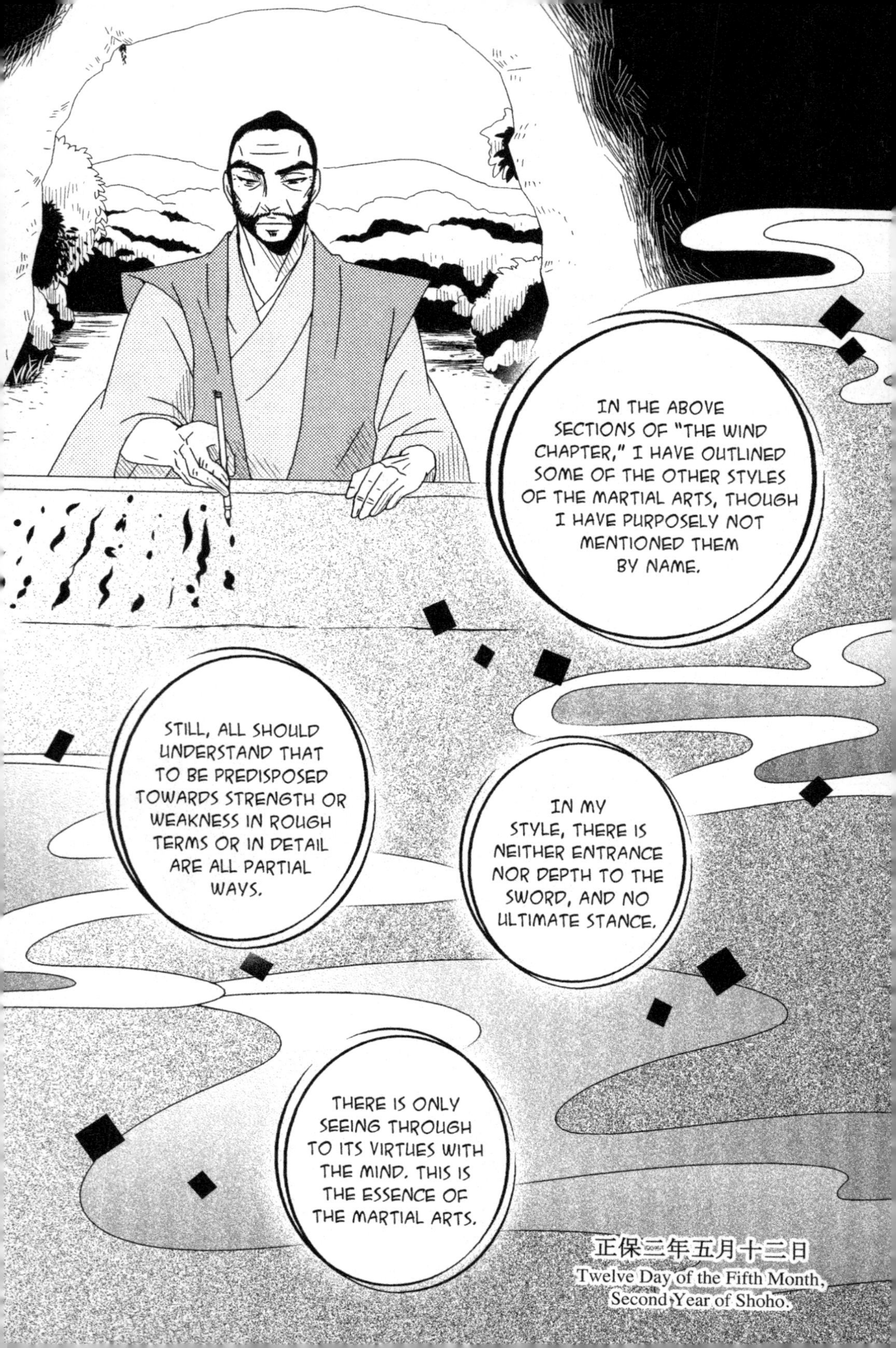
IN THE ABOVE SECTIONS OF "THE WIND CHAPTER," I HAVE OUTLINED SOME OF THE OTHER STYLES OF THE MARTIAL ARTS, THOUGH I HAVE PURPOSELY NOT MENTIONED THEM BY NAME.
STILL, ALL SHOULD UNDERSTAND THAT TO BE PREDISPOSED TOWARDS STRENGTH OR WEAKNESS IN ROUGH TERMS OR IN DETAIL ARE ALL PARTIAL WAYS.
IN MY STYLE, THERE IS NEITHER ENTRANCE NOR DEPTH TO THE SWORD, AND NO ULTIMATE STANCE.
THERE IS ONLY SEEING THROUGH TO ITS VIRTUES WITH THE MIND. THIS IS THE ESSENCE OF THE MARTIAL ARTS.
正保二年五月十二日
Twelve Day of the Fifth Month, Second Year of Shoho.

5
EMPTINESS

空

In Emptiness exists Good but no Evil.

Wisdom is Existence.

Principle is Existence.

The Way is Existence.

The Mind is Emptiness.

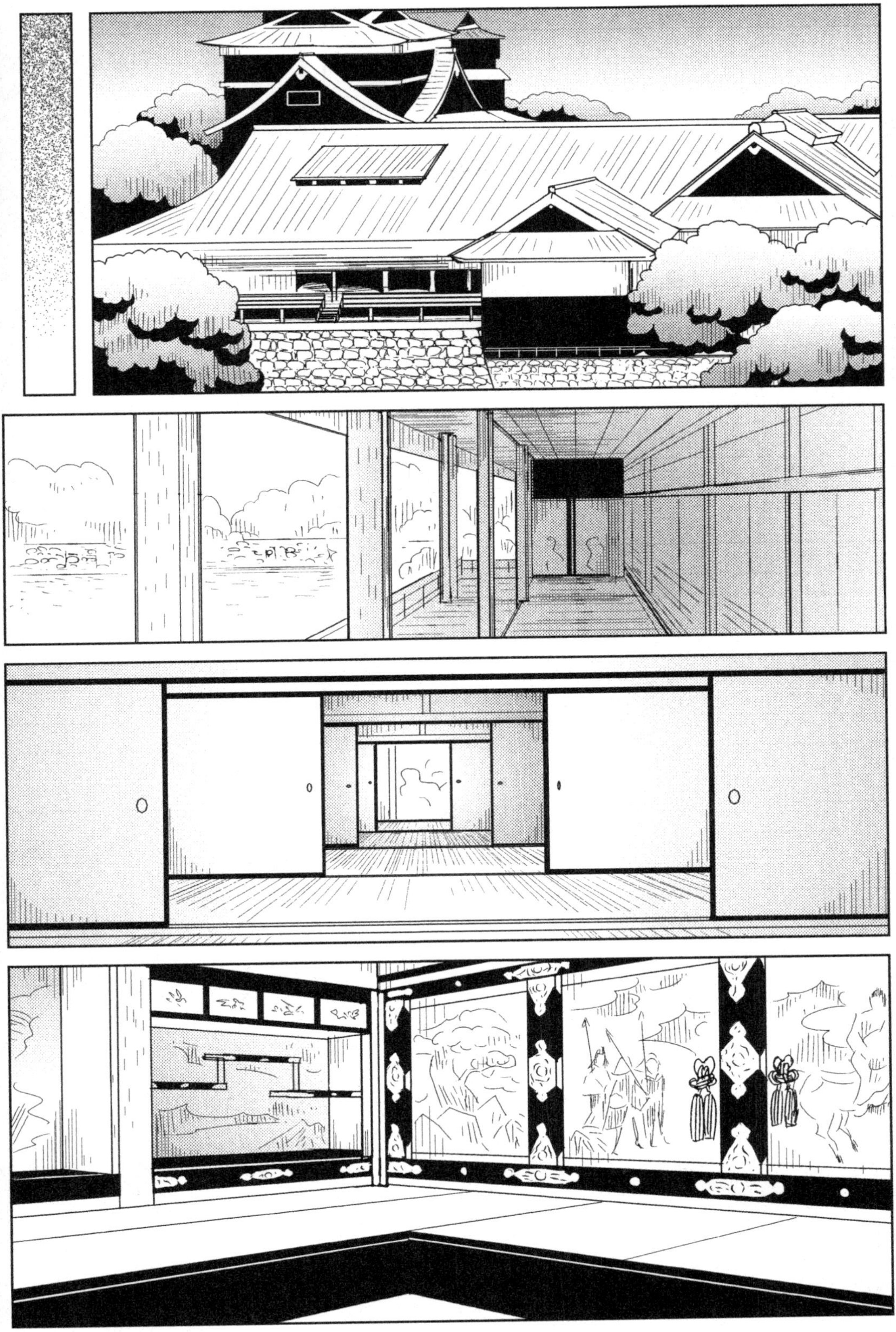

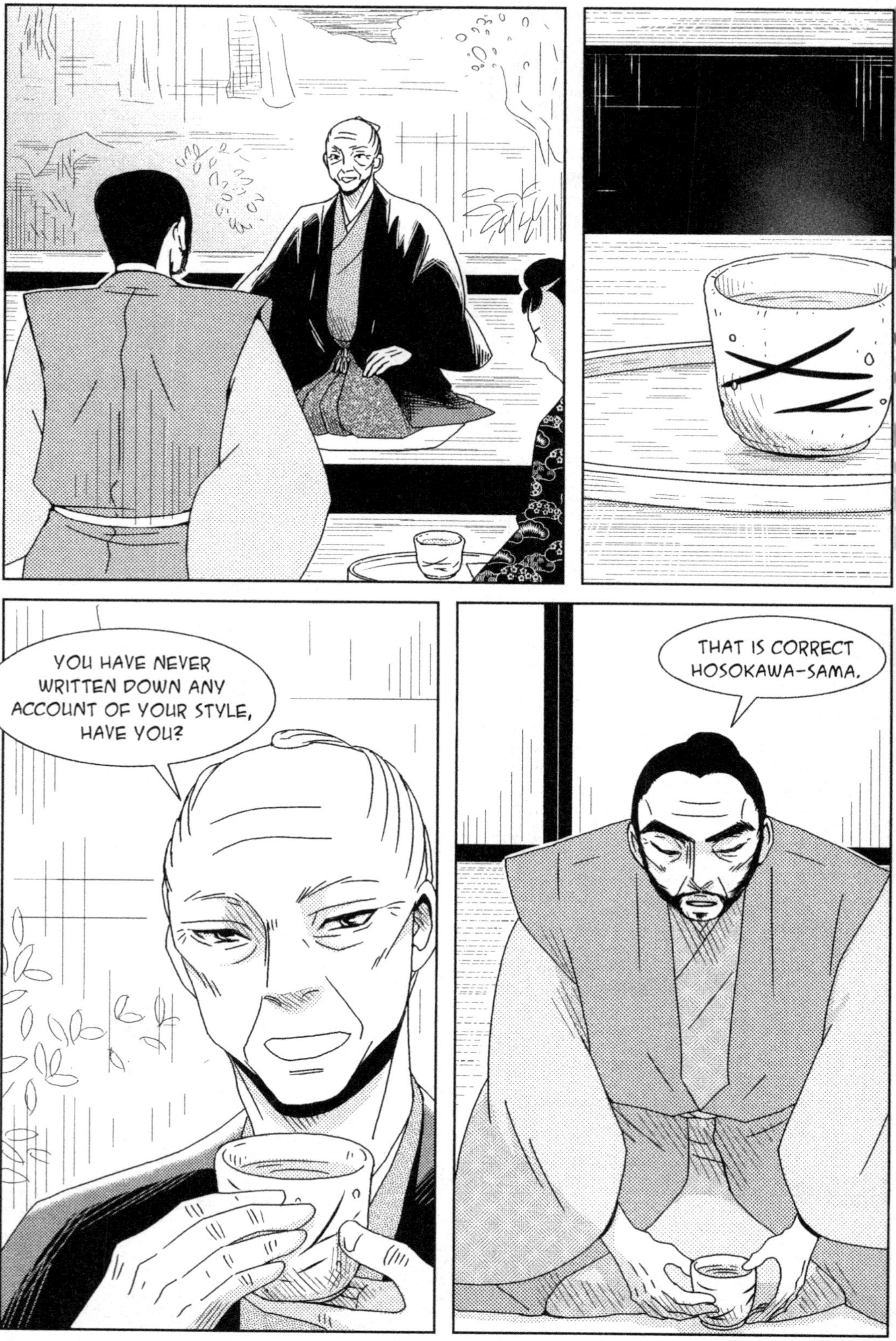
YOU HAVE NEVER WRITTEN DOWN ANY ACCOUNT OF YOUR STYLE, HAVE YOU?
THAT IS CORRECT HOSOKAWA-SAMA.

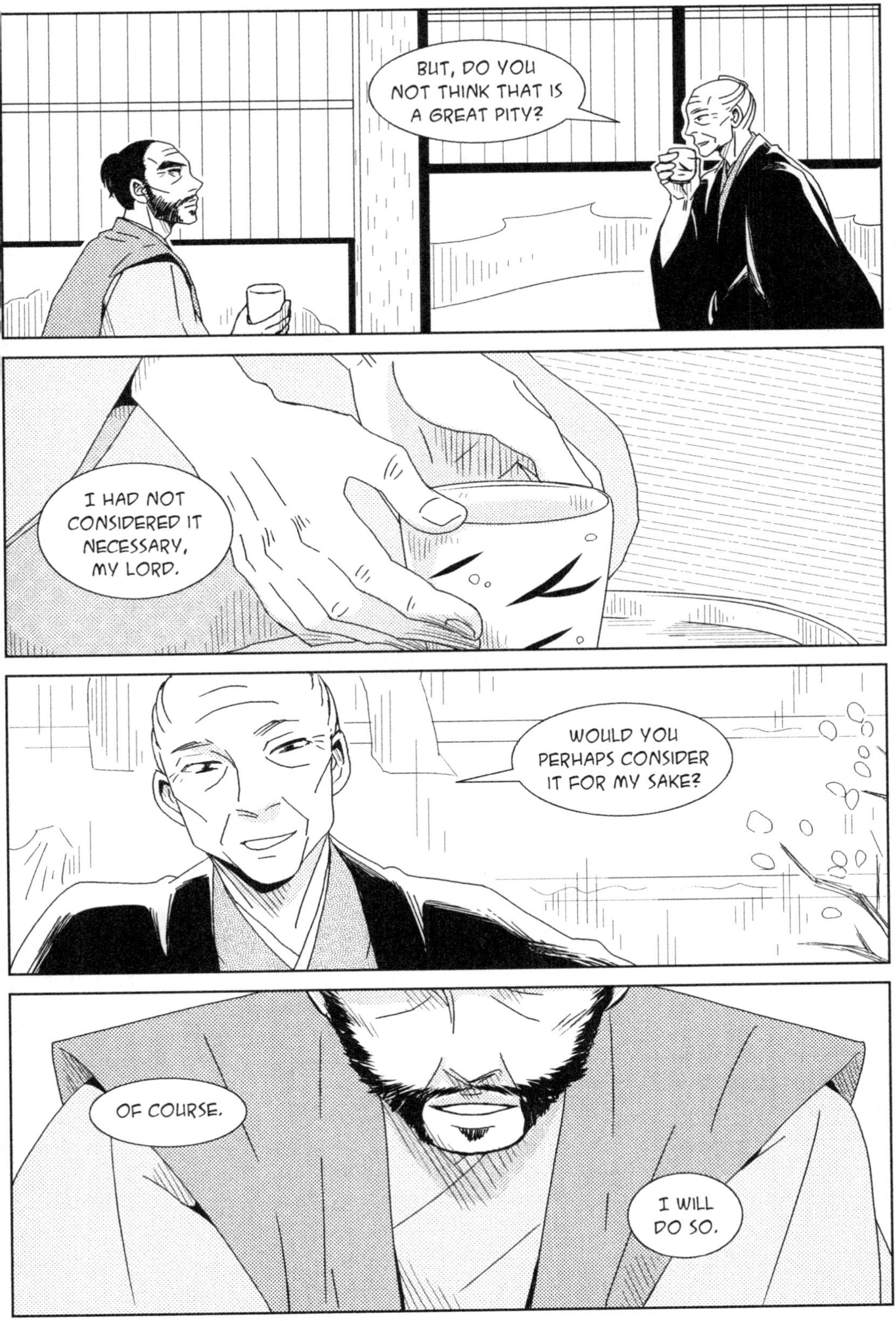
BUT, DO YOU NOT THINK THAT IS A GREAT PITY?
I HAD NOT CONSIDERED IT NECESSARY, MY LORD.
WOULD YOU PERHAPS CONSIDER IT FOR MY SAKE?
OF COURSE.
I WILL DO SO.

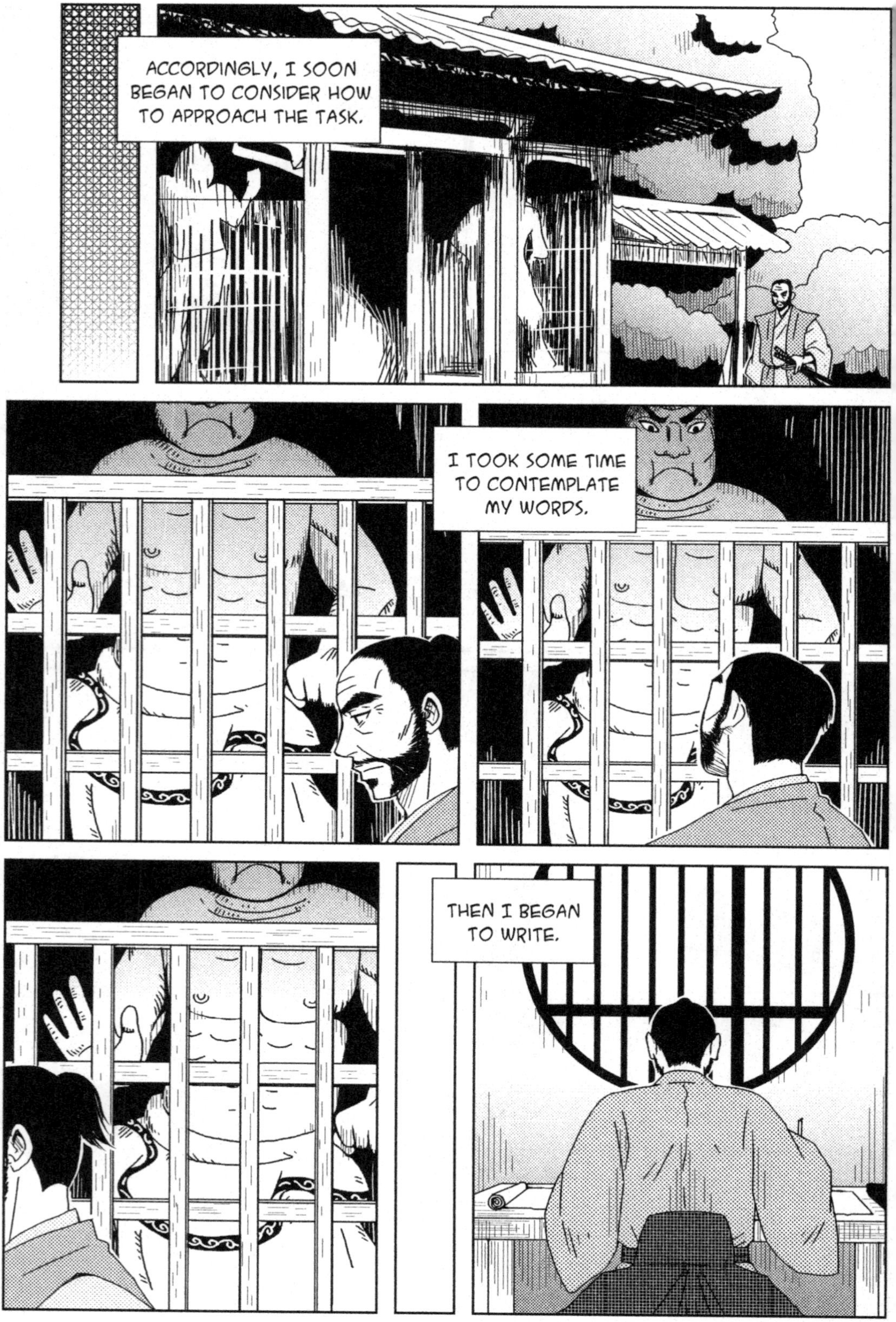
ACCORDINGLY, I SOON BEGAN TO CONSIDER HOW TO APPROACH THE TASK.
I TOOK SOME TIME TO CONTEMPLATE MY WORDS.
THEN I BEGAN TO WRITE.

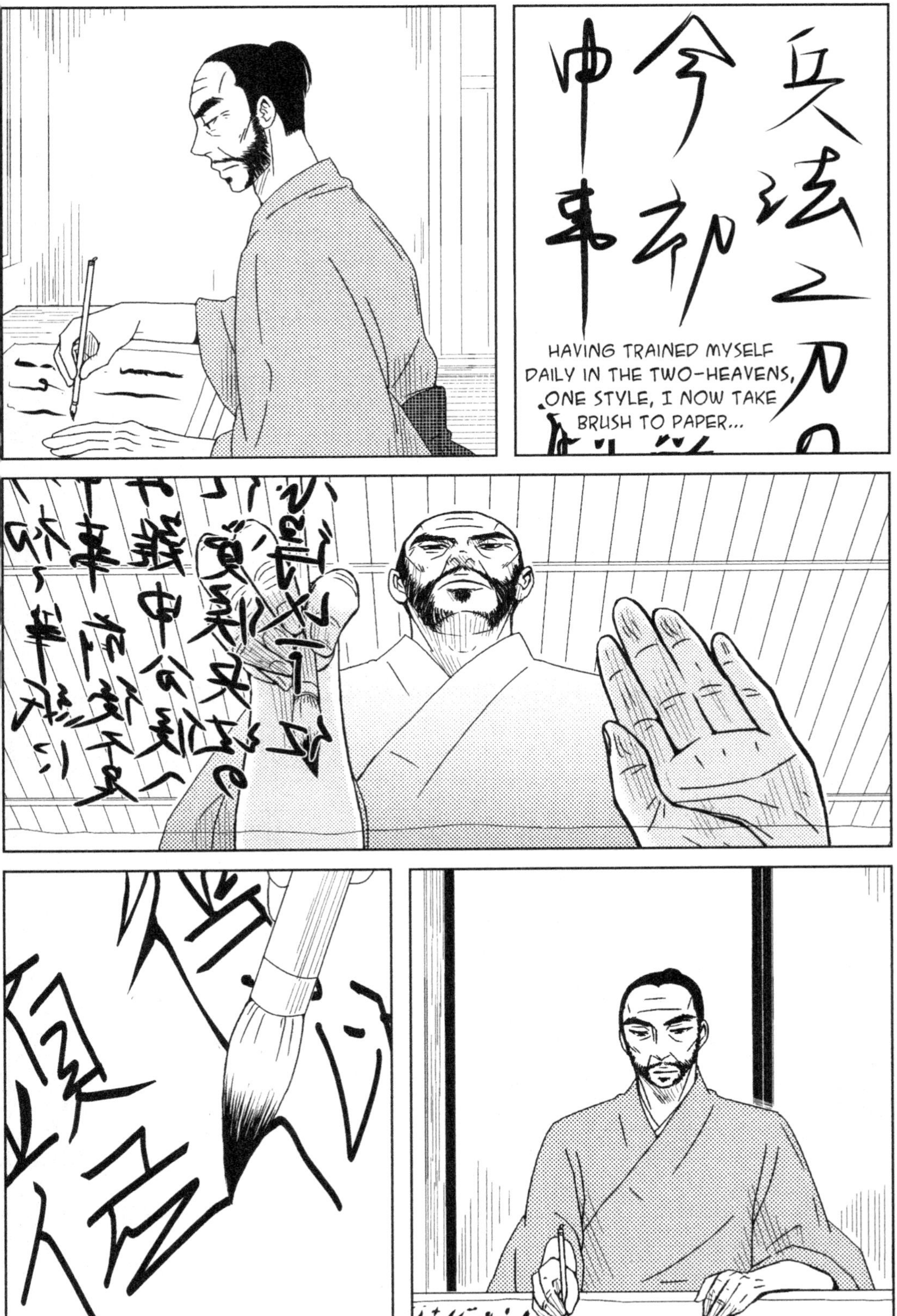
HAVING TRAINED MYSELF DAILY IN THE TWO-HEAVENS, ONE STYLE, I NOW TAKE BRUSH TO PAPER...

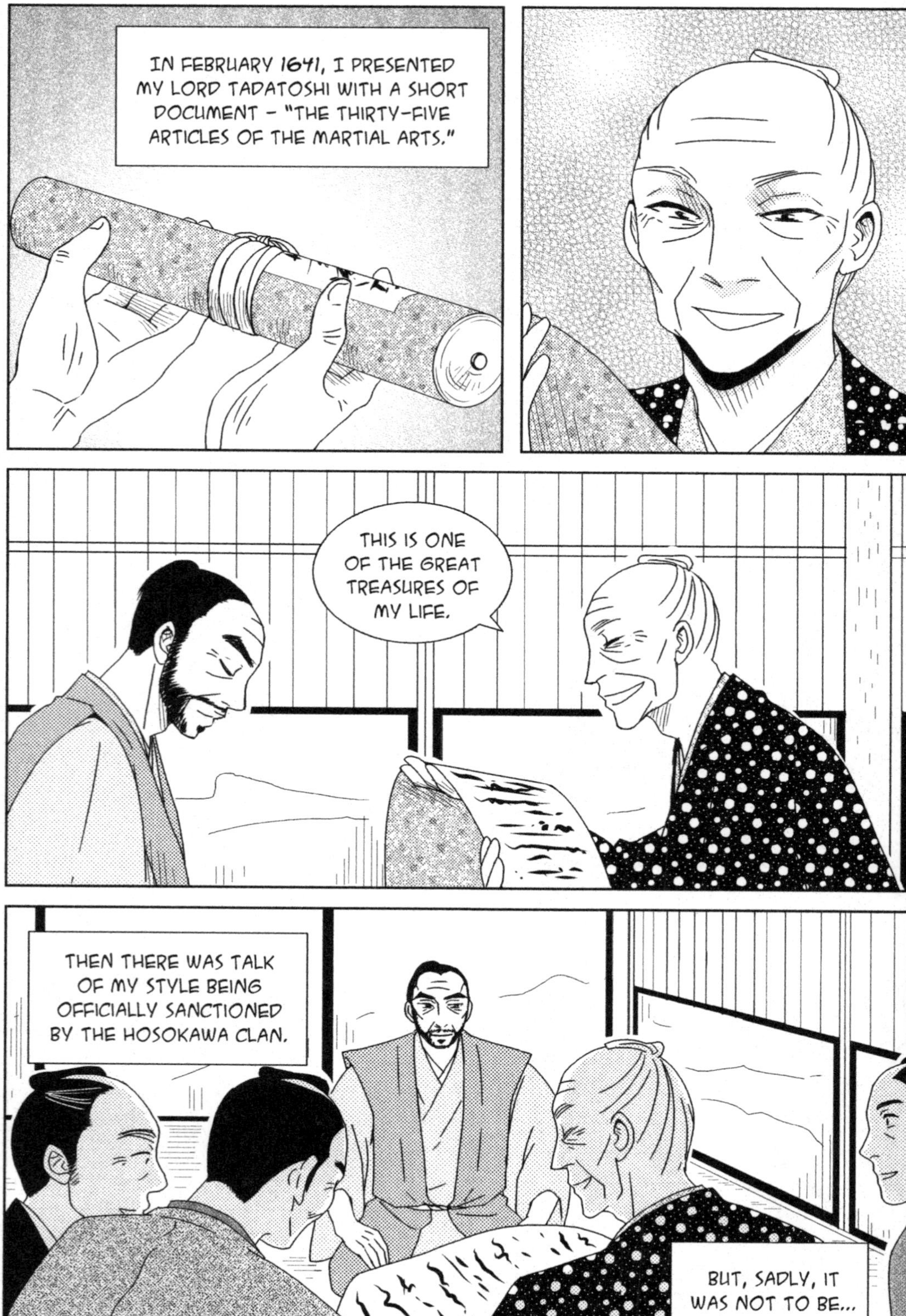

IN FEBRUARY 1641, I PRESENTED MY LORD TADATOSHI WITH A SHORT DOCUMENT – "THE THIRTY-FIVE ARTICLES OF THE MARTIAL ARTS."
THIS IS ONE OF THE GREAT TREASURES OF MY LIFE.
THEN THERE WAS TALK OF MY STYLE BEING OFFICIALLY SANCTIONED BY THE HOSOKAWA CLAN.
BUT, SADLY, IT WAS NOT TO BE...

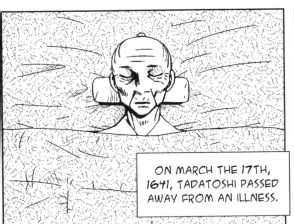

ON MARCH THE 17TH, 1641, TADATOSHI PASSED AWAY FROM AN ILLNESS.

LORD TADATOSHI WAS A FAMOUS GENERAL, PROFICIENT IN BOTH THE MILITARY AND LITERARY ARTS.

HE EXCELLED IN THE SIX ACCOMPLISHMENTS.

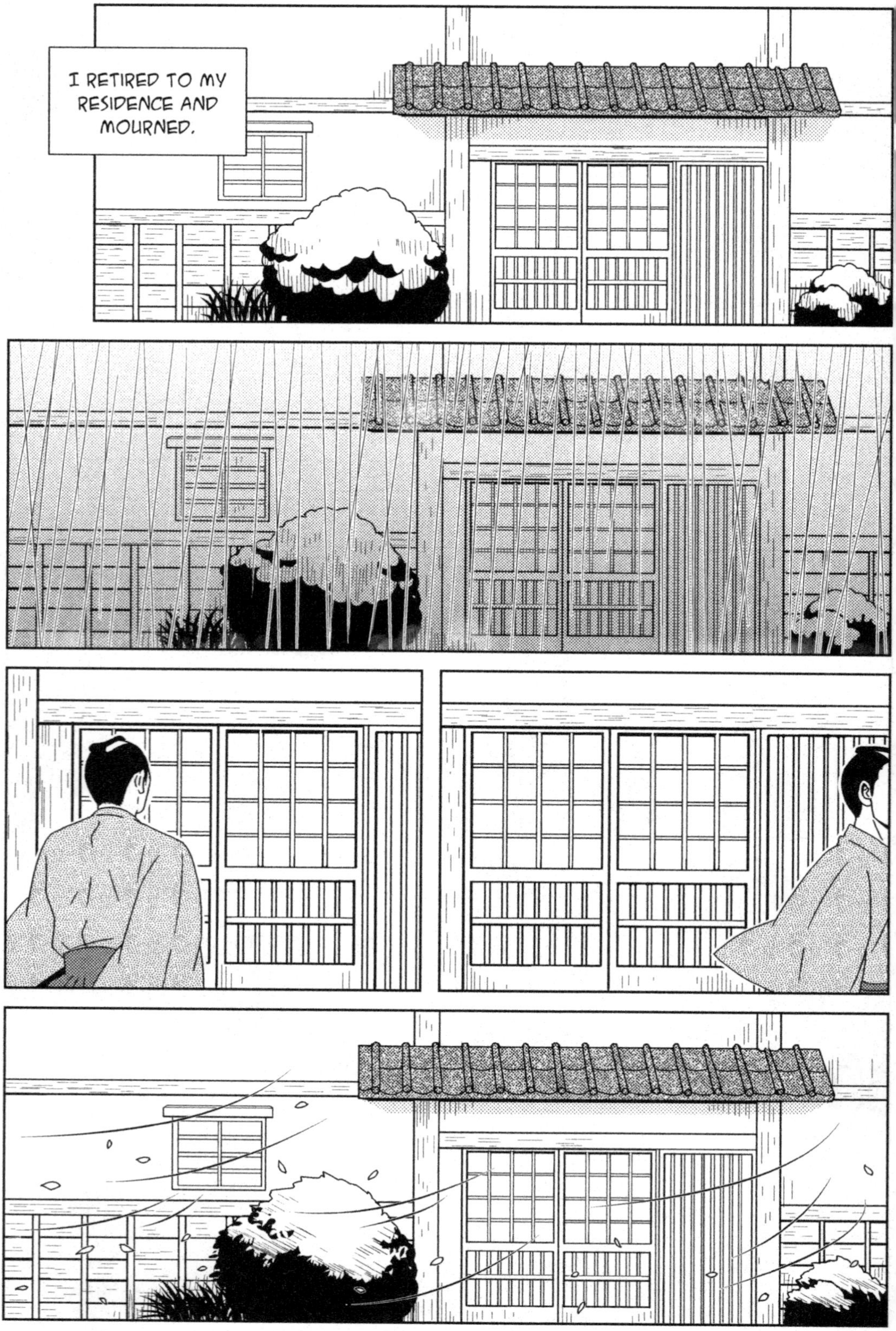
I RETIRED TO MY RESIDENCE AND MOURNED.

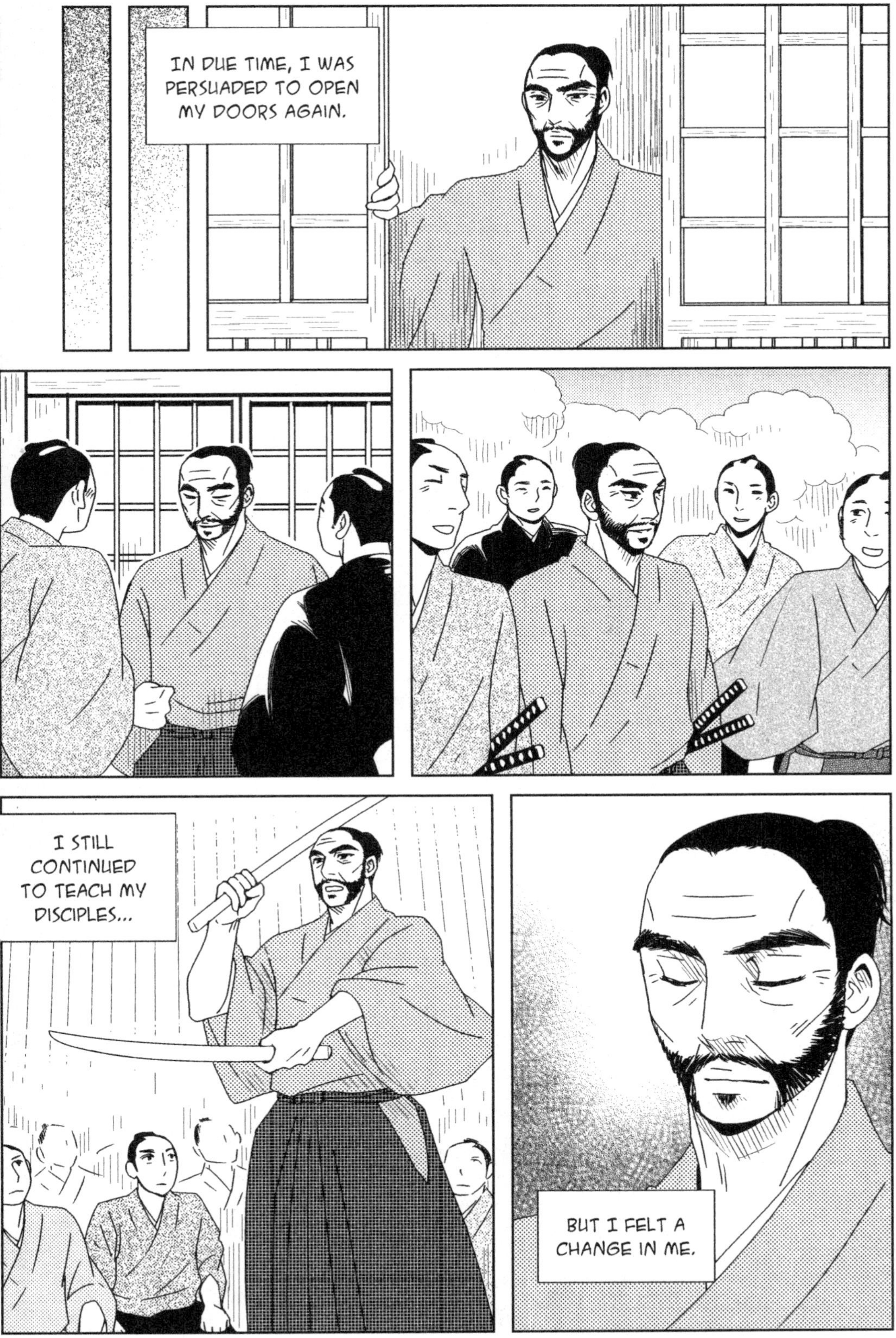
IN DUE TIME, I WAS PERSUADED TO OPEN MY DOORS AGAIN.
I STILL CONTINUED TO TEACH MY DISCIPLES...
BUT I FELT A CHANGE IN ME.

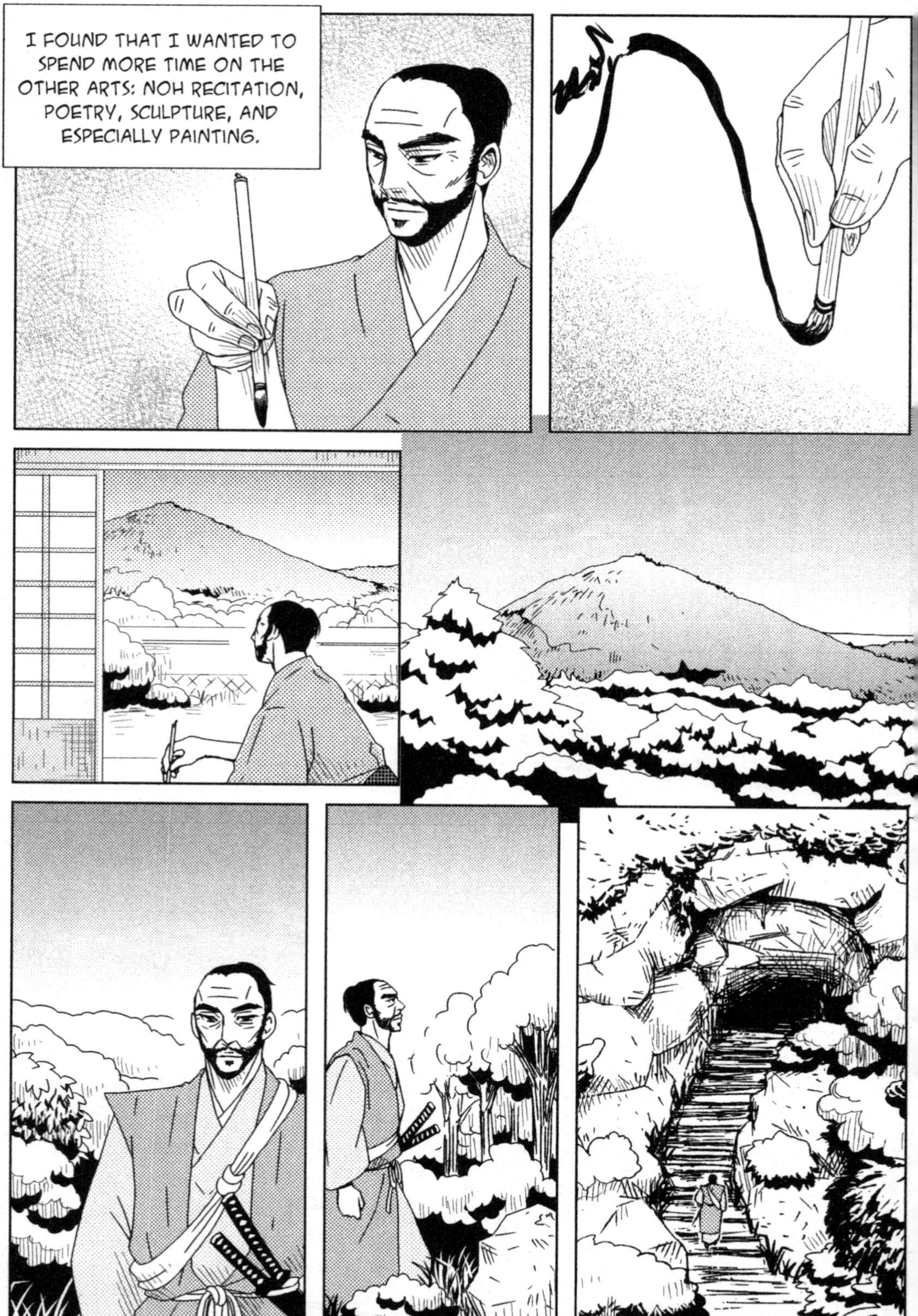
I FOUND THAT I WANTED TO SPEND MORE TIME ON THE OTHER ARTS: NOH RECITATION, POETRY, SCULPTURE, AND ESPECIALLY PAINTING.

IT IS IN "THE EMPTINESS CHAPTER" THAT I WRITE DOWN THE WAY OF THE MARTIAL ARTS OF THE TWO-SWORD STYLE.

THE HEART OF EMPTINESS IS IN THE ABSENCE OF ANYTHING OF FORM AND THE INABILITY TO HAVE KNOWLEDGE THEREOF. THIS I SEE AS EMPTINESS.

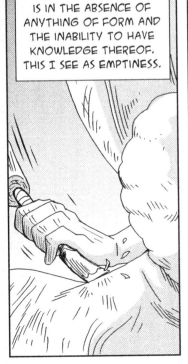

EMPTINESS, OF COURSE, IS NOTHINGNESS. KNOWING THE EXISTENT, YOU KNOW THE NONEXISTENT. THIS, EXACTLY, IS EMPTINESS.

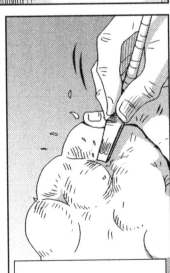

TO BE IN THE WORLD AND SEE THINGS POORLY, TO BE UNABLE TO DISTINGUISH ONE MATTER FROM ANOTHER AND TO REGARD THIS AS EMPTINESS — THIS IS NOT TRUE EMPTINESS.

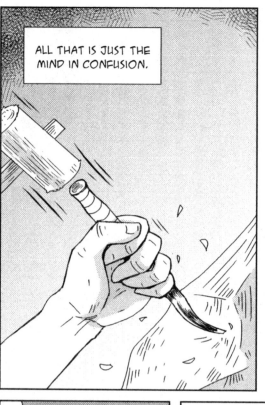

ALL THAT IS JUST THE MIND IN CONFUSION.

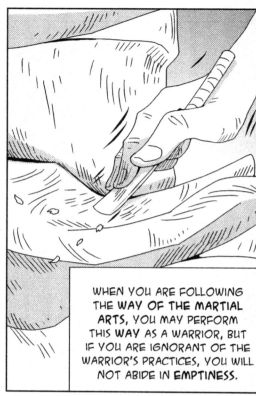

WHEN YOU ARE FOLLOWING THE **WAY OF THE MARTIAL ARTS**, YOU MAY PERFORM THIS **WAY** AS A WARRIOR, BUT IF YOU ARE IGNORANT OF THE WARRIOR'S PRACTICES, YOU WILL NOT ABIDE IN **EMPTINESS**.

YOU WILL BE CONFUSED AND WILL NOT DO THE THINGS THAT YOU SHOULD. THOUGH YOU TERM THIS "EMPTINESS," IT WILL NOT BE TRUE **EMPTINESS**.

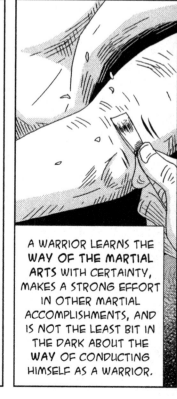

A WARRIOR LEARNS THE **WAY OF THE MARTIAL ARTS** WITH CERTAINTY, MAKES A STRONG EFFORT IN OTHER MARTIAL ACCOMPLISHMENTS, AND IS NOT THE LEAST BIT IN THE DARK ABOUT THE **WAY** OF CONDUCTING HIMSELF AS A WARRIOR.

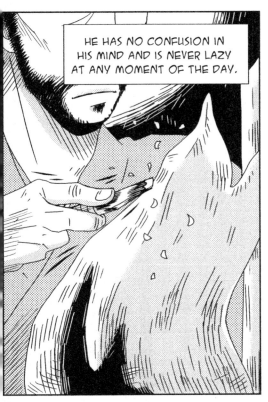

HE HAS NO CONFUSION IN HIS MIND AND IS NEVER LAZY AT ANY MOMENT OF THE DAY.

HE POLISHED THE TWO HEARTS OF HIS MIND AND WILL, AND SHARPENS THE TWO EYES OF BROAD OBSERVATION AND FOCUSED VISION.

HE IS NOT THE LEAST BIT DISTRACTED BY THE CLOUDS OF CONFUSION, BUT RATHER CLEARS THEM AWAY. YOU SHOULD KNOW THAT THIS IS TRUE EMPTINESS.

WHILE YOU ARE YET IGNORANT OF TRUE **EMPTINESS**, YOU MAY THINK THROUGH YOUR OWN CERTAIN **WAY**, RELYING ON NEITHER BUDDHISM NOR THE LAWS OF SOCIETY, AND THINK THIS IS GOOD.

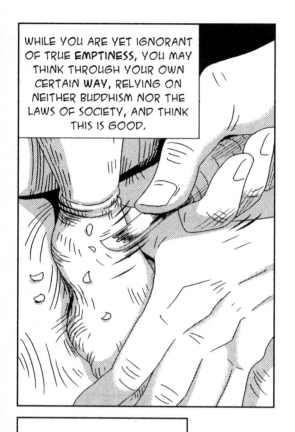

BUT WHEN YOU SEE THINGS FROM THE STRAIGHT **WAY** OF THE MIND, TAKING IN THE WORLD AT LARGE, YOU WILL SEE THAT EACH PERSON WILL HAVE THE PREFERENCES OF HIS OWN HEART, AND EACH EYE WILL HAVE ITS OWN DISTORTIONS. SUCH DISTORTIONS ARE TURNING YOUR BACK ON THE **TRUE WAY**.

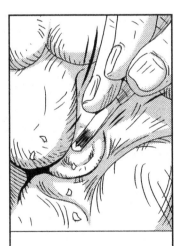

KNOW THE MEANING OF
THIS, AND MAKE THE
STRAIGHTFORWARD YOUR
FOUNDATION. MAKE THE
HEART OF TRUTH YOUR
WAY, PRACTICE A BROAD
SPECTRUM OF THE MARTIAL
ARTS, AND UNDERSTAND
THE EXPANSIVE CORRECTLY
AND CLEARLY.

ACCORDINGLY, YOU WILL
MAKE **EMPTINESS** THE
WAY, AND SEE THE WAY
AS **EMPTINESS**.

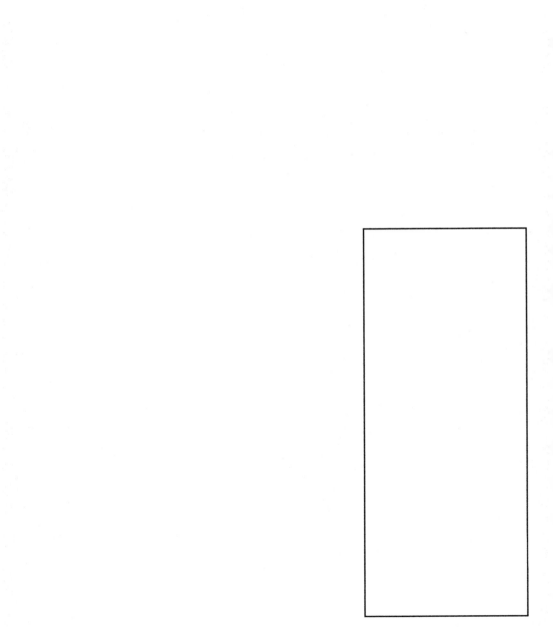

AFTERWORD

By the time Musashi moved to the cave where he would write *The Book of Five Rings,* his body was feeling the effects of nearly forty years on the road, and he was sick and progressively weaker with the beginnings of what would prove to be a fatal disease. Nevertheless, almost every day, he would climb to an open area above the cave and practice for several hours at a time, performing the same moves over and over again as he looked out over the Ariake Sea—the Sea of Dawn—from this "dojo," an outcropping of rock, high on Mount Kimpo. The famous swordsman was well past his days of wandering throughout the country, meeting other men of his art in combat, and perfecting his skills. His techniques, on which he put secondary importance anyway, were well established; and in the last number of years, most of the performance matches that had been pressed upon him by host daimyos or other aspiring swordsmen were characterized by his simply leading his opponent around in circles, demonstrating that the latter would get nowhere with him.

Why, then, at the end of his life, would Musashi continue to practice every day in this isolated place, far away from the public, with only the priest at the nearby Buddhist temple as his solitary neighbor?

The Meaning behind the Structure of *The Book of Five Rings*

When the monk Kukai returned to Japan from China in 806 CE, he brought with him an understanding of a new, esoteric form of Buddhism that he called the Shingon, or True Word, sect. Kukai was not only a devout Buddhist but a brilliant teacher and artist, and he taught that the esoteric meanings of Buddhism could be conveyed not in wordy explanations, but rather through art. This notion of Truth through Art had a direct appeal to Japanese sensibilities in general, and was one of the basic assumptions of Musashi's approach to life, found between the lines in every chapter of his book.

Most indicative of Musashi's understanding of Shingon Buddhism are the title and structure of *The Book of Five Rings* itself. Among the tenets of this sect is the assertion that the deeper esoteric teachings of Buddhism were taught by Vairocana, the cosmic Buddha, who in fact embodies the entire universe. Vairocana is manifested in a number of artistic forms, but in Japan he is often represented by the five-tiered pagoda, or *sotoba*, also called the *gorinto*, or Tower of Five Rings. This tower is usually constructed as follows: a square stone at the bottom represents the Earth element, or stability and the fundamental element of physical being; next, a round stone represents the Water element, or permeation and fluidity; a triangular stone represents the Fire element, or purity and unobstructed activity; a crescent-shaped stone represents the Wind element, or growth and perfect awareness; and at the top, a stone in the shape of a mani-jewel (wish-fulfilling gem) represents the Void element, space, or in Buddhist terms, Emptiness. Thus, the pagoda represents Vairocana himself, the very essence of the universe.

According to Kukai, these five elements are constantly interfusing to form the various manifestations of the universe, or Vairocana. The outward appearance of this eternal interplay is impermanence, but what is inherent in every single form, no matter how small, large, earthly, or ethereal, is Emptiness. Shingon teaches that, with constant meditation, these elements and their respective Buddhas will eventually result in unification with Vairocana, and thus in enlightenment.

The parallels of this system with the title and structure of Musashi's work are clear. Each chapter does indeed echo, reflect, and fuse with the others, as do the Five Elements. One chapter cannot be read to the exclusion of the others, or the full meaning will be lost.

"See Everything for Yourself"

Do not ride another man's horse;
Do not draw another man's bow.

It is interesting that, while the structure and exterior make-up of Musashi's book is based on an esoteric form of Buddhism, its interior has a firm foundation on the very exoteric Buddhism of Zen. One of Zen's first tenets is that one never truly knows water to be hot or cold until he puts his hand in it, and this point is repeated over and over again in *The Book of Five Rings* with the phrase "you must investigate this thoroughly." Musashi, who claims never to have had a teacher for any of the arts he so excelled in, would have us "train in the Way of the sword *with your hands*." And, while many of the famous swordsmen of this period claimed to have learned their art from dreams, gods, or demons, Musashi insisted that we must learn each move and technique as though we had discovered it on our own. This is the iron law of Zen that we "see everything for ourselves" (*issai jikan*: 一切自観), rather than hearing it from another—regardless of how famous a teacher he may be—or reading it in a book. Thus, *The Book of Five Rings* is only a stepping stone to self-discovery, to be abandoned much like the raft after one has crossed the stream.

"See everything for yourself." Practice, in this sense, must mean acute observation, and observation without prejudice. With this kind of practice, Musashi said, we gain real knowledge, and real knowledge implies freedom. Something only half-learned or taken in faith from another only hobbles the practitioner or puts blinders on his gaze.

Musashi lived for sixty years by the concepts of Zen, and besides *The Book of Five Rings*, left us with a number of fine India ink paintings that point to these same principles. One of these paintings depicts a cormorant, *a bird that swims underwater*, perched on a small ledge, perhaps looking over an unseen river. Musashi would have observed many of these birds on his travels, and admired their skill and singleness of purpose. Did he think, as he painted his subject, of the old Japanese saying, "The crow imitating a cormorant will drown?"

Summary of the Text

Although Musashi was heavily influenced by Zen and took a number of cues from Shingon, he could hardly be defined or limited by these sects. And, although a number of documents exist describing his activities and personality, their contradictory statements make it a difficult if not maddening job for the biographer to get a real handle on who he was. The best of all the original documents continues to be his slender volume, *The Book of Five Rings*, which was originally written down in five short scrolls.

As mentioned, Musashi was old (for that period in Japan) and terminally ill, and understood that this would be his final statement. So while the book is short, each section and each word was carefully deliberated upon and chosen. A brief summary is as follows:

The Earth Chapter

In this beginning chapter, Musashi explains the significance of the martial arts as he had come to know them over the course of fifty years, and stresses the necessity of knowing the advantages of the weapons one uses, and the fundamental principles of using them. He also insists that the martial artist must be practical: that partiality towards or bias against any weapon can be fatal. One should know what weapon is most fitting for himself, but should also be able to use any weapon at hand.

The Water Chapter

Here, Musashi relates the philosophy and practice of his own style of swordsmanship, the Niten Ichi-ryu. Included are practical measure and practices for mental attitude, body posture, use of the eyes and feet, and the various ways of striking with the sword. In this chapter, the imaginative reader will almost be able to visualize the bouts in which Musashi discovered these points for himself.

The Fire Chapter

In this chapter, Musashi writes about the strategies and practical applications of combat, and develops the extrapolation of the "large" martial art from the "small" martial art. It is here that he emphasizes the psychological techniques that are the foundation of his own martial art and its very point of departure: "In my martial art it is essential . . . that you bend and warp your opponent, taking the victory by twisting and distorting his mind."

The Wind Chapter

Musashi firmly believed Sun Tzu's statement that "If you know the enemy and know yourself, you will not be endangered in a hundred battles." Thus, in this chapter, he exposes the failings and contrivances of the other schools of swordsmanship that flourished in his time. Musashi despised the schools that charged money to sell "performance art" and advised his students not to be led astray by flashy techniques that were fine flowers but poor fruit.

The Emptiness Chapter

This chapter provides, in very few words, a frame of meditation for the preceding four chapters. In it, we sense Musashi struggling to put as succinctly as possible the summation of not only his swordsmanship, but of the Great Way in general. Emptiness is Existence, Existence is emptiness, and any attachment at all is the great heresy. It would seem that Musashi may have meant it as a sort of mantra to end his short work, similar to the mantra at the end of the *Heart Sutra.* "The Emptiness Chapter" brings *The Book of Five Rings* around in a full circle; it is the perfect *enso*, giving the work a center that is everywhere and that cannot be pinned down.

We may read *The Book of Five Rings* to study the insights that Musashi gained throughout the sixty-one years of his life. There are hundreds of martial artists, a number of Japanese businessmen, and at least one professional baseball player (a pitcher) in Japan who do so every year. Or we may read it to fill in the blanks of his life and to imagine how he worked through the most difficult and problematic matches of his years as a wandering swordsman, meeting others on the road and walking away having defeated yet another opponent. But we may also read this book in an attempt to grasp the mind of a man who lived his life with an intensity that few of us can equal, a man for whom discomfort and material poverty meant nothing compared to his art, and who has been held up as an inspiration to the Japanese people like few others. *The Book of Five Rings* is this man's brief but concise statement, and, after nearly four hundred years, it is still available to us today.

Go back now to Musashi, old and infirm, alone on the outcropping of rock, still practicing the moves he had learned for himself through his long career of observation and training. Each move he makes is as much an integral part of himself as his flesh and blood, and each posture a mudra of his own enlightened art. "You must investigate this thoroughly," not once or twice or a hundred times, but all your life. If you can do this, your life, like Musashi's, becomes Art itself.

As the thirteenth-century Zen priest Dogen wrote,

To study the Buddhist Way is to study the self. To study the self is to forget the self. To forget the self is to be actualized by everything in the universe. When actualized by everything in the universe, your mind and body, and the minds and bodies of all other selves drop away.

—*Genjo Koan*

The seventeenth-century Zen priest Takuan, to whom Musashi seems to have been well acquainted, added to this.

Presumably, as a martial artist, I do not fight for gain or loss, am not concerned with strength or weakness, and neither advance a step or retreat a step. The enemy does not see me. I do not see the enemy. Penetrating to a place where heaven and earth have not yet divided, where yin and yang have not yet arrived, I quickly and necessarily gain effect.

The student and Musashi are on the same Path. The signpost that Musashi left is *The Book of Five Rings*. What the student will leave is yet to be determined. But the means is right there, held in his hands.

The life of Miyamoto Musashi has been portrayed countless times over the centuries. Soon after his death, imaginative versions of his life were created by professional storytellers, and not long after his character began to appear in bunraku, kabuki, and even Noh plays. More recently, he has been the subject of numerous movies, his part interpreted by such prominent actors as Chiezo Kataoka, Toshiro Mifune, Tatsuya Nakadai, Kinnosuke Nakamura, and the great Ichikawa Raizo. Television, of course, has followed suit. Of the many novels that have been written about Musashi, the most famous is *Musashi*, by Yoshikawa Eiji. Written first as a serialized novel for the *Asahi* newspaper, and over four thousand pages in paperback, it has remained the high watermark of the fictionalized Musashi, the basis of many of the movies and television shows about the man, and has never been out of print. Finally, in the 1990s, the manga *Vagabond* appeared, and by the year 2000 there were over twenty-two million volumes of the series in print.

Now, with this manga version of *The Book of Five Rings*, we are provided for the first time with an artistic look into what Musashi wrote himself, insightfully adapted by Sean Michael Wilson, and illustrated with the dignity due the original author by Chie Kutsuwada. To those interested in Musashi, his art, and/or Japanese culture in general, I hope this engaging volume will prove interesting, instructive, and entertaining.

—*William Scott Wilson*